South African Music

South African Music

A Century of Traditions in Transformation

CAROL A. MULLER

A B C • C L I O

Santa Barbara, California   Denver, Colorado   Oxford, England

"Weskusklong," translated by Carol A. Muller, is reprinted with the
kind permission of David Kramer.

Songs by Thami Vilakazi are used here with his permission.

The hymns of Isaiah Shembe and Johannes Galilee Shembe were translated
by the late Bongani Mthethwa, with assistance from Themba Mbhele and
Sazi Dlamini of the University of Natal, and edited by Carol A. Muller.
They are reprinted with permission.

All photographs courtesy of the author.

Library of Congress Cataloging-in-Publication Data

Muller, Carol Ann.
South African music : a century of traditions in transformation /
Carol A. Muller.
p. cm. — (ABC-CLIO world music series)
Includes bibliographical references and index.
ISBN 1-57607-276-2 (hc : alk. paper) — ISBN 1-85109-527-6 (e-book)
1. Music—South Africa—History and criticism.
I. Title. II. Series.
ML350.M85 2004
780'.968—dc22
2004006533

04 05 06 07 ⁊ 10 9 8 7 6 5 4 3 2 1

This book is also available on the World Wide Web as an e-book.
Visit abc-clio.com for details.

ABC-CLIO, Inc.
130 Cremona Drive, P.O. Box 1911
Santa Barbara, California 93116-1911

Design by Jane Raese
Text set in New Baskerville

This book is printed on acid-free paper.
Manufactured in the United States of America

To Eric
for unconditional love

and Zachary
for your complete embrace of life

Contents

Musical Examples on Compact Disc

1. "Sometimes I Feel Like a Motherless Child," Sathima Bea Benjamin

2. "I Only Have Eyes for You," Sathima Bea Benjamin

3. "Windsong," Sathima Bea Benjamin

4. "Nations in Me, New Nation-a-Coming," Sathima Bea Benjamin

5. "Africa," Sathima Bea Benjamin

6. Isicathamiya "praktisa," Beatrice Street YMCA

7. Xolo Homeboys rehearsal

8. Zulu maskanda guitar with comb, Blanket Mkhize

9. Zulu maskanda concertina

10. Zulu maskanda violin

11. "Chuning," Thami Vilakazi

12. "Awusho Ndodana," Thami Vilakazi

13. "Kungcono Khona," Thami Vilakazi

14. Maskanda group accompaniment for gumboot dance, without dancers

15. Maskanda accompaniment for gumboot dance, with dancers

16. Liturgy for morning prayers

17. "Ameni! Oyincwele!"

18. Nazarite hymn with organ accompaniment

19. Nazarite hymn with piano accompaniment

20. Youth choir rehearsal singing in solfege

21. Youth choir performance in "classic" style

22. Nathoya Mbatha's gospel version of Shembe hymn

For additional information on each track, see Appendix Five.

Series Foreword

When Philip Bohlman, professor of ethnomusicology at the University of Chicago, and Alicia Merritt, acquistions editor at ABC-CLIO, first approached me in 1998 to ask if I would serve as editor for a new series of books on world music traditions, the prospect excited me greatly.

At that time, the monumental, ten-volume *Garland Encyclopedia of World Music* was on the verge of publication. Several academic publishers, including the University of Chicago Press, had developed extensive and impressive ethnomusicology lists. A handful of quality textbooks designed for introductory world music survey courses were already available, and a few other promising ones on the way. In short, in conjunction with the dramatic rise in the overall popularity of world music (a subject to which I will return), the related literature was growing rapidly and expanding on several different fronts all at once.

But for all of this growth and expansion in ethnomusicology and world music publishing, one special kind of book remained surprisingly rare: the accessible yet substantive introductory text on a specific world music region or area—and this was exactly the kind of book to which ABC-CLIO was now proposing to devote a series. I therefore enthusiastically accepted their series editorship invitation.

As I had expected, my enthusiasm for a series of such books on the world's diverse musical cultures and traditions was widely shared by my colleagues in the ethnomusicology/world music studies community. In short order, several leading experts, most of them teaching at major research universities with leading ethnomusicology programs (University of Chicago, University of Pennsylvania, University of Florida), were under contract to contribute volumes in their respective areas of expertise. This was a Dream Team of scholars, but even more importantly, these were highly gifted authors who were up to the series mission challenge that ABC-CLIO and I set before them: Write a book that is accessible to the non-specialist reader, that is highly informative without being overly technical, that is brought vividly to life by its illustrations and accompanying compact disc (CD), that conveys your own passion for the music it explores and the world in which that music lives, and that will engage the interest of a wide readership comprised principally of high school and undergraduate nonmusic students.

Beyond these requirements, the authors were asked to conceive of their works in accordance with a structured yet flexible model that directed each book through a telescopic progression from broadly general to increasingly specific vantage points, starting with a general introduction to the selected music area and topic covered, then moving to a more narrowly defined regional focus and an emphasis on key themes and issues, and finally concluding with an in-depth portrait of a particular musical community or phenomenon, a portrait based on the author's own principal field research. The model was developed with three specific objectives in mind: achieving a high level of consistency of presentation between volumes, striking of an appropriate balance between comprehensive breadth and focused depth within each volume, and engendering in readers an intimate sense of personal engagement with the music and its world. It has been highly satisfying for me as series editor to see these objectives splendidly realized in each volume to date.

Underlying the concept and vision of this series since its inception have been two important issues: the dramatic ascent of world music in recent years and the rather paradoxical term "world music" itself. Since these issues in a sense prefigured and continue to shape the ABC-CLIO World Music Series vision, I would like to devote the remainder of this foreword to a brief discussion of their significance.

The Dramatic Rise of "World Music"

The popularity of world music has grown by leaps and bounds here in the West in recent decades. It was not so long ago that the sounds of Indian sitars, Indonesian gamelans, Chinese pipas, and the like were largely unknown to the vast majority of Western listeners. Today, such sounds are to be heard just about everywhere: on the radio, on the Internet, in record stores, at concerts and festivals, even in shopping malls, supermarkets, and elevators. Whether or not you know to identify the source of the distinctive, "otherworldly" melody on your favorite Beatles or Ricky Martin CD as a sitar, it is there, permeating your consciousness and affecting your musical sensibilities. And that infectious Janet Jackson dance groove? Perhaps it's the one enlivened by a heavily processed, digitally sampled Balinese gamelan orchestra. Then, of course, there is the Internet, where thousands upon thousands of world music recordings and "sound file" sources are available at the click of a mouse to everyone, from major record producers and dance club DJs to soccer moms and teenage computer hackers.

Some of the musical traditions that fall within the eclectic domain of world music represent continuations and developments of musical practices and repertoires dating back centuries or even millennia, such as Indian *raga* and Japanese *gagaku*. Others, such as "world beat" and various cross-cultural fusion genres, are of recent origin or are emerging at this very moment, as music makers blend together resources, ideas, and musical materials from a variety of sources and inventively forge them into new expressions of their unique identities as individuals, as members of communities, societies, and cultures, and as human beings in the broadest sense of the term. All points on this spectrum are embraced within the pages of each volume of the ABC-CLIO World Music Series.

But what exactly *is* world music? There is no easy answer to this question. In actuality, *all* of the world's music traditions, or *musics,* as ethnomusicologists like to call them—past and present, traditional and modern, familiar and unfamiliar, Western and non-Western, classical and popular, folk and tribal—should rightly fall within the category of world music. Since all of the world's musics exist in the world, it makes sense that either all of them should be categorized as world music or that none of them should be. Any scheme that includes some musics within the category while excluding others is simply arbitrary.

And yet the popular meaning of the term "world music" is just that: arbitrary. It rose to prominence as a convenient catch-all classification for types of music that did not fit conveniently into existing

Western categories (jazz, rock, classical, etc.) and was subsequently embraced by bewildered record store owners seeking an appropriate designation for bins displaying such material. The "world music" category, as it is usually applied, includes only those musics that do not fit within the conventional categorical boxes that identify the Western musical "mainstream" (another slippery and ever-malleable term that today encompasses, among other musics, classical, jazz, rock, country and western, easy listening, rap, and hip-hop). Traditional musics of African, Asian, Aboriginal Australian, Native American, Central and South American, and Eastern European cultures are the prime candidates for inclusion. Western-influenced popular music styles built upon the roots of traditional musics of non-Western origin are also usually included, sometimes under the aforementioned subcategory of world beat. And certain musical traditions of North America and Western Europe—Irish traditional, Cajun, and so on—fit the bill of world music according to some people's lists but not others'.

The philosophy underlying the ABC-CLIO World Music Series, in step with current directions in the discipline of ethnomusicology and important recent publications such as *The Garland Encyclopedia of World Music*, endeavors to move away from the arbitrary inclusions and exclusions that are so often invoked by the term "world music" and to approach the study of world music instead simply as an exploration of selected musical traditions from around the world, wherever that exploration may originate and wherever it may take the reader along its multidirectional pathways. The geographical and cultural "hubs" of given musics—the places identified with their origins, the principal cultural groups with which they are connected, the musicians recognized as their leading representatives—are most certainly accounted for, but so too are the complex, intersecting webs of geography and culture that situate these musics in more broadly global, that is, in *world*, contexts.

Thus, for example, Philip Bohlman's volume on music and European nationalism privileges neither rural Eastern European folk music nor concert works by the well-known nineteenth-century Czech composer Antonin Dvorak one over the other, devoting serious attention to both; Carol Muller highlights the inextricable ties between indigenous Zulu musical traditions, Christian hymnody, and the global configuration of the modern popular music industry in her book on South African music; and Henry Spiller finds an essential continuity between the centuries-old tradition of Javanese *gamelan* music, on the one hand, and the Western pop music–inspired Islamic didacticism of the Indonesian *dangdut* genre on the other. In all cases, the concept of world music is treated by these authors not as an invitation to divide the world up in West-versus-the-rest style, but as a point of departure from which to explore musical traditions both at their most localized levels of identity and within the context of broad, overarching processes of globalization and modernization.

It is a great pleasure to bring this exciting series to your attention. I hope you enjoy reading these books as much as I have.

Michael B. Bakan

Preface

Via Africa:
Coming to South African Music

African music was and remains a music of encounters;
in this lies its attractive power.
—Manu Dibango (cited in Stewart 2000)

Africa: Fact and Fiction

All of us—those whose ancestors were born in Africa and those
whose ancestors colonized it, those of the old and new African diasporas, and those who know Africa and its music as cultural outsiders, come to Africa music with a particular set of ideas, imagin-
ings, and stereotypes. Many of us can tell some kind of personal
story of our first encounter with Africa and its music, regardless of
where we live or what our cultural or ancestral heritage is. Typically,
our understanding of Africa is shaped as much by what we see or
hear as it is by where we come from; in other words, our encounter
is culturally informed in at least two directions. But our wider
knowledge of Africa and its music is often filled with misconcep-
tions. This book on South Africa and its music is intended to dispel
three of these.

Misconception Number One: Africa is a country. People often talk
about Africa as if it is single place without cultural, linguistic, geographical, or historical differentiation. In fact, Africa is the second
largest *continent* on earth. It covers 28 million square kilometers,
and includes several islands to the west and east of the mainland.

The Kalahari Desert dominates the southern region, and the Sahara Desert the north. The equator lies in the middle and is surrounded by rainforests, with a combination of grasslands and plateau topography in other regions. Vast expanses of African land contain rich mineral resources that have been exploited, particularly in the last century, by colonial powers and more recently by heads of newly independent African states.

The African continent is home to 10 percent of the world's population, 25 percent of which is now urban. African people are divided into about 3,000 ethnic groups, and they speak close to 1,000 indigenous languages and thousands more dialects. Due to European colonial rule of Africa largely in the nineteenth and twentieth centuries (though this goes back to the mid-seventeenth century in South Africa), English, French, and Portuguese are commonly spoken in many urbanized areas of Africa. Several Asian and Arabic dialects, as well as a handful of new languages forged out of colonial contact, are also found.

South Africa is the country (the region is called southern Africa) in the southernmost part of the African continent. The Dutch were the first Europeans to settle in the area, starting in 1652, though the English and French played significant parts in the colonization of the region in subsequent years. South Africa now has eleven official languages, eleven more that are to be nurtured by the nation, and several additional languages spoken by its people. Afrikaans is perhaps the most significant language to have developed out of several languages in contact through the colonial period: Dutch, French, Portuguese, English, and German. Though the white Afrikaans-speaking community claimed the language as largely of and for Europeans, Cape Town Muslims were the first to write Afrikaans, and they did so in Arabic script (Austin 1988).

Misconception Number Two: Africa is a place and a people without history. This peculiarly Eurocentric notion assumes that because little has been written about the past, Africa has no history of note. Although this view is simply wrong, it did provide a convenient justification for the European colonization of Africa. Europeans convinced themselves that they were bringing "civilization" to "darkest Africa." The fact that the written record has been privileged over other archives and records of the past has also resulted in a peculiar kind of history: Africa's history has largely been written by non-Africans in the twentieth century.

The idea that Africa has no past has come under scrutiny in the twentieth century. For example, from the 1920s through the late 1990s, a series of discoveries of human remains excavated in South Africa place the origin of the human species firmly in the African continent rather than in Asia as was once thought. Since the 1960s, historians have revised their earlier ideas about Africa's past (or the lack of it), and found ways to recover a sense of Africa's long history by sharpening the methodological tools of oral history, tradition, and archeology, and by paying closer attention to the history of the continent produced by Africans themselves prior to the arrival of Europeans (White, Miescher, and Cohen 2001).

Alongside the mistaken view that Africa has no past is the equally erroneous view that Africa is only about the past, a view articulated possibly inadvertently by some African Americans in the United States. As a result of the violent and disruptive experience of slavery, and of not feeling fully integrated into the United States, a powerful body of ideas in certain sectors of the African-American community relegates Africa to cultural memory—Africa as the place that holds their past. In this view, there is little sense of Africa as a continent with a contemporary life or independent identity. This conflict of ideas about Africa is evident in the tensions that presently exist in the United States between those who have recently arrived from the African continent and African Americans whose ancestors came earlier. Though the idea of Africa as cultural memory works and is an important internal narrative in the United States, it is less useful for those who continue to live in Africa or who have left only recently. Twentieth-century technologies have made their way into contemporary life throughout Africa, particularly in South Africa, the most modern and technologically progressive country on the continent and, as the cradle of human life, the nation with the longest and most enduring past.

Misconception Number Three: Africa is a continent of drummers and complex drumming ensembles. According to this stereotype, if you want to know about rhythmic complexity articulated in dance and drumming ensembles, you must travel to Africa. In reality, drumming ensembles are common mostly in parts of the western regions of the continent. A range of other traditional instruments is typically part of African performance: the *mbira*-type instruments of southern and central Africa; the *kora*-type instruments of West Africa; and a host of whistles, rattles, harps, musical bows, and marimbas are found throughout the continent. Africa is also known for its fondness for the human voice, singing alone and collectively, in simple call and response and in more complex forms of vocal polyphony. In South Africa, it is certainly the human voice that is the original and most frequently used musical instrument.

Writing about Africa and Its Music

Like those who write about African history, those who write about African music are seldom people who were born there. Instead, they are people who have come to know Africa and its music through various forms of travel, and are more distant from African people and the music they make than cultural insiders might be. There are disadvantages to this kind of distance, such as not knowing the language or arriving with cultural biases. But these individuals typically reflect in their writing on their relationship to Africa, when and where that relationship began, and how it has developed. The reflection frequently takes a narrative turn—they tell stories about what Africa and its music have come to mean to then. Ultimately, Africa and its music become intertwined with the autobiographies of individuals from far-flung places.

Quite often those not born on the African continent are exposed to African music by first hearing it performed live in their own communities by African musicians who themselves have traveled. Often this music is staged on college campuses or in world music festivals (Berliner 1978). Many come to African music by hearing a recording or radio program. American journalist Banning Eyre (2000), for example, came to study and write about West African guitar music by traveling to the country of Mali in the 1990s. He studied Malian contemporary guitar music, which comprises translations of the traditional music of Malian *griots* or *jelis* onto the guitar. His decision to travel to Mali was shaped by a decade-long experience of listening to many recordings of African music available to him in the United States. Eyre has written about the experience of learning to play *griot*-style guitar from Djelimady, the leader of the Super Rail Band of Bamako, Mali (see Duran 1994 for discussion of this band).

Others engage with African music because they sense a connection through cultural or religious heritage. Ethnomusicologist Kay Shelemay traveled to Ethiopia in the early 1970s to study the music of Falashan Jews after reading that there was a black Jewish community in Ethiopia (1986). Shelemay is Jewish. African American musicologist Samuel Floyd has written about African "cultural memory" because he is of African descent (Floyd 1995, ch. 1), and he believes that that experience has shaped the sounds produced by African Americans like himself living in the United States. Many of those who have written about South African music, particularly from the 1960s onwards, have done so out of a political commitment to the struggles of people of color living inside and outside of South Africa.

Many who write about Africa and its music in the latter part of the twentieth century convey their profound sense of compassion and admiration for the music and peoples of Africa. Each traveler recounts observations of suffering humanity, but also of an awesome humility found in the face of enormous struggle. Reading these accounts, I have been struck by a particular quality in the writing about Africa, its people, and their music: it is the quality of total love for the continent and its peoples. Chris Stapleton and Chris May begin their book, *African Rock,* in a confessional tone, conveying the "respective enthusiasm of two British writers who, independently, fell in love with the music of Africa in the early 1970s." They continue by saying that when they returned to Britain after working in two separate development agencies, they "fell with evangelical zeal to the task of converting anyone within reach to the magic of African music" (1990, Introduction). The passion of writers who have stayed a while in Africa, to record, and perhaps even learn the music, stands in stark contrast to the kinds of images produced by the mass media about Africa in the twenty-first century. These portray the continent as a place rife with starvation, warfare, disease, drought, famine, ethnic conflict—a continent of victims unable to help themselves.

Those hearing African music outside of Africa respond in various ways to the music. Some celebrate its rhythmic complexity, others its elements of sociability, still others its complete simplicity. The process of engaging with African music, is however, not uncontested. Paul Berliner, an ethnomusicologist who has written a comprehensive account of the history and culture of *mbira* playing in Zimbabwe, includes an experience he had in which a Zimbabwean musician talked about how Europeans viewed Zimbabwean music relative to European classical music. Berliner first heard *mbira* music performed at a lecture demonstration conducted by the late Dumisani Maraire, the Zimbabwean *mbira* expert who visited Seattle, Washington, in the 1970s. Berliner recalls how Maraire demonstrated the educational methods of the Christian missionaries to the crowd.

> [Maraire] walked onto the stage carrying a round-box resonator with a fifteen-key instrument inside. He turned toward the audience and raised the round-box over his head. "What is this?" he called out. There was no response. "All right," he said, "it is an mbira; M-B-I-R-A." Now what did I say it was?" A few people replied, "Mbira; it is an mbira." Most of the audience sat still in puzzlement. "What is it?" Maraire repeated, as if slightly annoyed. More people called out, "Mbira." "Again," Maraire insisted. "Mbira" returned the audience. "Again!" he shouted. When the auditorium echoed with "Mbira" Maraire laughed out loud. "All right," he said with good-natured sarcasm, "that is the way the Christian missionaries taught me to say piano." (Berliner 1978, 8–9)

Berliner explains that "Dumisani Maraire was reacting to the fact that people from the same culture that supports missionary education in Africa continually referred to his instrument in ethnocentric terms as 'finger piano,' 'thumb piano,' or 'hand piano,' and showed little interest in learning its African name" (Berliner 1978, 8–9).

My own love for Africa and its music combines a sense of both distance and closeness in what might seem at first to be a strange way. I was born in the southernmost part of Africa, in Cape Town, South Africa, in the early 1960s, a period in South African history when all things African were being either completely suppressed by the government or dismissed as having little value. African music was made available only to those people who were the bearers of that particular strand of musical culture. Zulu-speaking people living together in Zulu territory were supposed to listen only to Zulu music, and Xhosa-speaking people to Xhosa music. This was made complicated by the fact that there are so many languages spoken in South Africa: to understand much of the music one had to know the language of its performers. African languages were not usually taught to South Africans of European descent in schools at the time. Because my father was a minister in the Presbyterian Church, my first real exposure to any kind of African music was through the church. Then as an undergraduate ethnomusicology student, I began to look for "African music." One weekend in 1984, a fellow student, Janet Topp Fargion, and I set off for a Catholic mission station in the Eastern Cape to find African music. And we found it—integrated into the Catholic mass with Zimbabwean-introduced marimbas and the liturgy in Xhosa traditional style. This was the start of the journey into the African-made music of South Africa described and discussed in this book.

African Music as Compositional Resource

African and non-African composers frequently draw on African music for inspiration and as a compositional resource. Anglo-African classical cellist Tunde Jegede, for example, was exposed by his father, a Nigerian sculptor living in England, to the musicians and artists of the African diaspora residing in and traveling through Britain. One of these was Jamaican reggae king Bob Marley; the other was a well-known *kora* player from West Africa. Transformed by these experiences, Jegede traveled to the Gambia in West Africa in the 1990s to find his musical and cultural roots among *kora* players in that region (Jegede 1994 and 1995). He felt he found his soul in Africa, after which he was able to compose art music in a new style, one that combined his European and African classical training.

French-speaking Afropea (the blending of African and European heritage) singer Marie Daulne and her family fled the Belgian Congo when she was a child (Feld 2000 and de Villiers 1994). Like Jegede, Daulne studied composition and ethnomusicology in Europe. In the process, she came across recordings of the people commonly labeled pygmies (though they prefer to be labeled linguistically, Bayaka or Babenzele, for example) made by ethnomusicologist

Hugo Zemp. Daulne recalled that before her family escaped the civil war in Congo, the pygmies her Bantu-speaking mother had befriended protected Daulne and her siblings from warring Congolese until they could leave the country. In the 1990s Marie Daulne visited Central Africa to record pygmy performances. On returning to Europe she formed an a capella ensemble called Zap Mama. She has produced several CD recordings of original vocal performance, the first of which features a track of "pygmy" sounds created by the women of Zap Mama.

British-born music explorer David Fanshawe traveled to four countries in Africa, mostly on foot, in the early 1970s to record African music (Muller 2002 and Fanshawe 1976). He has used this recorded material as an integral resource for making his own music. *African Sanctus,* which combines field recordings with live renditions of British choral settings of the Latin mass, is perhaps the best known of these compositions. One of the most widely publicized integrations of African musical techniques and aesthetics from South Africa is the 2002 Opera Africa production titled *Princess Magogo.* It was composed by South African Mzilikazi Khumalo with the libretto in the Zulu language written by Themba Msimang. The world premiere of this opera was aired live on PBS on May 4, 2002.

Songwriters on Africa

Songwriters in Africa have created word images of Africa in both sound and text. These images are sometimes intended to represent Africa as it really is, but also as they desire Africa to be for them. I have selected four examples to illustrate how "Africa" has been represented in song texts. First, Brazilian jazz vocalist Flora Purim of the group Fourth World sings about longing for the continent of Africa as a place where there is rhythm, the freedom to run and to dance, and a sense of communal unity. South African jazz singer Sathima Bea Benjamin composed a song called "Africa" while moving in and out of Africa in the early 1970s. Hers, too, is a song of longing for a place of warmth, gentle breezes, the smell of the earth, the laughter of children, and indeed, a profound sense of home. South African Afro-pop musician Johnny Clegg (known in

France as *Zoulou-blanc*, the white Zulu) wrote a song several years back in which he talked about Africa as having the "mbaqanga man," the South African musician with a special kind of music that enables people to keep moving forward. Finally, Tanzanian popular singer Remmy Ongala provides contrasting images to the idealism of the previous songwriters. In one song, Ongala writes about Africa as a place where his people listen to each other and love one another. In another, he comments on what it is like to be African and poor, to have no voice and no sense of political rights. (The full texts of Ongala's songs are quoted in Grebner 1997, 114–115.)

Distinctive Elements of African Musical and Cultural Style

It is impossible to fairly represent the music and or culture of an entire continent in a book, and certainly not in a few lines. Nevertheless, certain musical and textual characteristics constitute a sense of African-ness when compared with other styles in the world.

Characteristics of African Music

- *Call-and-response.* In this musical form, the call is generally articulated by a soloist and the response comes from a group, but the phrases of the musical dialogue overlap, so that the leader's line continues as the group responds, and their line continues as the leader re-enters.
- *Cyclical structure.* Tied to the idea of call-and-response, a cyclical structure means there is no clear sense of a beginning, middle, or end. Instead the song or instrumental performance is repeated over and over.
- *Rhythmic complexity.* Much of the music of Africa is rhythmically complex. Scholars have called this music polymetric and polyrhythmic, and these textures also include cross-rhythmic interplay and hemiola patterns. Rhythmic complexity of parts symbolizes the complexity of social relationships that exist in traditional African cultures (Andrew Tracey cited in Andersson 1981).

- *Relative pitch.* In many African communities, there is no sense of a universal and fixed pitch as there is for example, with piano tuning; pitch is relative to the skills of singers and the desires of instrument makers.
- *Tuning.* Because performance is so tied to the human voice and to language itself, musicians in Africa will frequently use a wide spectrum of sound for individual pitches, often sounding "out of tune" to the musical outsider.

African Music and Language

- *Tonal language.* Language plays a central role in the articulation of melodic lines and rhythms in African music. Many African languages are tonal languages, which means that a single word can have quite different meanings depending on how the word is sounded out—using different combinations of high, medium, and lower pitches for each syllable.
- *Nonverbal utterance.* In some instances words are not as important in song performance as the interactive polyphony and rhythms generated by the lines singers improvise.
- *Words articulate life experience.* In contrast to the use of words for rhythmic purposes, words in much African popular and traditional music are used to tell others about the plight of the poor, to reflect on the powerless, and to criticize the powerful.

Music and Dance

- The body is central to all performance. The rhythm of the body expressed in individual and communal dance is integral to powerful musical performances in many parts of Africa. Typically the rhythms produced by instrumental performers exist in tension with the rhythms of the dancers in the same musical performance.

In South Africa, several of these more traditional elements of African performance exist, if not in drumming ensembles, then frequently in the more improvised vocal performances of traditional wedding ceremonies and religious practices. A fair proportion of the music performed and produced in contemporary South Africa has been deeply reshaped and influenced by European and American religious and popular music, particularly from the mid-nineteenth century onwards. This music came to South Africa in live performances of musicians who traveled the world in the nineteenth and twentieth centuries, through the missionaries, and in the form of musical objects distributed in the channels of the global entertainment industry. Some of this music has traveled back to the metropolitan centers of London, Paris, New York, and Los Angeles, but it has done so transformed by the sounds and aesthetic ideals of South Africans musicians.

Coming to South African Music

Despite the circulation of music and musicians between South Africa, Europe, and the United States in the twentieth century, South African music might seem a long way from your own musical experiences at first. But you might be more familiar with it than you realize. If you own Paul Simon's *Graceland* album, you have heard South Africans performing. Perhaps you have seen Michael Jackson's *Moonwalker* video; the group singing and dancing at the end of the video is Ladysmith Black Mambazo, the close-harmony male choir first heard globally on the *Graceland* album. Perhaps you have sung the words "In the jungle, the mighty jungle . . ." from the song popularized by the Weavers called "Wimoweh" in the United States and "Mbube" in South Africa. If you follow world music releases, you might be familiar with Johnny Clegg's group, Juluka, and the more commercial-sounding follow-up band, Savuka.

You may also have heard South African music in films, both fictional and documentary, produced in the last two decades. In the mid-1980s British documentary filmmaker Jeremy Marre produced *Rhythm of Resistance,* a film about black South African music that was shown on BBC television and at numerous public gatherings in Europe and the United States. In 1987 Richard Attenborough directed the film *Cry Freedom,* a story about South African Black Conscious-ness leader Steve Biko's friendship with white South African journal-ist Donald Woods. The music there was co-written by American George Fenton and South African Jonas Gwangwa. In 1992 John Avildsen directed *The Power of One,* a film about a white English-speaking South African boy's experiences of apartheid in the 1930s to 1950s in South Africa. Numerous tracks of South African music are used in this film. More recently, the 1996 Oscar-nominated doc-umentary film titled *Mandela: Son of Africa, Father of a Nation* show-cased a wide range of South African popular music in its soundtrack. In 2002 *Amandla! Revolution in Four Part Harmony* won an audience award at the Sundance Film Festival. This film about black resistance music features the work of several South African musicians: Abdul-lah Ibrahim, Hugh Masakela, Miriam Makeba, and Vusi Mahlasela.

If you are a jazz fan, especially of jazz from around the world, you may have heard the music of South African pianists Abdullah Ibrahim (also known as Dollar Brand), Chris McGregor and the Brotherhood of Breath, Winston Mankunku, and Bheki Mseleku. You may also have heard the singing of Sathima Bea Benjamin, Miriam Makeba, or Thuli Dumakade. You might recall hearing the group Malombo in New York City at the World Music Institute con-certs in the 1980s. Perhaps you know the trumpet playing or com-positions of Hugh Masekela.

Perhaps you are a hip hop and rap consumer who listens beyond the borders of the United States and are familiar with Prophets of da City, the hip hop group from Cape Town that has localized the sounds of African American roots hip hop to speak to the musical preferences and verbal messages of their Cape Town constituency (see Watkins 2001).

Maybe none of these musical examples is in your own personal archive or soundscape yet. If not, you have an exciting musical jour-ney ahead of you. Your challenge in reading this book will be to ex-pand your own world of sound across the African continent to its southernmost tip, where South Africa lies. To start your musical trav-els, we begin with some vital statistics about South Africa, and a brief discussion about twentieth-century South Africa's changing relation-ship to the African continent, musically, politically, and culturally.

Vital Statistics

Eleven official languages: English, Zulu, Xhosa, Afrikaans, Pedi, Tswana, Sotho, Tsonga, Swati, Venda, and Ndebele.

Nine provinces: Western Cape, Eastern Cape, Northern Cape, KwaZulu Natal, Free State, Gauteng, Mpumamlanga, Northern Province, and Northwest Province. In the apartheid era there were six self-governing territories called Gazankulu, KwaNdebele, KaNgwane, KwaZulu, Lebowa, and Qwaqwa. There were four "independent countries": Transkei, Ciskei, Bophutatswana, and Venda.

Three capitals: Pretoria (executive), Cape Town (legislative), Bloemfontein (judicial).

Education: through 1954 all education for black South Africans was by the Christian mission; in 1954 Bantu Education by the government made all black education for servitude. Post-1994: education is for all.

Population: 43 million people.

Racial categories under apartheid: African, Coloured, European, Asian.

The "New" South Africa

On April 27, 1994, South Africans stood in long lines and waited patiently, some for many hours, to cast their vote in the first democratic elections held in the country's history. On May 10, South Africa's first black president, Nelson Mandela, was sworn into office, and the world witnessed the birth of a "new," fully democratic South Africa. One of the many significant outcomes of that historical moment was that South Africa realigned its relationship with the African continent, and South Africans began to ask themselves, first, what it meant to be a nation, and second, what it meant to be situated in the African continent.

These may seem strange questions to those not familiar with South Africa's political history, but they make sense when you consider that South Africa was colonized by Europeans beginning in

1652 with the arrival of Dutchman Jan van Riebeek in what became the city of Cape Town. For the next four hundred years, the people of South Africa, both those of African and European descent, were involved in continual contest, and frequent conflict, over land ownership, religious practice, political power, education, and certainly over musical and cultural tradition and practice. In fact, as we shall see, South Africa's colonial history has had an enduring impact on its people and their music.

Although 1994 was certainly a moment of triumph for all, it was also a time of enormous uncertainty about how the future of South Africa might work itself out. From the South African perspective, the twentieth century must therefore be understood as a period of enormous challenge—a time of great hope, but also of considerable stress and, for many, deep distress. Even positive changes in the country were accompanied by anxiety and the sense of traveling uncharted waters.

As you read this book, you might keep in mind these questions: How is traditional music defined in twentieth-century South Africa? What happened to musical traditions in the numerous moments of societal transformation? How did black South Africans respond musically to the power of the colonial mission and its ideas about African music? What were the consequences of apartheid for South African musical traditions? What alternative musical models came to South Africa, and how did South Africans respond to the possibilities presented in Hollywood films and recordings of jazz that traveled to South Africa from other parts of the world? What is the history of the transatlantic connections sensed between African Americans and South Africans of African descent and mixed racial heritage?

Keywords/Key Concepts
in the Study of South African Music

I have created an extended list of key words and core ideas or issues that may help you to navigate through the chapters of the book and to answer some of the questions posed above.

Music and

- tradition: invented, appropriated, borrowed, hybrid
- travel: movement of musicians and musical commodities; real, imagined, virtual
- colonialism and the "civilizing" process
- mass media
- modernity, with and without democracy
- politics: racial, cultural, and gendered
- exile
- the body and the voice
- kinds of listening
- orality and literacy
- language
- the sacred
- contact
- imagination
- art or culture
- the entertainment industry: local and global
- covers and copies
- collaboration
- nation building: the state and the law

Chapter Outline

This book is shaped in large part by my personal experiences and intellectual interests in Africa and its music. Much of what I write about in subsequent chapters is performance I have directly experienced; very little pertaining to the music of South Africa is simply book knowledge. In the remainder of this book, I examine a range of musical styles drawn from contemporary South Africa in order to understand something of what it means to be a South African who makes and consumes music in that country. This includes discussion of black South African performance and the music of people of mixed racial (Coloured) heritage. It is about the music of those who perform only in the country, as well as the music of those who have traveled, or allowed their music to travel, outside the country. This will be a narrative about great joy and continual struggle for local and international recognition.

Chapter One provides an overview of South African political and media history, focused on the twentieth century and the problem of apartheid, or legalized racial discrimination. Chapter Two, the first of four case studies, examines a pivotal moment in South African music history and in South Africa's relationship to American-made popular music through a discussion of the 1986 *Graceland* recording, the well-known musical collaboration between Paul Simon and several South African musicians. Chapter Three presents the second case study: Cape Town Jazz from the 1950s through the present time, viewed from the perspective of South African jazz singer Sathima Bea Benjamin. Chapter Four, the third case study, looks at three music/dance genres performed by migrant workers largely from KwaZulu Natal: *isicathamiya, maskanda,* and gumboot dance. The fourth case study, presented in Chapter Five, focuses on the indigenous religious community of Isaiah Shembe, *ibandla lama-Nazaretha,* examining the hymn repertory as both written and performed repertory, and explores changes to the repertory through the course of the twentieth century. The book concludes with a brief examination of the film *The Power of One* as a focal point for reiterating the key issues in a study of South African musical traditions in the twentieth century.

Acknowledgments

In many ways, writing this book has been a personal journey retracing the steps of a significant portion of my adult life as a South African. Although I ultimately left the country physically, I never left it emotionally. Writing this text has taken me back to that twenty-year period in South Africa, gently reminding me of a way of life that no longer exists but that has profoundly shaped my intellectual and musical understanding. There are so many whom I would like to thank for walking parts of this path with me, and many who crossed that path at particular, crucial moments, even if very brief.

Two of my teachers, now colleagues, introduced me to the study of ethnomusicology early in my life: Christopher Ballantine (University of Natal) and Veit Erlmann (University of Texas at Austin). Later Kay Shelemay (Harvard University) enabled me to pursue graduate study at New York University. Thank you to the three of you for opening the doors to me. Eleanor Preston-Whyte, Jim Kiernan, Deborah James, Jeff Thomas, Kevin Volans, Darius Brubeck, Bev Parker, Betsey Oehrle, and so many others shaped my thinking as an undergraduate ethnomusicology student at the University of Natal.

When I returned to the University of Natal to teach in the early 1990s, I developed a deeply valued collegial relationship with my colleague Bongani Mthethwa and his wife, Ntombemhlope, and their daughter, Khethiwe. They were warm and willing to share the Shembe space with me. Thank you. Many of my students at UND talked with me, engaged with me in the pursuit of ethnomusicology, and taught me much about life in South Africa and KwaZulu Natal specifically—lessons I will value for the rest of my life. Those were heady, exciting times, as we struggled through the early days of forging a new nation, addressing the educational and epistemological issues together.

To all those who welcomed me so warmly into *ibandla lama-Nazaretha,* the Shembe community, particularly Samu Nthini and her parents and friends in KwaMashu's F Section, my heartfelt appreciation for the kindness and protectiveness you showed towards me in some quite frightening moments in Inanda in the early 1990s.

Coming to know Sathima Bea Benjamin, Abdullah Ibrahim, and their two children, Tsidi and Tsakwe, has been a precious gift. As Sathima, in particular, has shared her music, her life, and its struggles with me, I have come to a deeper understanding of intellectual problems of exile, diaspora, and the creative process, not just in their lives but indeed in my own. I can say the same for my gumboot dance teacher, Blanket Mkhize, and my dearest friend, gumboot dance partner, and colleague, Janet Topp-Fargion.

And now to those who have supported my work in the United States. I am so indebted to New York University, to Edward Roesner, Stanley Boorman, David Burrows, and Donna Buchanan for the strong support they provided, both financially and intellectually, as I pursued what was at the time a very unusual dissertation topic for NYU's music department. Faye Ginsburg and Bambi Schieffelin in anthropology at NYU and Julia Keydel in the film school provided rich learning environments for me in the early 1990s.

Later, at the University of Pennsylvania, Emma Dillon and Christopher Hasty (my erstwhile colleague now lost to Harvard) are the two in the music department who have provided me with the most sustained intellectual engagement. It has been wonderful to have Tim Rommen join the department this year. Maryellen Malek, Laura Chen, and Margie Smith have given emotional and administrative sustenance at key moments in the past year. More recently, both my undergraduate class and graduate seminar read versions of this text. Both classes were forthcoming with advice and responses. The undergraduate students are Toni Peebles, Eric Liederbach, Julia Gottlieb, Evelyn Protano, Chris Kazacs, and Alex Dodson. The graduate seminar included Marie Jorittsma, Laurie Silverberg, Mae Campanella, Charles Carson, Jennifer Ryan, Jennifer Noakes, Cynthia Murtaugh, Greg Robinson, Tim Ribchester, and Kate Thomas.

Phil Bohlman of the University of Chicago invited me to participate in this book project, and Michael Bakan has been a patient and supportive series editor. Alicia Merritt and Michelle Trader at ABC-CLIO have been superb at every level, as has the copyeditor,

Carol Estes. Eugene Lew at the University of Pennsylvania has once again outdone himself with technical guidance and absolute kindness in enabling me to compile the compact disc.

Research over the past decade has been generously funded by the Center for Science Development (Pretoria), the University of Natal Research Foundation, and the University of Pennsylvania's Research Foundation and Department of Music. None of these institutions is responsible for views expressed in this book.

Finally, my immediate family. My parents, Douglas and Avril, have been extremely supportive, spending numerous days and weekends taking care of my son Zachary so that I could write more intensively during the semesters. My husband, Eric, and Zachary have spent huge amounts of time together in the past few months as I have scrambled to get the book completed. My deepest sense of love and gratitude extends to the two of you. And we await with eager expectation the possibility of welcoming another child into our family in the near future.

South African Music

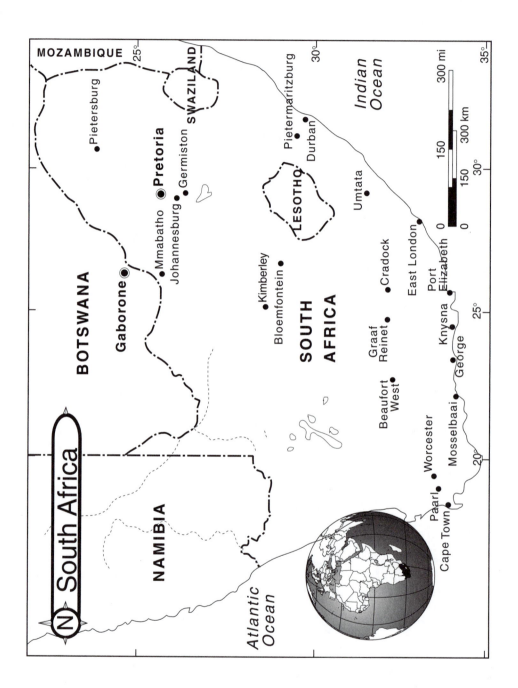

South Africa

MOZAMBIQUE

SWAZILAND

BOTSWANA

NAMIBIA

SOUTH AFRICA

LESOTHO

Pietersburg

Pretoria
Mmabatho
Johannesburg
Germiston

Gaborone

Kimberley

Bloemfontein

Pietermaritzburg
Durban

Umtata

Cradock
Graaf
Reinet

East London
Port
Elizabeth
Knysna
George

Beaufort
West

Mosselbaai

Worcester

Paarl

Cape Town

Atlantic
Ocean

Indian
Ocean

25°

30°

35°

30°

25°

20°

N

300 mi

300 km

150

150

0

0

Chapter One

South African Music

A Century of Traditions in Transformation

Transforming Musical Traditions

The year 1994 must surely stand as a momentous year in South African and, indeed, in global history, for it was the year that South Africa finally moved towards a fully democratic dispensation for all her people. With this date in mind, I begin this chapter by referring you to the photograph on the book's cover. It is a picture of a group of black South African women singing, their hands extended in the air. The singers are dressed in brightly colored robes. The choir uniforms are not just arbitrary colors, however. These women have wrapped their bodies in the design and colors of the South African flag, the symbol of the birth of a new nation in 1994. This newly designed flag is also a reminder of the new South African constitution, one of the most progressive in the world, which was hammered out in the 1990s to protect men, women, and children of all races and creeds from violation by other citizens and by the state itself. Both the constitution and the flag are signs of newfound rights and freedoms, mostly achieved at great cost: many people were injured, abused, or killed in the fight for a new political dispensation in South Africa. Wrapping their bodies in the design and colors of the flag symbolizes the protection women hope will be guaranteed by the new flag. Both the flag and the constitution are now held to be sacred by all South Africans.

Because we are limited by what a visual image can tell us about song performance, the specific repertory being sung by these women is not self-evident. Nevertheless, from my deep knowledge of the history and abundant activity focused on vocal performance in contemporary South Africa, I suggest there are two interrelated possibilities: *makwaya* (South African choral music) and gospel. Their roots in nineteenth-century South African culture are the same. In the first context, the women are completing a longer choral performance by singing South Africa's new national anthem, a blending of two previously distinct anthems. The first, "*Nkosi Sikelel'iAfrika*" ("God Bless Africa"), composed by the relatively obscure nineteenth-century composer Enoch Sontonga, is sung in a combination of three South African languages: Zulu, Xhosa, and Sotho. The second, "Die Stem" ("The Call"), was composed in the early twentieth century and is sung in both English and Afrikaans (a South African language that developed out of cultural contact with Europeans in the colonial era). While both anthems draw on aspects of the European hymn, arranged in four-part harmony, South African composer Mzilikazi Khumalo skillfully combined these two anthems into a single unit as South Africans united into a new nation in 1994.

In the second scenario, these women are singing religious music in a gospel style, drawing on the models of African American gospel music heard on radio and television, especially in the last decade, but made to sound more South African through the use of local languages and singers. From the buildings I can see in the background, I am guessing that the performance may have occurred on the steps of the Great Hall at the University of the Witwatersrand in Johannesburg, particularly important in the struggle against apartheid as a site where people invoked the principles of academic freedom to fight battles against racial segregation. It might also have been situated on the steps in front of the Union Buildings in Pretoria, a monument initially built to celebrate the unity of English- and Afrikaans-speaking peoples of European descent in the early twentieth century, but now a building that has been covered afresh with the memories of the inauguration of the first black South African president, Nelson Mandela, on May 10, 1994, mass mediated to the wider world through the channels of Cable News Network (CNN) and the South African Broadcast Corporation (SABC). (To grasp a sense of the significance of the event, watch the Mandela documentary, *Mandela: Son of Africa, Father of a Nation* [1996].)

Choral performance—sacred and secular—has a long history in South Africa. Collective singing was a central dimension of life in pre-colonial Africa. With the arrival of the first missionaries from Britain, Europe, and later the United States, it assumed a more specific kind of arrangement: the four-part harmony structure of the European Christian hymn and its various incarnations manifest in the Great Awakening spiritual movements of the eighteenth and nineteenth centuries in England and the United States. This means that for almost two centuries in some parts of South Africa (the Eastern Cape in particular), black South African school children and churchgoers have been immersed in the religious and classical repertories of Europe. Through the travels of various entertainers and artists to South Africa and local copies of and improvisations on these performances, the sacred and secular popular songs of nineteenth-century America have became intertwined in South African performance history and practice.

In 1994, I caught a glimpse of the complexity of this history, with its mix of nineteenth-century popular and religious choral repertories, the ones brought to black South Africans by European and American missionaries. My father, a Presbyterian minister, was inducted as Moderator of the Presbyterian Church of Southern Africa in the Great Hall at the University of the Witwatersrand. In an attempt to articulate a kind of racial and cultural reconciliation, a more African form within the largely Scottish-derived rituals and traditions of the Presbyterian Church, my father asked me to help him "Africanize" the induction. We planned three kinds of performance.

First, we invited a marimba ensemble from a Catholic seminary in KwaZulu Natal. Marimbas, a musical tradition borrowed from Zimbabwe, were used to re-Africanize Catholic liturgical practices in that country, and also initiated by then-Catholic priest (now secular ethnomusicologist) Father Dave Dargie in the Eastern Cape to create a similar kind of liturgical practice there. Father Dargie was also responsible for introducing to 1990s European world music festivals the overtone singing of Xhosa women from his parish in the Eastern Cape.

Second, I arranged a version of a recorded segment of the *Missa*

Luba, a hybrid mass written by a European missionary working in Kenya but drawing on vernacular language and musical style. A racially diverse choir representing several Presbyterian churches performed the arrangement.

A black South African choir from Mamelodi Presbyterian Church was asked to sing a piece of their own choice as the third element in our attempt to created a more hybrid, or culturally inclusive style for the induction. All three traditions inserted into the induction were "invented" or appropriated, borrowed, or indigenized in some way.

It was this last segment, the "own choice" piece, that was most revealing in articulating the relationship between mission and popular culture in the nineteenth century. The choir performed all their music at our joint rehearsals using tonic solfa, that is, all pitch was rendered using the syllables doh re mi fah soh la ti doh. At the final rehearsal, the day before the induction, the choir finally sang the words of their song. To my surprise, they had selected a completely secular piece, a Stephen Foster song about love and romance, for a truly sacred context. I was taken aback, having expected a selection with religious words. The choice, nonetheless, was a gentle reminder to me of the relationship between nineteenth-century mission work and the "civilizing" project, what anthropologist Jean Comaroff (1985) has termed the "colonization of consciousness." Mission work was not simply about converting black South Africans to Christianity but to the ways of European "civilization" as well. Because it was the same people who introduced Stephen Foster songs and mission hymns, how were black South Africans, who did not draw the same boundaries between sacred and secular as we have created, to make the distinction? All "civilized" singing, sacred and secular, was foreign at the outset. The same four-part harmony style was used in both sacred and secular songs: it was only the words that differed. Those who did not speak English did not understand them anyway. We can begin to understand why those in contact with early missionaries simply did not draw a distinction between repertories. This relationship between mission work and the civilizing project is one of the themes that is central to an understanding of much South African performance in the twentieth century.

For much of the twentieth century, then, European and American forms were the models for black South Africans singing in four-part harmony with bodies taut and voices strained. In the 1980s, however, youth choirs began to select their music from the mass media, opting for what has been defined as the "more African" gospel performance, which allows for greater bodily movement, vocal inflection, solo performances with group support, and increased freedom in the use of the voice. In this image the African body and voice, so often beaten and silenced by the old regime, are similarly symbolic of newly achieved political, cultural, and musical power. In the 1990s, flowing, robe-like choir uniforms began to replace the tighter fitting, less flexible "European" buttoned blouses and skirts of earlier, more formal choirs. The clothing has become freer, more "African." Similarly, the choral repertory and style have shifted in the last decade. Both the body and the voice imagined in the photograph on the book's cover signal newly found social and political liberation.

Defining Twentieth-Century Musical Tradition and Travel

Clearly South African music, even in the most hallowed performance traditions, is what Cameroon saxophonist Manu Dibango calls "a music of encounters." In other words, "traditional" music cannot be thought of as music that never changes. While a few South African traditions remained fairly intact through the early twentieth century, relatively isolated from major forces of change, some music labeled "traditional" in the 1990s was music that sounded quite different from its ancestral forms performed earlier in the twentieth century. This is particularly true with the music that moved to the cities and was transformed by urban experience. This music called "traditional" by South Africans may in fact seem to be quite "modern" to those of us outside of South Africa. So, for example, gumboot dancing and *maskanda* guitar playing are two genres of performance South African musicians define as "traditional" that may not sound so to our ears. After all, gumboot dancers wear black Wellington boots, which are something like the rubber work boots or fishing boots used in the United States. *Maskanda* performers play on non-African instruments like the guitar and the concertina.

These are not "pure" tradition, but more hybrid forms of traditional performance that have emerged out of encounters, some good, some bad, with European music. Some might call these "invented" traditions, that is, traditions with roots in the local environment but clearly transformed or inserted anew into a particular cultural milieu at a specific historical moment, often for political purposes. Nevertheless, it is important that we respect the views of cultural insiders in our encounters with this music, even if we can see that a larger historical narrative might need to be added to understand the claim of "traditional" performance.

Related to this idea of "tradition" as always in flux, constantly responding to changes in the larger political, economic, and cultural environment, is the central notion of travel. If you know nothing about South Africa, you might be surprised by how cosmopolitan its citizens are, even the most rural of people. Let me give you a brief example of what I mean. In July 2002 I returned to South Africa to visit *ibandla lamaNazaretha,* the religious community I had worked with in the early 1990s. As I entered the village, one of a handful of white South Africans on the site, someone called out to me, "Hey, what about September eleventh?" I was stunned. Out in the remote regions of KwaZulu Natal, among people I had no idea knew anything about what had happened in the world at large in the past twelve months, I was confronted by the amazing sense of a world beyond the borders of South Africa. If I had been in rural America, I would not have been surprised, but this was rural South Africa. I wondered how many people in rural parts of other countries would know, for example, who Nelson Mandela was. It was a gentle reminder to me of the depth of openness of South Africans to the outside world, a characteristic of the country and its citizens, particularly from the 1990s on. But that openness is also a result of the long history of European colonization and engagement with South Africans from the mid-seventeenth century. This engagement might be thought of as a plethora of forms of travel: in person, in product, and more recently, virtual travel.

Europeans who began traveling to South Africa in the seventeenth century came on their way to other places. First explorers and traders, then fortune seekers and entertainers arrived with stories of faraway places. These experiences and encounters began to be mapped onto the South African landscape and culture. So Bushman rock painters provide records of the encounters between Europeans and Bushman, between gun cultures and bow cultures. The global travels of Christy Minstrels in the nineteenth century have marked themselves indelibly into the performance consciousness of all kinds of black migrant musical cultures (Erlmann 1992). Eventually, Europeans came to colonize, and missionaries came to proselytize. Each arrival brought new ideas, new languages, and new cultural practices. Some were coercive, some less obtrusive, but all became entwined in the shaping of what we now call South African music and culture.

Travel in all its forms—physical, imagined, and virtual—might be a central characteristic of what it means to be South African, but the right to travel has not always been uncontested. Under the apartheid government, freedom of movement was curtailed by the state. It was monitored, policed, and closely guarded. For black South Africans this was true inside the country, as the state controlled the movement of migrant workers and people from different ethnic groups who desired to gather together. But it was also true for those seeking to travel abroad. Gifted scholars, performers, and athletes were frequently denied the right to travel when the state refused to grant them the appropriate documentation.

In this book, the travel motif assumes two contrasting possibilities, in music on the one hand, and in language on the other. The degree to which music, particularly from Europe and the United States, has traveled to other places during the twentieth century, particularly music recorded, broadcast, and, more recently, distributed through satellite networks. The combination of Hollywood's use of the nineteenth-century romantic orchestral format for its early sound tracks, the pervasiveness of the Christian hymn and its use of functional harmony in a homophonic texture, and the dissemination of American popular music created a homogenous musical language for global consumption. The stylistic homogeneity, coupled with the vivid images and store of human narratives produced in Hollywood, enabled many in the world to begin to think about music as a universal language, a language they could learn and make their own regardless of their home or place of origin. South Africans were some of those who absorbed this music and indigenized it in all manner of creative and imaginative ways. In this book, you will begin to see how this happened.

Contrasting with the near universal appeal and consumption of European and American music as a universal language is the problem of local languages that did not readily travel across the globe. South Africa has eleven official languages; English is just one of these. Even so, South African English is now so distinctive an *Oxford Dictionary of South African English* has been published, suggesting that English itself is only partially universal in its use and meanings. Thus, while South Africans might be open to taking in new sounds and styles from the outside, their own creative endeavors would not have traveled back to those metropolitan centers as easily if they used languages other than English. On the positive side, this lack of linguistic travel has led to the richness and diversity of South African languages that have kept South Africans and their music deeply rooted in their home culture. Though many have learned English as a second, third, or even fourth language, there remains a strong sense of culture and locality in knowing South African vernaculars like Zulu, Tswana, and Pedi. These languages are not conceived of as languages of international trade and travel—have you ever seen a Berlitz language course that taught Zulu or Pedi language skills? Although Zulu is not an international language, it is, nevertheless, the first language of at least five million South Africans, spoken by several million more, and related to two other languages, Ndebele (Zimbabwe) and Xhosa (Eastern Cape).

What are the consequences for South Africans of all this travel?

- South Africans generally have a remarkable sense of a world beyond the borders of their own country.
- They have a deep pride in the physical beauty of their country in comparison with other places.
- Those who lived through the 1990s are grateful for the relatively peaceful transition to democracy and exuberant about having Nelson Mandela as a world leader and hero.
- It is sometimes surprising to realize the profound sense of South Africa's relationship to global powers. South Africans will regularly compare their own achievements with those they imagine beyond their geographic borders.

- South Africa is a complex country, a place in some ways seemingly behind the times, but in others, remarkably prophetic. When they hear of the struggles abroad for movement towards multicultural democracies, South Africans have a sense that they have already been through these transformative moments and may be able to help others through the process.
- In the past decade South Africa, like so many other countries, has engaged with the new technologies of virtual communities: it is a country with culture and music on display through the worldwide web.
- South African traditions rarely remain the same: they are always fluid, in flux, and open to new possibilities.

South Africans have lived through tumultuous times. They live with great abundance on the one hand, and extreme impoverishment on the other. It is my belief that traditions of all kinds, and those of music specifically, have helped to stabilize and enable individuals and groups to move forward with a certain sense of rootedness and place.

South African Music and Apartheid

Ideas about and understanding of tradition, travel, and transformation in South African music provide a strong introductory framework for understanding this country and its musical performance. But it is surely apartheid that has had the most profound impact on all South Africans, and certainly on all musical traditions and production in the past century. Apartheid, legalized racial discrimination, was established by a body of laws made by a minority of people of European and British descent in response to their fears of living in a country where the majority of its people were of black African descent. The white minority was largely educated, while most black South Africans had had very little exposure to European forms of education. British mining interests controlled a large portion of the economy, and from 1948 through 1990, those of European descent, called Afrikaners, ran the government.

Any real understanding of musical performance in the twentieth century has to factor in the making and dismantling of the apartheid system of government. There can be no real understanding of twentieth-century South African performance without knowledge of the politics and struggles of everyday life. This means we must examine musical performance as situated in historical, cultural, and political contexts. For the remainder of this chapter I focus on the problem of apartheid and the complicity of the mass media in its structures. I begin with an introduction to the apartheid government: how it came into being, something of what it was like to live under its laws, and how it was finally dismantled. I then examine the use of the mass media in shaping the apartheid project—in some ways it was a very modern though certainly not progressive project, principally because of the way in which radio was positioned to reinforce state ideology (television first came to the country late in 1975). The music industry, though not state controlled, fit in with state ideology in order to survive economically. Films were largely imported, but the government monitored and censored all entertainment in the apartheid years.

Apartheid Legislation[1]

The year 1948 marked the coming to power of a group of Europeans whose ancestors had begun to settle in South Africa from the mid-seventeenth century. This period of settlement and colonization in South Africa is considerably earlier than in many other parts of Africa, an important point if you are to gain some sense of the depth of "Europeanization" of the region on one hand, but also in some ways, for the degree of "Africanization" of parts of its settler communities on the other. By extension, it means that African musical traditions are often deeply imbued with European musical instruments or forms, even though these traditions are now viewed as more African than European. Noteworthy, too, is the fact that while it is often assumed that apartheid has defined South Africa for its entire history, it did not become state policy until 1948 and began to be officially dismantled in the late 1980s. The political environment in South Africa, like that of the United States, underwent continuous transformation in the course of the twentieth century. Musical performance often reflected, resisted, or predicted these changes in remarkable ways. It is true, nonetheless, that ideas about linguistic, cultural, and racial difference and frequently extremely racist sensibilities characterized the colonization by Europeans of various parts of Africa, Asia, and the Americas, mostly in the nineteenth century.

The new rulers in 1948 called themselves the Afrikaner Nationalist Party; their goal, however, was not to forge a single nation out of the enormous diversity of South Africa's inhabitants. Even though white South Africans had fought a bloody conflict with each other in the Anglo-Boer War (1899–1902), where the English had confined many boer or Afrikaans women and children in concentration camps, killing thousands, the two groups created the Union of South Africa in 1910. In 1948 the Nationalist government sought to build on that union of people of British and European descent a nation for "white" people only. Building on earlier legislation made by the English-dominated South African government, the Nationalist plan for Bantu-speaking peoples, the numerical majority in South Africa, was to use them as labor in a rapidly growing modern economy based on agriculture and industry, but not to allow them permanent residence in white urban areas. This was modernity without its accompanying practice of democracy. While they might spend most of their lives working in the urban areas, the status of the Bantu-speaking people was always "temporary" and even that was permitted only with the correct documentation: all non-Europeans were required to carry the infamous "pass" on their person at all times or face jail time or deportation back to their "homeland."

The policy of apartheid has been called a kind of social engineering because what the Nationalist government increasingly forced on South Africa was the opposite of the more natural processes of social practice, of people engaging with each other despite racial, cultural, and linguistic differences. Where early South African history suggests far more racial and cultural mixing or creolization, particularly after the arrival of Europeans in what became the city of Cape Town, the Nationalist government in the mid-twentieth century stressed racial purity and separation to divide South Africans. It drew on ideas current in Germany with the emergence of

Adolf Hitler: national socialism, racial purity, and superiority. To expedite the creation of a society that conformed to these ideals, the Nationalist government introduced a series of laws starting in 1950 that tightened restrictions on non-Europeans and established strict geographical boundaries between people of different races, language, and culture.[2] By 1960, the framework of the apartheid regime was in place, even though apartheid was not comprehensively enforced until March of the year, when state forces massacred more than sixty black South Africans protesting against the pass laws, in what is now remembered as the Sharpeville Massacre.

You might be wondering why non-European South Africans allowed apartheid legislation to pass. There are several reasons. They were not equipped to beat the superior military force of the government, and they had no rights to protest because they were no longer considered citizens of the white parts of South Africa. Government-controlled radio was used as a weapon of apartheid, constructing a "Bantustan" mindset in its listeners, and vast illiteracy meant that few could read materials either in English or their home languages to acquire a sense of world opinion on apartheid. But this compliance is also partly explained by the sense of optimism amongst urbanized black South Africans and other people of color in the post-war period. Having just participated in the war effort on the side of the Allies, many were hopeful that South Africa would become more racially and culturally integrated. After all, there is nothing like a war to foster national sentiment and the longing for home by those sent abroad. Many South Africans were taken by complete surprise at the Nationalist Party victory in the 1948 elections; and the early apartheid legislation was not initially rigidly enforced.

So under the apartheid plan, the "real" homes of people of African descent were found in one of the nine "Bantustans" or "homelands" created by the Nationalist government on a small portion of the total landmass of the country: at one point, 80 percent of the population inhabited only 13 percent of the land. Those employed in urban areas entered the city and its surroundings under a series of laws aimed at "influx control," which at the very least, required all black South Africans to carry "passbooks" on their person at all times. (The nearest parallel in the United States is the use of one's driver's license as a form of identification that one carries around,

Apartheid Legislation, Made and Unmade (1948–1998)

1948   English-dominated United Party loses election and Afrikaner Nationalists come to power.

1949   Prohibition of Mixed Marriages Act is passed; mission schools for black South Africans come under scrutiny of Nationalist Party government.

1950   Immorality Act forbids sexual relations between whites and any people of color; Population Registration Act introduces legalized racial classification—White, Coloured, Native, and Asiatic; Group Areas Act divides the country into residential areas based on racial classification; Suppression of Communism Act defines "communist" as anyone hostile to the government; South African Communist Party dissolves; many join the African National Congress.

1951   Government legislation removes Coloureds from voters' roll; Bantu Authorities Act creates tribal and territorial authorities, re-tribalizing the African/Bantu population.

1952   Native Laws Amendment Act extends influx control to all urban areas, meaning all non-Europeans are required to carry a reference book (called "dompass"—stupid pass) of 96 pages detailing work and residence rights; the Defiance Campaign, in which women protest the pass laws, begins.

1953   Public Safety Act enables governor general to declare states of emergency and rule by decree.

1954   Native Resettlement Act allows for forced removal of black residents from Sophiatown, Johannesburg, over five years. Bantu education legislation removes black education from the control of the missions and places it in the hands of the apartheid government.

1955   African National Congress draws up Freedom Charter.

1956   South African Amendment Act removes 45,000 Coloured voters from electoral rolls; Industrial Coalition Act reserves certain skilled jobs for whites; government tries 156 ANC activists for treason in what becomes known as the Treason Trial.

1957   Union Jack is removed as dual official flag of South Africa.

(continues)

Apartheid Legislation (continued)

1958   National Party wins large majority in first all-white election; women protest the pass laws, and about 2,000 are arrested.

1959   South African president Hendrik Verwoerd launches the "independent homelands" project creating separate areas for each tribal/cultural group: for example, Transkei for Xhosa, Zululand for Zulus; Extension of University Education Bill excludes all "nonwhites" from white universities and creates separate universities for blacks, Indians, and Coloureds; Pan Africanist Congress (PAC) is formed with strong black-consciousness focus.

1960   Police fire on PAC-inspired march against pass laws (Sharpeville Massacre), killing 60, wounding 178; Bantu Radio is established; United Nations Security Council calls on South African government to end apartheid.

1961   South Africa is proclaimed a republic; ANC president Albert Luthuli receives Nobel Peace Prize; Treason Trial ends after four years, with all 156 ANC members found guilty.

1963   General Law Amendment Act allows police to arrest and detain suspects for 90 days without trial; police capture ANC underground leadership, including Nelson Mandela, Govan Mbeki, and Walter Sizulu, and all are charged with sabotage (punishable by death without appeal); Transkei becomes self-governing.

1964   Mandela and others are sentenced to life in prison; South Africa is banned from participation at Olympic Games because of apartheid.

1965   Bantu Laws Amendment Act denies 7 million black people the right to live inside South Africa except as temporary dwellers.

1967   Defence Amendment Act requires white South African men to undertake military service; Terrorism Act defines terrorism as anything that threatens law and order, and gives government unlimited power to arrest, detain, and try without jury.

1968   Black Consciousness Movement is constituted with Steve Biko as its first president.

Apartheid Legislation (continued)

1969   Bureau of State Security is established with wide investigative powers; newspapers are prohibited from reporting on
Bureau activities.

1970–1980s   Trade union and anti-apartheid activity; South
African Defense Force activity in surrounding countries.

1970   Bantu Homelands Citizenship Act makes all black South
Africans citizens of a tribal homeland, regardless of their
place of birth.

1972   Bophutatswana, Ciskei, and Lebowa become independent
homelands, with the KwaZulu part of present-day KwaZulu
Natal as semi-autonomous.

1976   Television comes to South Africa; Soweto schoolchildren
protest Afrikaans as medium of instruction (Soweto Uprising) and police fire on them, killing many and sparking
months of protest countrywide.

1977   Steve Biko is detained under Terrorism Act and dies in jail
of brain injuries.

1983   United Democratic Front (UDF) is formed to coordinate
resistance inside South Africa; United Nations resolves to
blacklist foreign entertainers traveling to South Africa and
Sun City.

1984   Archbishop Desmond Tutu is awarded Nobel Peace Prize;
Tutu and others renew call for economic sanctions against
South Africa.

1985   Political protesters are fired on; indefinite state of emer-
gency declared; Congress of South African Trade Unions
(COSATU) is formed; Paul Simon travels in secret to South
Africa to record with South African musicians.

1986   Pass Laws, Prohibition of Mixed Marriages, and Prohibition
of Political Interference acts all abolished; U.S. Congress
resolves to declare blanket economic sanctions against
South Africa; *Graceland* album released.

1987   Political turbulence in KwaZulu Natal intensifies.

1988   Church leaders begin to assume role as spokesmen for
political organizations.

(continues)

Apartheid Legislation (continued)

1990   State president F. W. de Klerk unbans political organizations, including ANC and PAC, announces release of Mandela; Separate Amenities Act repealed; state of emergency lifted.

1991–1992   CODESA I and II (Convention for a Democratic South Africa), vehicle to guide South Africa towards a democratic dispensation, is succeeded by the Negotiating Council, the council that will draft the new constitution.

1993   With old government still in power, Transitional Executive Council is formed to oversee transition to democracy.

1994   First free democratic elections held April 27–29; Nelson Mandela is elected first black president of South Africa, inaugurated May 10.

1995   Truth and Reconciliation Commission is called for by Mandela and legislated by South African Government of National Unity with the Promotion of National Unity and Reconciliation Act, No. 24, 1995.

1998   Thabo Mbeki is elected second black South African president.

---

but "non-Europeans" in South Africa were constantly asked for their documentation and immediately punished by police if they failed to produce it.) Black South Africans were allowed to stay in the urban areas only if they had had ten years of permanent employment with a single employer, had lived in the area for fifteen years (and could prove it), or had been born there. If they fulfilled none of these requirements, they were not permitted to stay longer than seventy-two hours, after which they would be "deported" back to the "homeland."

The rhetoric used by the Afrikaner Nationalists was one of "separate development": each cultural group would develop along its own lines and on its own terms in its separate areas. Each "homeland" was identified by language and culture: Zululand was for Zulu people, who must speak Zulu as their mother tongue and practice Zulu customs and traditions; Pondoland for the amaMpondo people;

Transkei for the Xhosa people; Bophutatswana for the Tswana. To this end, the government appointed "tribal" chiefs and administrators of these "homelands." They were paid by the Nationalist government and were largely puppets of the white government. At times, their political power was reinforced with the military power of the Nationalist government, though this was not acknowledged publicly.

European South Africans owned most of the land in South Africa, in both rural and urban areas. Since agricultural production constituted a core piece of the South African economy, farms required black labor to function efficiently. So the apartheid government created a set of laws that enabled white farmers to employ black laborers while monitoring and controlling their movement. A black South African could stay on a white farm (that is, a farm located in areas designated for whites only) if employed by a farmer, but there was a quota system to control the numbers of black workers on farms. It was on these farms that many of the more traditional Zulu-speaking men first heard the sounds of the banjo, ukelele, guitar, concertina, guitar, and violin. Typically, they heard European folk music on these instruments; some might even have learned to play this music for the Europeans. Ultimately, it was this encounter between the Afrikaans farmer, or "boer," and his black laborers (often house servants), that came to constitute one strand of the history of *maskanda,* a genre of migrant performance discussed in Chapter Four.

Even those considered racially and culturally closer to whites—officially labeled "Coloured" and "Asiatic" by the government—were separated from their white neighbors in urban areas by Group Areas legislation. Coloured people were primarily those of mixed racial heritage, many of whom had come as slaves from Central Africa and Asia but who were born out of interracial relationships with European settlers in South Africa. The Asiatic group was largely comprised of Indians from India who had initially arrived in the nineteenth century, either as indentured laborers or as free passengers. The Group Areas legislation allowed them to reside and work in urban areas, but they lived largely in racially segregated residential spaces.

To effect these new social divisions, millions of South Africans were forcibly moved from racially integrated into segregated areas. By 1972, 1.8 million people of African descent; 600,000 categorized as Coloured, Indian, and Chinese; and 40,000 whites had been removed to facilitate the Group Areas Act. The government had brought into being about twenty separate laws that enabled forced removals, the harshest of which prevented black South Africans from requesting a court interdict to prevent their removal. Sophiatown (Johannesburg), District Six (Cape Town), and Cato Manor (Durban) are perhaps the best-known communities destroyed through these processes. Composers have inscribed the memory of at least two of them in musicals written about District Six and Mkhumbane (Cato Manor).

State Broadcasting

In his much-cited book *Imagined Communities: On the Origins and Spread of Nationalism* (1983), Benedict Andersson argues that the sense of being a part of a nation is something that people imagine rather than really experience, and they do so through the mass media. No one can actually know everyone in the country, and there is little face-to-face interaction between citizens. Instead, citizens imagine connections through participating in collective rituals at the same time of day, albeit not in the same place. So, for example, many in the nation read the same news in the daily newspapers on the same day. Alternatively, the six o'clock news is listened to by millions of people simultaneously, each in their own spaces. Everyone consumes the same news and shapes their understanding of the world based on the same information. The knowledge garnered through the citizens' habitual, common activities fosters an imagined sense of national unity.

Andersson's theory works for the apartheid government's idea of the nation insofar as it is an idea promulgated by the media. But instead of newspapers (most South Africans were illiterate), radio was the medium that the apartheid government used to engineer a new kind of social order. Rather than articulating national unity, however, radio was used to articulate difference between smaller groups of people, largely determined by language use. It was a remarkably expensive policy, because so many languages are spoken in South Africa (recall that the new political dispensation lists eleven official languages and many more unofficial ones). Each language had its own radio station and program content. This idea of the nation hearkened back to nineteenth-century ideas of a cultural and linguistic community: all Zulu speakers, for example, were thought to practice the same traditions and were targeted as a single radio audience on what eventually became Radio Zulu. This idea of national boundaries might be likened to that of the present day European community: German-speaking people live in Germany, Italian speakers in Italy, French speakers in France, English speakers in England.

Zulu-speaking announcers were used on Zulu language programs, reinforcing the sense that the news, music, and ideas were truly "Zulu" rather than "European" because they were spoken in the Zulu language. Listeners identified with the announcer, not because they knew him or her personally, but because they identified more generally with the sound of the voice and the language of the message. Strict rules governed performers' behavior, program content, and mode of presentation. There was a hierarchy of value attached to whiteness over blackness, and much greater economic support provided for the media and cultural interests of whites than for the "traditional practices" of black South Africans. Although not every black South African bought into the ideologies of apartheid expounded on Bantu Radio, it is not difficult to understand why a significant proportion did.

Radio Music and Apartheid

There were two distinctive agendas for European and "non-European" radio programming as set out by the South African Broadcast Corporation (SABC). Using the British Broadcast Corporation's (BBC) class-based model for radio, the SABC sought to educate and enlighten its audiences, to maintain social control by not engaging with any political troublemakers, and to program according to Christian values and morals. In addition, all events in South Africa were portrayed positively, and programs were developed that celebrated the excellent heritage and culture of Europeans. Any negative event in South Africa was blamed on outside forces, especially the infiltration of communists and their ideology into the country.

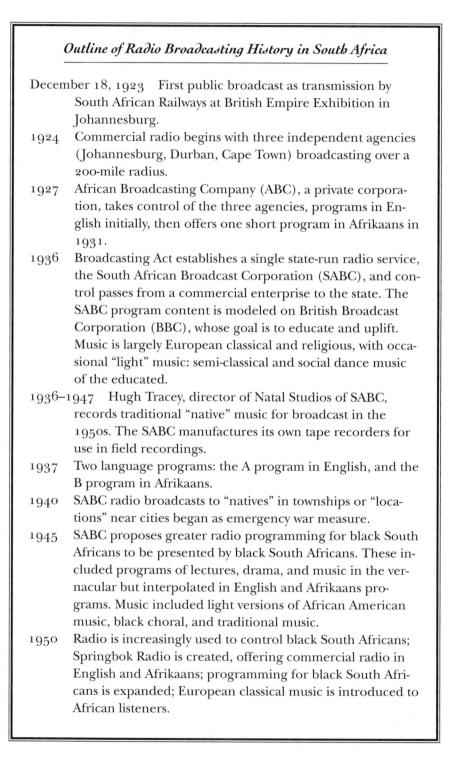

Outline of Radio Broadcasting History in South Africa

December 18, 1923   First public broadcast as transmission by
South African Railways at British Empire Exhibition in
Johannesburg.

1924   Commercial radio begins with three independent agencies
(Johannesburg, Durban, Cape Town) broadcasting over a
200-mile radius.

1927   African Broadcasting Company (ABC), a private corporation, takes control of the three agencies, programs in English initially, then offers one short program in Afrikaans in
1931.

1936   Broadcasting Act establishes a single state-run radio service,
the South African Broadcast Corporation (SABC), and control passes from a commercial enterprise to the state. The
SABC program content is modeled on British Broadcast
Corporation (BBC), whose goal is to educate and uplift.
Music is largely European classical and religious, with occasional "light" music: semi-classical and social dance music
of the educated.

1936–1947   Hugh Tracey, director of Natal Studios of SABC,
records traditional "native" music for broadcast in the
1950s. The SABC manufactures its own tape recorders for
use in field recordings.

1937   Two language programs: the A program in English, and the
B program in Afrikaans.

1940   SABC radio broadcasts to "natives" in townships or "loca-
tions" near cities began as emergency war measure.

1945   SABC proposes greater radio programming for black South
Africans to be presented by black South Africans. These included programs of lectures, drama, and music in the vernacular but interpolated in English and Afrikaans programs. Music included light versions of African American
music, black choral, and traditional music.

1950   Radio is increasingly used to control black South Africans;
Springbok Radio is created, offering commercial radio in
English and Afrikaans; programming for black South Afri-
cans is expanded; European classical music is introduced to
African listeners.

Radio Broadcasting History (continued)

1952   Rediffusion service for elite black South Africans, to "provide native with entertainment in his own home . . . to contribute to prevention of crime . . . and towards the education of the Bantu" (cited in Hamm 215). Traditional music
is used to keep a record of dying traditions and maintain
pride in culture. No black working-class popular music is
aired until 1960. Initially, 4,300 homes subscribe to rediffusion service; by 1956, 14,000 homes subscribe.

1959   Promotion of Bantu Self-Government Act, with radio integral to this process. Radio viewed as "constant companion
of man in modern times in all his activities, moulds his intellect and his way of life." Radio broadcasting to express
"unique South African way of life" (SABC Annual Report
1959, 4).

1960   Bantu Radio established with revised Broadcast Act. Cre-
ation of Bantu Program Control Board expands Zulu and
Xhosa services; new services to Sotho, Tswana, Venda, and
Tsonga listeners; increased reception areas for all services.

1962   Black South Africans own 103,000 radio receivers; by 1968,
2 million own sets.

1966   Forty-five percent of high school seniors listen to LM Radio
broadcast out of Lourenco Marques in Mozambique, cir-
cumventing the controls of SABC, which refused to play
British and American rock and pop music as LM Radio did.
Twenty percent listen to Springbok Radio, nineteen percent to Afrikaans Radio, and four percent to English radio
stations.

Late 1960s   Bantu Radio broadcasts in seven African languages,
twenty-four hours a day.

1972   SABC takes control of LM Radio and renames it Radio 5.

1976   Television comes to South Africa with two hours of evening
programming, English- and Afrikaans-language programming on alternate evenings (7–9 P.M.). No significant television music programming at this stage.

Late 1970s   Bantu Radio's audience is 5 million listeners.

(continues)

Radio Broadcasting History (continued)

1980s   SABC plan to completely dominate the airwaves is fully functional, molding the intellect and daily life of South Africans. But independent radio stations begin to broadcast from so-called independent states, or Bantustans, including Capital Radio (1979) from Transkei, Music Radio 702 from Bophutatswana, numerous Christian radio services, the BBC, and Voice of America on shortwave.

1990s   A complete turnaround for the SABC, which now airs previously silenced voices of musicians and political figures from liberation movements on SABC radio.

1994   Creation of Independent Broadcast Authority, established to work through the transition to democracy.

1995   Proposed legislation for introduction of local music quotas by Independent Broadcast Authority to promote the local music industry in South Africa and ward off the recolonization of airwaves by foreign music and companies. (Adapted from Andersson 1981, Baines 1998, and Hamm 1996)

This was the Cold War period, the era of McCarthyism and the fear of communism in the United States.

During this period, music comprised a fair proportion of radio programming for all constituencies. For those of European descent (English- and Afrikaans-speaking) it consisted of religious and European classical music, along with some American and British popular music. In the 1950s, rock 'n' roll was considered morally unacceptable, so it was not permitted on radio. Instead, light music from the pre-rock times was regularly played. Program titles from the period focused on beautiful melodies, particularly those embedded in the swing dance era. Only the more commercial Springbok Radio, which broadcast in English and Afrikaans, aired contemporary South African and international popular music, though it also steered away from rock 'n' roll. Jazz occupied a complex position on European radio in South Africa. The traditional Dixie and swing eras were adequately represented, but with the arrival of bebop, the more experimental "black" form from the United States, jazz programming went in and out of favor with radio producers and the team of censors working behind the scenes.

In devising radio programs for black South Africans, the SABC promoted differences between black and white South Africa. These distinctions carried economic and political benefits. Politically, Bantu Radio was of strategic importance to Prime Minister Hendrik Verwoerd's plans for implementing what has come to be known as Grand Apartheid, beginning in 1958. Radio's purpose was to make black South Africans concede to their place in the Bantustans, where they should relish their traditions and not create political havoc. Radio was also used as a medium to increase the sale of commodities to a growing number of black consumers. However, radio was a new technology to black South Africans, and listening habits were completely foreign. To draw black listeners to the radio, the SABC, with loans from the government, installed high-quality, good-reception radio technology in the mid-1960s to expand the reach of the radio propaganda. And they did so using the newer FM transmission, because it allowed a number of radio frequencies to be used simultaneously.

Music on Bantu Radio stations differed in purpose and style from that played on European stations. Like the European programming, black radio had to adhere to Christian ideals and not undermine national interests. Music played on Radio Zulu should be culturally consistent with a reified idea of Zulu tradition and culture. So, too, for Sotho and Tswana music. Only Zulu language song texts were used for Radio Zulu, Xhosa for Transkei Radio, and so forth. All song texts were subject to scrutiny from a control/censorship board before being aired. The goal was to make the music appealing to listeners so that black South Africans would tune in, digest the messages about traditional culture and homelands, and buy the products advertised.

The 1962 SABC Annual Report summarizes the musical content of Bantu Radio programs in three categories: popular, traditional, and choral music. As Charles Hamm (1996) remarks, enormous amounts of airtime were given to traditional music, the perfect music to articulate one's "tribal" identity. The SABC invested significant resources recording and broadcasting the traditional music of groups represented by its stations. The idea was to capture the ears of traditionalists in rural areas or migrant workers moving between rural and urban areas. Urbanized black South Africans had largely rejected their traditional pasts as a result of the mission influence. They were fed two kinds of more Westernized music: choral performances in the vernacular and popular music. The most important South African genres aired on Bantu Radio from the early 1960s were *isicathamiya* (but without any political references in the lyrics); the close-harmony vocal music of groups like Joseph Shabalala's Ladysmith Black Mambazo; African jazz; the more commercial sounds of American swing jazz and film music (often translated into the vernacular); *kwela* music, the hugely popular pennywhistle music developed in the streets of Johannesburg that became popular in Britain and the United States in the 1960s; and finally, the radio-produced sounds of South African "jive" (later known as *mbaqanga*). This is the music that best served the needs of Radio Bantu: the text-less instrumental music was without political inference, and the vocal jive drew on the traditional images and language of a group to reinforce "tribal" identity.

Though ethnomusicologists have not specifically addressed the manner in which Bantu radio shaped the lives of the thousands of migrant workers, particularly from the 1960s, there can be no doubt that with the availability of personal wireless systems, radio created vital connections between urban and rural homes. Black South African migrant workers moved between rural and urban areas, never really belonging in the place where they spent most of their lives. They owned no property and often had no place of residence. The place where you were supposed to belong, the "homeland," you only visited for a maximum sustained period of one month a year. Longing for home is a common theme in the lyrics of the primary musical genres of migrant workers: *isicathamiya*, gumboot dance, and *maskanda*. Radio united the two social spaces. Migrant men and women heard the same radio programs at home in the city and at home in the reserve. The presence of Radio Zulu/Ukhozi Radio in the living and workspaces of people I have worked with in my research suggests that radio is central to everyday life in both town and countryside. I remember hoping, when I spent time with Shembe girls in *ibandla lamaNazaretha*, that I might hear them singing together as they went about their daily tasks at *Ebuhleni*. But the only voices I heard in song through much of the time I spent with them in July 1991 were those streaming from Radio Zulu!

In post-apartheid South Africa, the focus of radio broadcasting has shifted dramatically. In addition to continued programming in English and Afrikaans, nine African language radio stations were designated by the Independent Broadcast Authority (IBA) in 1994. This meant that stations like Radio Zulu continued to operate using Zulu as the primary medium of communication, but in an attempt to distance the stations from the prior associations with language, culture, and "national" identity, the stations changed their names. So Radio Zulu became Ukhozi Radio, the station of the Black Mountain Eagle. These radio stations are now programmed to reflect greater cultural diversity (Radio Zulu began producing programs that dealt with African indigenous religion, Christianity, and Islam over the exclusive focus on a narrowly defined Christianity under apartheid). The continued focus on African languages reflects a concern for the nurturing of linguistic diversity and development.

A major challenge in post-apartheid South Africa has been to generate local music products that can compete with, and perhaps be sold to, international markets (Baines 1998). Musically, the IBA recommended in 1994 that the nascent music and television production industries be protected from foreign competition with the introduction of local music quotas required of public and commercial radio and television stations. The problem with much English-language radio broadcasting of popular music has been its dependence on foreign music imports for local music consumption. One of the problems in the growth of a specifically South African music scene, as we will explore below, has been the lack of music industry support, particularly from Gallo Records, the recording company with the longest history in South African musical production and consumption.

Imported Musical Entertainment

South Africa is a country whose population has felt rupture and division as a consequence of the government legislation listed above and the movement of peoples, either locally through labor migration or transnationally through immigration. But the gaps have frequently been closed and division transcended through the mass media and the products of the global entertainment industry. Purchasing products from the global centers of entertainment enabled South Africans to imagine alternatives to what increasingly became a politically oppressive and controlled social environment. As long as these media continued to be imported, South Africans still had a sense that they had some freedom of choice in the music they consumed and in the cultural milieu they participated in.

Nevertheless, South Africans responded in two ways to the impact of foreign music and media on the local scene: celebration and anxiety (Feld 2000).

On the celebratory side, the importation of foreign recordings and movies by the dominant recording interest, Gallo (Africa), and African Consolidated Theaters in the mid-twentieth century, for example, meant that South Africans could connect to the world outside. Local performers imitated the recordings and cultural models seen in Hollywood movies shown around Cape Town or Johannesburg, and these communities prided themselves on having their own Nat King Cole, Frank Sinatra, or Elvis Presley. American jazz, available for decades on local radio and on recordings, developed layers of meaning in South Africa. For liberal, English-speaking veterans of the World War II entertainment corps, jazz signified membership in an enlightened international community. For South African Indians, jazz suggested degrees of Anglicization and modernity. For mixed-race Pan-Africanists, it represented collective suffering, and for Afrikaner nationalists it embodied the devil. Knowledge of the jazz repertory gleaned from recordings also enabled South African musicians to connect with the international jazz world when they went into political exile in the late 1950s and early 1960s. Finally, jazz represented a force for integration of all race and language groups, a vision of the possibilities of a "rainbow nation" in both the middle and later years of the twentieth century.

On the darker, more anxious side, the mass media and recording industry were manipulated in very particular ways by the apartheid government: to limit South Africans' access to information and the outside world, to selectively record musicians, and to silence non-compliant voices. We now take a closer look at how commercial forms of sound recording and film worked in twentieth-century South Africa.

Sound Recordings

In his landmark study on black South African urban performing arts, *In Township Tonight!*, David Coplan suggests that from the earliest days, the transnational entertainment corporations realized the commercial potential of the urbanizing black workforce. On one hand, British but especially American films became a core part of the working-class experience among urban dwellers, across racial groups, from the 1920s. On the other, record companies like Pathe, HMV, Columbia, Decca, Brunswick, and Polydor all established subsidiaries or marketing channels in South Africa as early as the 1920s. Though there was only minimal recording of African traditional music in the early twentieth century, scholarly interest was sparked by the work of British- born South African Hugh Tracey. In 1929, Tracey, a musicologist, initiated his recording of African music with a field trip to Mozambique and Zimbabwe (see http://www.ilam.ru.ac.za). In the next two decades he would extend his recording significantly, working for the SABC and Gallo, funded by Ford and Carnegie. Clearly, commercial and scholarly interests overlapped considerably, even in the work of a musicologist like Tracey. At one point, Gallo agreed to fund Tracey's recording projects on condition that potential "hit" recordings would be given to Gallo to exploit commercially. Ultimately Tracey created an archive of his own, the International Library of African Music, as a resource for recording and research in African traditional music, separating out commercial from scholarly goals in his recording projects.

The South African Broadcast Corporation (SABC) also played a central role in recording local traditional music through its Transcription Series, geared towards radio audiences rather than the sale of recordings. Consistent with the ideology of apartheid, the SABC focused its efforts on Afrikaans folk music and *Boeremusiek*, local Afrikaans-language music for romantic crooning and social dancing, European classical music, and the folk music of "tribal" peoples. A writer for the SABC reported in 1952 on a recording trip made into the rural areas of present-day Northern Province. The ideas then current about "native tradition" are illustrated in the following excerpt—that the African and his singing were "tribal" and "pre-modern," while the European and his technology were modern and sophisticated.

> The South African Native has a song for everything . . . and everyday of the sun-baked year these melodies echo and re-echo through our hills and fade-away into the distance of the plains. . . . To do this [recording of traditional native music] successfully, we traveled in the giant recording van of the SABC to where the various tribes of the Bapedi nation have their towns . . . Only when one sees it personally can one appreciate the extent to which singing plays a part in the native national life. . . . We captured on magnetic tape about a dozen songs . . . Chief Maserumuli called his singers together with the aid of the microphone in the recording van. We came back laden with treasure for we had captured in that area of great scenic beauty something even greater. Contained in a dozen rolls of magnetic tape we had something [that] was far more dear to the Native heart than anything a camera could possibly produce. (*SABC Magazine,* September 26, 1952)

The mainstay of the local music-recording and publishing activity in South Africa in the twentieth century was Gallo (Africa). Eric Gallo began Gallo Records in 1932 when his father purchased the Gauteng agency of Brunswick Records (USA) in Johannesburg. Hugh Tracey of the International Library of African Music published his 200 LP series, *The Music of Africa,* with Gallo. Because the white, English-speaking purchasing community has always been quite small and closely allied with its "home" culture in Britain, Gallo rarely recorded original music in the English language, preferring to either import superior British recordings or, at most, to use South African voices singing British and American hits under license from the parent companies in Britain and the United States. Because of the relatively small consumer base, it simply was not profitable for Gallo to record English-language performance in South Africa. This is not to say that white South Africans did not use music as a vehicle for social and political protest. But those who did were never given recording contracts by Gallo, because the market for this music was too small to make a profit, and when performers did articulate any kind of criticism of the apartheid government, the music was immediately either censored or banned outright, foreclosing potential markets for this music.

Foreign recordings were first advertised in South Africa in 1912. These included several English language titles and one Afrikaans-language song, "Vat Jou Goed en Trek, Ferreira" (Trewhela 1980, 44). Although Gallo began experimenting with record pressing in the mid-1930s, all local recordings continued to be pressed in Britain and shipped to the port city of Cape Town, where they were distributed across the country by land or later by air travel. During World War II, it was almost impossible to import any foreign musical products. In 1949, Gallo opened its first pressing plant. In the first two months of production, Gallo manufactured 500,000 records (Trewhela 1980, 45). From the early 1950s, local production of foreign music, much of it translated into Afrikaans, created a vibrant market for sale to white Afrikaners in particular. In 1953 African Consolidated Sound Industries near Johannesburg opened a new Hi Fidelity record-production plant. This meant that by the early 1950s, the local market was shaped by both South African and imported products. There are advertisements in the local press for the international corporations including Columbia, Decca, EMI, His Masters Voice, Capitol Records, and South Africa's Gallo Records.

Independent Labels, Archival Reissues

Independent labels began to play a critical role in expanding the possibilities for recorded music in South Africa. Perhaps the most important label in the 1980s was Shifty Records, but there were numerous others. David Marks is an independent recording artist and producer in Durban. He has been involved in the recording of South African artists since the 1960s and has now an expansive archive of South African performance that was not aired nationally in the dark days of apartheid.

In post-apartheid South Africa, multinational entertainment corporations like Sony (Japan), BMG, and EMI Records, scared off by the cultural boycott and economic sanctions imposed in the 1980s by many countries, including the United States, have returned to South Africa. But numerous independent and locally owned labels emerged in the 1990s, and the Internet and worldwide web are used by those who have the computer and financial resources for advertising their groups, narrating histories and biographies, and selling their products. This book would have been very different if it had been written in the pre–worldwide web days. There is now much information available for perusal by anyone with Internet access.

One of the really interesting projects of Gallo Records in the 1980s and 1990s is the series of reissues the company created as a means of recuperating the lost voices of South Africa's musical past—voices lost both directly, through the harsh years of censorship and silencing of much musical performance by the apartheid government (see Allen 1996), and indirectly, when much of South Africa's rich musical heritage and abundant talent disappeared from public hearing with the move into exile of numbers of South African musicians from the late 1950s and through the early 1990s. The archivist at Gallo, American Rob Allingham, has made a significant contribution to the recuperation and revision of South African music history with his often collaboratively written liner notes enclosed in reissues in compact disc format of what remains of the highlights of South Africa's musical heritage.

Film

Although South Africa has never had a thriving state-supported film industry, there have been numerous film projects by South Africans about South African life and experience. For the most part, South Africans were fed a regular diet of British- and American-made films, from the times of the silent movies right through the apartheid era and into the present day. But in the late 1940s and 1950s, a handful of films were made by South Africans—white producers and directors of black talent—a few of which have recently been reissued and distributed through Villon Films in Canada. These films provide a rare glimpse into the vibrant performance culture created by black South Africans in response to their avid viewing of Hollywood films.

The postwar period was a period of enormous optimism, exuberance, and remarkable achievement for black South Africans. Many people of color had undertaken military service, traveling north into various parts of Africa to serve on the side of the Allies. They were optimistic that the freedoms they had witnessed in other parts of the world would soon be theirs. Several had participated in the Entertainment Corps and returned brimming with enthusiasm about the exciting music they had played and the skills they had acquired in the process. Many South Africans think of the 1950s as the pinnacle of artistic, literary, and cultural development of the country as a whole. It was the decade of growing collaboration musically between people of different racial groups. Few believed that the government would actually enforce the new apartheid legislation. After all, even political marches and rallies that called for equality and fairness for all South Africans were tolerated by the government in the 1950s.

Though they lacked formal institutions for music and dance training, South Africans' ears were finely tuned from generations of aural transmission, they listened closely to the records available for purchase, and they watched the gestures and costuming of American performers on the silver screen. These foreign models of performance were re-enacted live in South Africa's communities, often translated into vernacular performance aesthetics and languages.

White South Africans sought to harness this talent and enthusiasm on film and to export it to Britain in the postwar era in three films: *Jim Comes to Joburg/African Jim* (the Zulu man migrates from the rural to urban areas, encounters African Jazz and the commodities of recorded music, and becomes a performance star); *Song of Africa,* showcasing the "Zulu jazz" performance of a man who migrates from the rural areas to the urban, learns jazz, and teaches it, via the purchase of a gramophone and discs, to his rural people; and *Zonk!,* a film showcasing African variety and jazz performances typical of the 1940s and 1950s.

These films are treasured witnesses to a remarkable era in South African performance history brutally silenced by the apartheid government. They were, nevertheless, profoundly shaped by Hollywood versions of black performance culture, as was the case with the *Graceland* album, examined in the next chapter. Ideas about

"Africanness" in the modern world that traveled to the United States from West Africa were transformed through a period of two hundred years, then taken up by white performers, and finally returned to South Africa in a highly mediated version. In the twentieth century these were in turn taken up by black South Africans looking for models of new, more modern forms of Africanness. The impact of the Hollywood versions of black performance in South Africa are easily understood if you juxtapose a viewing of *Cabin in the Sky* with *Zonk!*, for example. In its time, *Cabin in the Sky* was one of the most popular films shown in South Africa.

Foreign Music Live

In the twentieth century, imported and locally produced recordings and the fairly regular visits of foreign musicians worked together to shape local culture in quite profound ways. I provide two examples here to illustrate the appeal to some South Africans of live performances "from overseas" on the one hand, and of new forms of sound-recording technologies on the other. They illustrate audience responses in two decades: the live performance in the 1930s and the recorded performance in the mid-1950s, though until the mid-twentieth century, both forms of imported performance intermingled in South Africa, especially for those in the growing urban centers. In Chapter 3 we discuss further the different ways in which various modes of performance shaped the musical experiences of musicians in 1950s Cape Town. In the two excerpts here we are given a rare glimpse into audience/consumer responses to both live and mediated musical cultures, of how the individual imagination worked in the process of listening to the music.

The first account is derived from the memories of white South African Percy Tucker on the visit of Gracie Fields to the country in the 1930s (Tucker 1997, 10). Percy Tucker was one of the central figures in shaping white South African entertainment in the twentieth century. He was involved in the world of local and international show business through most of that century, and in 1997 he published a thick book of his memories of his life. At the beginning of the book is a moving account of his first encounter with a living performer from Britain, Gracie Fields. Fields came to Tucker's hometown, Benoni, situated just outside of Johannesburg, and performed in the local movie theater, a common practice of the period.

Tucker recalls the palpable excitement he and his peers felt at the prospect of a live performance by Gracie Fields, of the absolutely transformative moment in his life when Fields entered the cinema stage.

> The lights dimmed, and the orchestra struck up. I don't remember what they actually played, but the entrance of Gracie Fields is as vivid in my mind as if it were yesterday. Tall, fair-haired and wearing a long blue dress, which sparkled under the spotlight, she seemed to me, aged seven, the most glamorous of creatures. (In reality, she was quite a plain woman, but with a very strong and inviting personality.)
>
> I suppose Gracie Fields was the first person to win my heart. As her clear and resonant voice soared over that cinema auditorium, my love of vocal music, which was to expand and embrace the whole spectrum of music over the years, was born, and my young soul was filled with total happiness. There was no holding me back after that. (Tucker 1997, 10)

The second is an account by black South African journalist Gideon Jay writing in *Zonk! The African People's Magazine* in the 1950s about how he listens to his recordings.

> Is there anything so wonderful as a gramophone record? That hard, flat circular piece of inert material that comes to life when you spin it and put the point of the needle in the groove. It comes to life and plays on your emotions, bringing joy or sorrow: you tap your feet or you shed a tear . . . How do you listen to YOUR records? In my case, I sit alone and spin the discs (usually in the small hours of the morning). I get the feeling that the artists come to me through the loudspeaker of my radiogram. They step out, take a bow and sing or play, and then step back through the speaker and the curtain comes down as the automatic switch clicks the turntable to a standstill. And I am left again with a cold disc. (*Zonk!*, December 1952, 45)

Gideon Jay's evocative description of his relationship to sound recordings gives us a wonderful sense of the ways in which memories of live performances were generalized to fit individual listening to similar kinds of performances, not as live but as recorded experiences.

Television

You might be wondering why there has been no discussion of television as a medium for propagating the ideals of apartheid. The simple reason is that television was not introduced into South Africa until the end of 1975 for white South Africans; a black television channel began broadcasting in 1982. Numerous explanations have been suggested for the absence of television. These include the view that the apartheid government did not want black South Africans to see any interracial relationships on television and that they did not believe that television was necessary in a country where people spend large amounts of time outdoors (the climate is conducive to outdoor activity almost year round), and that there was not a large enough consumer base (of white people only) to pay for the cost of introducing television and sustaining programming.

But the question of television for South Africans had been debated ever since it was first introduced in the United States. There is, for example, a lovely description of a television screen in a white South African entertainment magazine in 1954. Take note of the real awareness the writer displays of what is happening in the English-speaking world beyond South Africa.

> In the homes of millions of American, Canadians, and Britishers, particularly in the living room, there rests an innovation that has become an integral part of their mode of living—the television set . . . As you approach the receiver there is found a large grey area, round on some sets and rectangular on others. This area is framed by a light colored border and then a metallic frame. Commonly called the TV screen, this area is the face of a cathoid ray tube. It is covered by a plate of glass that extends to the metallic frame that is set into the cabinet. Below, or beside, the tube there are two dials. (*Bandstand Magazine*, April 1954, 16)

When television did finally come to South Africa in 1975–1976, the SABC-TV offered two hours of programming each evening between 7 and 9 P.M. The programs alternated between English-language shows and Afrikaans-language material. There was no significant music programming at that time other than the national anthem at the end of the transmission. Many of the Afrikaans-language programs were imported, largely American programs, whose English-language sound tracks were dubbed into Afrikaans. (When Zulu-language programs were introduced in the 1980s, it was not uncommon to see a show like "Love Boat" dubbed into Zulu—that is, a pleasure boat filled with white people all talking to each other in Zulu!) Most contemporary television programming, with the exception now of the growing number of satellite television channels, remains under the control of a much-transformed SABC. There are one or two local cable television channels available for those who wish to purchase the service. Music Television (MTV) is not generally available in South Africa, despite promises to the contrary, except on satellite channels. Since 1994, television in South Africa has been profoundly reshaped by the Independent Broadcast Authority's concern for the nurturing and protection of African languages, and the use of television as an educational tool for language development. The most popular television programs include local music programming, soap operas (foreign and local), game shows, and talk shows.

In the 1980s, the only music aired on television was found in imported films of European and American symphony orchestras and local Afrikaans *boeremusiek*—piano accordion music with a drum kit, bass, guitar, and singer, strongly influenced by the sounds of east European folk music translated into local idiom and language. But increasingly, local music has found its way into the channels of the national network. Sunday morning television features religious music of local and African-American gospel performers, along with popular music of the Asian diaspora. Several nights a week South African traditional music, including choral performances, *maskanda, mbaqanga,* other local-global fusions, and a wide selection of current, imported acts from Europe and the United States are made available to local viewers.

NOTES

1. While I provide a map, a schematic outline of South African political history, its human and physical geography, and a guide to significant musical and cultural moments of the twentieth century in the boxed text, you might be interested in more general accounts in, for example, the Lonely Planet's *South Africa, Lesotho, and Swaziland* (2002) on one hand, and Reader's Digest's *Illustrated History of South Africa* on the other, resources selected because they are accessible both in the presentation of content and availability for purchase. There are now literally thousands of websites, a small selection of which are listed and annotated in Appendix 3.

2. This process is enacted in *The Power of One* (1992) and *Mandela: Son of Africa, Father of a Nation* (1996).

REFERENCES

Allen, Lara. "An Archive of Black South African Popular Music: Recently Released Reissues." *British Journal of Ethnomusicology,* 5 (1996): 177–180.

Anderson, Benedict. *Imagined Communities: On the Origins and Spread of Nationalism.* London: Verso, 1983.

Baines, Gary. "Catalyst or Detonator? Local Music Quotas and the Current South African Music 'Explosion.'" *Social Dynamics,* 24/1 (1998): 66–87.

Comaroff, Jean. *Body of Power, Spirit of Resistance.* Chicago: University of Chicago Press, 1985.

Erlmann, Veit. *Music, Modernity, and the Global Imagination.* New York: Oxford University Press, 1999.

Feld, Steven. "The Poetics and Politics of Pygmy Pop." In *Western Music and Its Others,* edited by Georgina Born and Desmond Hesmondhalgh, 254–279. Berkeley: University of California Press, 2000.

Hamm, Charles. *Putting Popular Music in Its Place.* Cambridge: Cambridge University Press, 1995.

Reader's Digest. *Illustrated History of South Africa: The Real Story.* Expanded third edition, completely updated. Cape Town: Reader's Digest, 1994.

Trewhela, Ralph. *Song Safari.* Johannesburg: Limelight Press, 1980.

Tucker, Percy. *Just the Ticket! My 50 Years in Show Business.* Johannesburg: Jonathan Ball Publishers, 1997.

Chapter Two

Graceland

A Contested Musical Collaboration

Introduction

There are two recordings central to this discussion that you should listen to or view: Paul Simon's *Graceland* album issued in 1986 by Warner Brothers, and reissued (with new, much more comprehensive liner notes and as an enhanced CD) in 1996. The 1998 DVD/video titled *Paul Simon: Graceland, Recounting the Journey of a Legendary Music Recording* would greatly expand your understanding of the making of the music and the album, and of the response of some of its musicians to the process. A third, *Graceland: The African Concert,* filmed in 1987 in Harare, Zimbabwe, presents the only live version of the *Graceland* music and is extremely useful, even though several excerpts from that video have been used in the *Paul Simon* DVD/video.

Paul Simon's *Graceland* project, which generated considerable international controversy when it was released, provides a perfect entrance into a discussion of South African musical traditions in transformation. For much of the twentieth century, South Africa and its music remained cut off from the African continent and the rest of the world. The sense of isolation was due in large part to the policies of apartheid, the laws that enforced racial segregation and discrimination on the basis of racial and cultural difference. Because of the timing of its release, *Graceland* occupies a pivotal moment in South African music history With this album. Paul Simon brokered a sense among South Africans that it was once again possible to reconnect internationally and perhaps even work collaboratively inside the country. It evokes several of the major themes and issues pertinent to an understanding of South Africa and its music in the contemporary world. These include the relationships between music and politics, music and travel, the voice and the body, and music and technology, along with the ongoing dialogue between South African and American musical production. The album also articulates differences between musical cultures in the global centers and their margins.

Released in 1986, the *Graceland* album showcased, among others, the music of American star Paul Simon with South African musicians Joseph Shabalala and his a capella *isicathamiya* group Ladysmith Black Mambazo, guitarist Ray Phiri, pennywhistle player Morris Goldberg, bass player Bakhiti Khumalo, drummer Vusi Khumalo, percussionist Makhaya Mahlangu, singers General MD Shirinda and the Gaza Sisters, piano accordionist Forere Motloheloa, and the township group, Boyoyo Boys. The album was controversial in part because of the charged nature of the political and musical climate into which the recording was inserted.

The mid-1980s in South Africa were the most repressive years in apartheid history, a period in which the government expelled foreign journalists and declared numerous "states of emergency" because political resistance to apartheid, inside and outside of the country, was at its peak. As a result, state security forces were everpresent in black townships and white urban areas, and thousands of mostly black South Africans, including hundreds of children, were arrested and detained without access to legal representation, let alone a free and fair trial. It was also the era of the mega "charity rock" concerts like Live Aid, Farm Aid, and We Are the World, which were beamed by satellite to the world from London and the United States. In these events the stars of the entertainment world presented themselves, and were marketed as, socially conscious musicians. This was the moment in which American rock musician and producer Little Steven released the collaboratively created *Sun City: Artists United Against Apartheid* video, album, and book package. The music video had been made with MTV audiences in mind and aired on that site (the American Public Broadcasting Service, PBS, had refused to air the video for fear of alienating its largely white viewers, and there was no Black Entertainment Television [BET] at the time). *Sun City* was not just a moneymaking event; it was designed to raise people's consciousness and to get them thinking about South African policies of apartheid and reflecting on parallels in their own experience of racism in their own countries.

To comprehend the controversy generated by *Graceland,* we must consider four points: 1) the international cultural boycott that had been called for by South Africans in exile in Europe and the United States and applied against South Africa—its government and its people; 2) "Sun City," the entertainment center in South Africa that symbolized the evil of the apartheid regime; 3) *Rhythms of Resistance,* a video documentary on black South African music directed by British filmmaker Jeremy Marre in 1979; and 4) the musical collaborations across racial divides that had begun to form inside South Africa in the 1980s.

Cultural Boycott

The history of cultural boycotts against South Africa reaches back beyond apartheid to the 1940s. As early as 1946 the American Actor's Equity resolved to discourage its members from working in South Africa because of racial discrimination. India initiated the first boycott in 1947, but it was an Anglican priest, Father Trevor Huddleston, who had worked in Sophiatown, Johannesburg, when the government decided to destroy that community, whose call for a boycott against South Africa achieved international media attention in the 1950s. The poignancy of his message was reinforced with the Sharpeville Massacre in March 1960. In response, Equity, the British Actors' Union, and the British Musicians' Union refused to allow their members to perform in South Africa from the late 1950s. Nobel Peace Prize winner and President General of the ANC Albert Luthuli invoked United Nations principles to call for an even larger boycott in the 1960s. In 1965, sixty-five actors pledged to refuse to perform in South Africa, including Harry Belafonte, Sammy Davis, Jr., and Nina Simone.

In 1969, the United Nations resolved to encourage member states to suspend all ties with the South African government: racial, sporting, and cultural. When television was introduced to South

Africa, no British shows were aired because of the boycott. By the 1980s, South Africa had become quite isolated from the international cultural and sporting arenas.[1] In the early 1980s the United Nations declared that it would blacklist any performer who traveled to South Africa. The boycott did not just include popular artists, but classical performers and conductors as well (Shifrin 1989). Essentially, the United Nations' cultural boycott meant that there would be no exchange of performers or performances between that country and the rest of the world. (Nevertheless, since the boycott could only be policed in terms of entertainers traveling in person, recordings of many famous artists continued to be sold in South Africa through the 1980s.)

By traveling to South Africa in 1985, at the height of public awareness of the evils of apartheid, Paul Simon broke the terms of the cultural boycott, which was supported not only by the United Nations, but also by numerous arts organizations the world over. Simon had not acquired permission from the United Nations or the African National Congress, the two organizations at the forefront of the boycott, to travel to South Africa or to work with the musicians. The international anti-apartheid community feared that if someone as powerful as Paul Simon did not abide by the principles, the struggle against the South African government would crumble.

Sun City

Sun City is the Las Vegas–style casino and entertainment center created by Sol Kerzner and funded in part by the South African government. South Africa's equivalent to Donald Trump, Kerzner built the casino in the "independent" homeland of Bophutatswana, north of Johannesburg. Overseas entertainers were lured to the site with offers of significant financial packages and the assurance that Bophutatswana was not part of South Africa, but rather, an independent state. The problem was that Bophutatswana was just one of the official "Bantustans" into which black South Africans had been relegated, so most of the black residents of the homeland lived in dire poverty, in contrast to the significant resources the South African government covertly poured into the entertainment oasis.

So in 1985, American and British musicians worked together to create the MTV-targeted music video *Sun City: Artists United Against Apartheid* and a series of other recordings made in the spirit of the international anti-apartheid movement. Recordings included the song "Biko" by Peter Gabriel, "Apartheid Is Wrong" by Stevie Wonder, "Nelson Mandela" by Youssou N'dour, "Tutu" by Miles Davis, and "No Easy Walk to Freedom" by Peter, Paul, and Mary. The music video, book, and record package articulated the collective resolve of musicians not to be coerced into playing at Sun City. *Sun City* was issued in 1985, the same year that Paul Simon quietly traveled to South Africa to record tracks with three groups he had heard on a cassette titled *Gumboots: Accordion Jive Hits Vol. II,* given to him by a friend. It was this display of blatant disregard for the cultural boycott, and what many read as a disregard for the suffering and plight of the same black South African musicians Simon was working with, that made the world point its fingers at this very privileged white American performer. But negative media attention did not hinder record sales—*Graceland* has sold millions of copies the world over.

Rhythm of Resistance

In an effort to build sympathy for black South African performers abroad, British filmmaker Jeremy Marre traveled to South Africa in the late 1970s to make a film on black South African performance. Titled *Rhythm of Resistance: Black South African Performance,* this film, made before the cultural boycott, fleshed out the politics of musical performance and production in the apartheid period. Ladysmith Black Mambazo was one of the groups featured on this video, which was frequently shown at anti-apartheid gatherings in Britain and the United States in the 1980s. Marre, who also produced the video/DVD titled *Paul Simon: Graceland* (1998), a documentary on the making of the *Graceland* album, interspersed clips from *Rhythm of Resistance* into the new video. Marre's agenda in the film was to expose the hidden forms of street and studio performance of black South Africa, labeled "tribal" music, that otherwise were seldom heard by white South Africans or beyond the borders of South Africa (see Chapter Four).

Collaborations across the Racial Divide

Rhythm of Resistance provides the first glimpses of the kinds of musical collaborations that South Africans themselves had begun to form anew in the late 1970s, such as that of the singer–song writer duo of white South African Johnny Clegg and black migrant worker Sipho Mchunu. I remember discovering the music of the duo, called Juluka, and the band they subsequently formed—and dancing the night away with my friends to recordings of this music in the mid-1980s. But I also recall attending one of their performances in the Durban city hall at about the same time—the sheer presence of black and white men performing together in public was reason for the stage to be guarded by South African police, who stood in the wings the entire performance to quell any public unrest that might be generated by the interracial group. Fortunately, the only thing generated by the performance was huge enthusiasm for the sounds streaming from the stage.

Soon other groups also began to transgress the racial ideologies of apartheid. Later in the 1980s, Mango Groove, an interracial ensemble, recorded and performed South African popular music, integrating the sounds of *kwela* and *marabi,* sounds that evoked a deep nostalgia for a bygone, pre-Grand Apartheid era. (See *African Wave: Mango Groove.*) The African Jazz Pioneers was the third group, made up largely of black South African musicians who had played jazz in the 1950s but who re-formed as an interracial group (by including a white trombonist) in the 1980s. (See *African Wave.*)

The Graceland Album

A great deal has been written about the *Graceland* album since its release in 1986—much of it in response to the controversy itself.[2] But since the recording and the controversy are already almost twenty years old, my purpose here is to use *Graceland* to flesh out the many meanings and interpretations that are generated by a single musical recording. The *Graceland* case study should enable you to reflect on the relationship between South African music history and that of the United States, on one hand, and more generally on some of the

Documenting South African Music

The thirteen-part video series *African Wave: South African Music and Its Influences* (1998) tells the stories of thirteen South African musicians/groups whose lives intertwine in the aftermath of the *Graceland* album. Countering the separate development images of South African performances under apartheid, this series stresses the "multicultural music of South Africa, its major musicians, and the traditional and contemporary influences that color their work" (Video cover 1998). Included in the series are those who have recorded with Gallo Records: township pop singer Brenda Fassie; the contemporary queen of popular music in Africa, Yvonne Chaka Chaka; African Jazz Pioneers leader Ntemi Piliso; Ladysmith Black Mambazo; Ray Phiri; Sipho Hotstix Mabuse (the latter three all tied into the *Graceland* narrative); white rock copies Little Sister; South African reggaeman Lucky Dube; interracial popular group with a distinctive South African sound Mango Groove; hybrid Soweto duo Marcalex; hip hop artists Prophets of da City; and the late great Zulu dancer and growler Mahlathini. The most pervasive themes in the series are 1) market crossover, which in South Africa means racial and genre crossover—that is, groups that sell to more than one group of consumers defined by race/culture and language; 2) covering and borrowing sounds and styles from abroad; and 3) the significance of *Graceland* to their music.

issues raised by the *Graceland* collaboration and the production of what the industry and the academy call "world music," on the other.

At its core, *Graceland* is a musical collaboration between Paul Simon and a host of other musicians. These included Cajun zydeco music of Rockin' Dopsie and the Twisters, the Chicano Rock of Los Lobos, the Everly Brothers in the United States, as well as a large contingency of South Africans, with Joseph Shabalala and Ladysmith Black Mambazo, and Ray Phiri and Stimela in the foreground. *Graceland,* the album, included a different set of musicians than did *Graceland: The African Concert* (presumably for logistical reasons, but the changing personnel and the difference between studio production and live performance are important in coming to terms with the ownership of *Graceland*).

Like so many recordings, including *Sun City*, the *Graceland* album was the result of numerous studio recordings creating multiple tracks of sound that were then combined to create the single texture we now hear as the final *Graceland* product. And these recordings occurred in Johannesburg, in London, in Los Angeles, and in New York City. One of the criticisms of the album is that even though Simon was showcasing musicians to the world, they were not properly credited for their creative contribution. By all accounts they were well paid as studio musicians but were not compensated as artists. Responding to this accusation in Marre's video, Paul Simon talks not so much as a musician but as a producer, shifting the idea of musical collaboration to one where he and his engineer collected raw materials in South Africa that required refinement for the popular market.

There are eleven tracks on the compact disc, to a greater and lesser degree incorporating or shaped by South African vocal and/or instrumental performances. Excluding the Zulu texts of Joseph Shabalala, the words of all the songs are attributed to Paul Simon. The most explicitly South African–sounding tracks are discussed in detail on the Marre DVD (1998), *Paul Simon: Graceland, Recounting the Journey of a Legendary Music Recording*. These are: Track 1, "Boy in the Bubble," the least South African of all tracks; Track 2, "Graceland"; and Track 8, "Homeless," the most easily locatable as a South African sound. Four more tracks discussed and showcased are Track 9, "Crazy Love Vol. II"; Track 7, "Under African Skies"; Track 6, "You Can Call Me Al"; and Track 5, "Diamonds on the Soles of Her Shoes." Five of the eleven tracks are analyzed to varying degrees below.

Marked differences in the liner notes contained inside the 1986 original and 1996 reissue are revealing in light of changes made to the front and back cover images. The expanded notes in the 1996 reissue, written by *Billboard Magazine*'s editor-in-chief, Timothy White, discuss the making of the album and its political context since 1985. The photographic image of Paul Simon leaning against a wall, alone, which was originally on the front of the album, is moved to the back in 1996; the "more African" image, the Ethiopian print of King George on a horse, has moved from back to front. All the musicians who contributed in some way to the making of *Graceland,* and their record companies, are carefully listed and acknowledged in the same way in both sets of notes. In short, a recording made and distributed globally in 1986 primarily as an American masterpiece written in the first person by Paul Simon, with a brief personal narrative of how it all came about, is completely reframed in 1996. The personal journey is gone. In its place is a politically informed story that relates the *Graceland* album and its production more intimately to South African music and political history, and places Paul Simon firmly into that archive, along with the South Africans who worked with him. Even if our response two decades later is to shrug our shoulders and say "So what?" to 1980s racial politics, it is clear that the controversy generated by the *Graceland* in 1985 forced Paul Simon and Warner Brothers to reevaluate and reconfigure the presentation of the product for the global marketplace.

The Paul Simon Video: Making *Graceland*

Unlike the *Graceland* album, which was made in the dark days of apartheid, Jeremy Marre's video, *Paul Simon: Graceland, Recounting the Journey of a Legendary Music Recording* (1998), was released well into the post-apartheid era. Its contents, like the liner notes of the 1996 *Graceland* release, reflect the concerns of the mid-1990s cultural production. Although some cynically call it an atmosphere of political correctness, the era is at least characterized by a heightened sensitivity to the politics of musical production, especially between so-called first- and third-world musicians.

In this environment musicians like Paul Simon have become far more aware of relationships of power, the need for mutual respect between all musicians, appropriate payment and accreditation for multiple layers of musical sound that collectively constitute the final product, and the proper acknowledgment of musical collaboration. Since the mid-1980s, the view of third-world musicians as sources of inspiration has shifted to viewing them as co-creators. One might argue that the *Graceland* controversy not only raised awareness of the political plight of black South Africans, but also highlighted these issues. This shift is certainly evident in the two narratives (1986 and 1996) told about Simon's motivations for the *Graceland* project. In the first, Paul Simon began his journey to South Africa naïve about the fine lines one might draw between inspiration and collaboration, between influence and appropriation, between writing and recording, and between jamming and composing. It is clear from his narrative that he began the journey looking for new sources of compositional inspiration: it was a personal quest. In the second, the international media, arts organizations, the United Nations, and many others publicly scrutinize the individual journeys of powerful musicians. In this narrative, these musicians are held accountable and the individual search for artistic inspiration becomes inseparable from larger issues of power and compensation.

The brief chronology of recording the album runs like this. Paul Simon spent several weeks listening to a cassette, a copy of *Gumboots: Accordion Jive Hits, II,* given to him by a friend, Heidi Berg, in the summer of 1984. Simon, then in something of a personal and creative slump, was looking for personal and compositional renewal. He heard in this music strange but familiar musical ideas. He asked Warner Brothers to track down the source of the cassette. They made contact with record producer Hilton Rosenthal in Johannesburg, who sent about twenty recordings of the gamut of black South African performance. Rosenthal set up a recording date with Paul Simon and three groups that performed on Simon's cassette: Tao Ea Matsekha, General M.D. Shirinda and the Gaza Sisters, and the Boyoyo Boys bands. (Clips from these recording sessions are included in the Marre video.) Paul Simon and his engineer, Roy Halee, quietly traveled to South Africa in February 1985.

Soon after the Johannesburg recording session Paul Simon sent a letter and tape to Joseph Shabalala with some compositional ideas for what became "Homeless," and Shabalala and Ladysmith Black Mambazo traveled to London to record with Simon. Simon then returned to New York and over the next few months invited several other musicians, including Nigerian pedal steel guitarist Demola Adepoju and Senegalese singer Youssou N'dour, to record rhythmic and vocal tracks that would be dubbed into the recording mix. Some of this recording took place in Los Angeles. Although the album was scheduled for release in the summer of 1986, Warner

Brothers delayed until the fall. The South African musicians were in New York City because Ladysmith Black Mambazo and the Soweto Rhythm Section were to appear on "Saturday Night Live." The South Africans went into the studio with Paul Simon in New York City and recorded "Diamonds on the Soles of Her Shoes," which was never intended to be on the original album, in a very few takes.

Two ideas form the core of Marre's video on the making of *Graceland:* "collaboration" (see Meintjes 1990 for a thoughtful exploration of this idea in *Graceland*) and "composition" in the artistic sense. These two concepts work in tension with each other because a truly collaborative project would have required Simon to give artistic (and royalty) credit to the other artists, whereas the composition of a work of art by an individual composer enabled Simon to take the credit and royalty checks.

Marre integrates video footage from a range of sources: live interviews with musicians and technicians; footage from his own archive as used in *Rhythm of Resistance;* excerpts of the *Graceland: The African Concert* (filmed in Zimbabwe in the late 1980s); news footage of political turbulence under apartheid; still images of 1950s black South African performance, particularly of pennywhistle *kwela;* studio footage from Johannesburg, London, and New York; footage taken from "Saturday Night Live"; and several music video clips that both illustrate the words of the songs and present a single track ("You Can Call Me Al") with Chevy Chase lip-synching the words in a humorous rendition of the song.

Analyzing *Graceland*

There is a pervasive sense in the *Graceland* video that when Paul Simon initiated contacts with and traveled to South Africa in 1985, he was on a personal journey as an artist out to expand his creative resources. It does not appear to have been a journey with a political motivation, as Maree's *Rhythm of Resistance* video so clearly was. His intent was not to expose South Africa's music to the world or to speak for or about South Africa and its music or racism. His was a singularly artistic process—initially, anyway—one in which art/music and politics did not mix. But it ultimately proved impossible for him to separate the two, because in the South Africa of the late twentieth century, the personal, political, economic, and even musical were inextricably intertwined.

In addition to telling of the politicized character of the "journey of a legendary music recording," as the video claims to do, it contributes to an understanding of South African music in the global economy in ways that are important to ethnomusicologists. First, it provides rare footage of the inside of a recording studio, and not just one but several studios. Second, the video reveals the complex layers of compositional process, from Paul Simon's jotting of words onto paper, to the "jam" sessions held with South Africans, to the careful crafting of the final mix. Third, we witness some of the interaction between Paul Simon and the South African musicians as the tracks are laid. The voices of the musicians are woven into a narrative that displays different perspectives on a single process and portrays the complex negotiation that occurred as *Graceland* came together. Finally, the footage of engineer Roy Halee provides a rarely heard voice from inside the industry itself. Both men, Simon and Halee, are presented as thoughtful and frank in their discussion of the musical and traveling experiences that ultimately resulted in this remarkable recording.

Simon's narrative of how he came to record *Graceland* and the processes by which he selected and multi-tracked the final product are key organizational nodes in the film. About halfway through the video an educational segment on South African music deconstructs the layers of South African sounds in the musical product. Perhaps the most useful information we glean from the video is how specific musical tracks were created, what parts were specifically South African, and what parts came directly from Paul Simon. Let us take a more in-depth look at three of these musical tracks.

The Boy in the Bubble

The opening measures of the album not only introduce to the audience strands of the familiar but strange sounds of southern African migrant worker performance; they also represent the whole concept of *Graceland* sonically. It was a social and musical experiment, collaborative to its very core, inspired by the sounds of accordion, guitar, drums, and bass on *Gumboots: Accordion Jive Hits, II.* The song starts out with several measures of solo piano accordion playing, and the powerful beats of the drum enter to place the beat firmly in its 4/4 frame. For almost eight measures these two instruments establish the groove that carries Paul Simon's voice and lyrics through the remainder of the track.

"I think we always knew that this would be the start of the album. It began so unusually, and the sound of those drums sounded so 'African.' It was really an announcement that said you haven't heard this before. . . ." Simon says. For engineer Roy Halee the song suggested the uncertainty of the moment, musically and politically. "It represents that whole experience: a very dark, very brooding quality about it. It most represents the whole trip, the whole concept, the recording in that studio" (Marre DVD 1998).

The song text, particularly in its refrain, explains the recording project as a connection created between the center and its "distant constellation," a "long distance call," urging its mainstream audience to think globally, to extend their listening ears to the place of "lasers in the jungle" (even though there is no "jungle" in South Africa). Retrospectively, the stress upon "miracles and wonder" has an eerie prophetic sense to it. But as Paul Simon remarks on the video, he knew that political change would eventually come to South Africa, but it seemed, in the mid-1980s, a very remote possibility. It is significant that the narrative about the radical political transformation of South Africa in the 1990s also used words like "miracles" and "wonders."

Homeless

The most removed in sound and musical arrangement from the experience of mainstream popular music audiences is the eighth track of the *Graceland* album, "Homeless." This is the track that most powerfully demonstrates the possibilities of musical collaboration between South African musicians and Paul Simon, even though they come from extremely different musical traditions. This track is also the most authentically "South African" in its sound—

dear to many South Africans, but certainly the most remote to cultural outsiders.

The song begins with Joseph Shabalala intoning the "call" and Mambazo men "responding" in traditional African style. They sing Simon's original ideas in Zulu but do not directly translate his words. Of all the South African musical traditions represented on *Graceland,* the unaccompanied four-part harmony vocal arrangements of *isicathamiya* is the one most flexible in meeting the requirements of the recording while remaining faithful to the tradition. *Isicathamiya,* which means "to walk stealthily, like a cat," or "to walk on tiptoes," traces its roots to mission hymnody (the four part—soprano, alto, tenor, bass, or SATB style) and the visit of African-American performer Orpheus McAdoo and the Virginia Jubilee Singers to South Africa in the 1890s.[3] As the performance aesthetics of *isicathamiya* shifted in the twentieth century, so has its name. Once called *Mbube,* it was subsequently called *ibombing* because of the loud, near shouting style of its performance. Under Joseph Shabalala it has assumed a softer, sweeter, more harmonious sensibility, and is now performed with *isteps,* soft, stealthy dance routines reminiscent of nineteenth-century minstrel performances that took place all around South Africa.[4]

As you listen to "Homeless," try to separate the distinctly "African/South African" aspects and those that are more familiar, more "mainstream" in American popular music. In thinking about the idea of familiar but different, an idea that characterizes the music on this album, think first about language. While Mambazo and Simon both sing in English, listen to the intonation of black South African English. How does it differ from the American accent? The structure of the piece is largely sung in a call and response format—sometimes Joseph Shabalala is the leader, calling for a response; at other times Paul Simon assumes leadership, and Shabalala's voice is subsumed into the larger choral response.

Isicathamiya, as we have seen, is about four voices—soprano, alto, tenor, and bass—in harmony. Is this texture African or Western? This is an important question. Because of the long history of European, and more recently American, colonization of South Africa (largely through the missions and more recently through the entertainment industry), the musical texture of the mission hymn has become so much a part of black South African performance practices, not only in *isicathamiya* but also in other styles of choral music, that it is now considered African. Clearly, appropriation of musical styles and ideas has not been a one way process, Americans of African styles, but indeed, an ongoing feature of the musical exchange between the two continents throughout the twentieth century, and in some cases, even earlier.

But as it has indigenized, the SATB texture has taken on its own peculiarities. In the *isicathamiya* context, the soprano and alto voices usually sung by women are missing—the women are back at home in the rural areas, left behind by men who migrated to the cities for work. When migrant men began to form vocal groups and sing in the mission style, they adjusted the sound to a bass-heavy texture. In *isicathamiya* most voices sing bass, then tenor. Typically only one or two higher male voices sing alto, and the leader sings the soprano line. This is what you hear in Ladysmith Black Mambazo's singing both on *Graceland* and numerous other recordings they have made over the past four decades.

Finally, notice the creative, perhaps unusual use of the human voice on this track. Near the beginning of the song, we suddenly hear something that sounds like "rrrrrp rrrrp shek shek" in one of the voices. These are sonic signs of sounds Joseph Shabalala recalls hearing in his childhood on his family farm. A little later one of the men, perhaps Shabalala, ululates—a high-pitched articulation typically done by women to express approval and joy in performance. Near the end of the song, the English phrase "Somebody say" is juxtaposed with alternating English words and syllables that are purely rhythmic in function: "ih hih ih hih ih." In all of these instances the human voice is used both melodically and rhythmically—a key feature of much vocal performance in South Africa. These are the "exotic" elements of *isicathamiya* performance that make it sell to a world music audience.

If you listen carefully to the Zulu lyrics near the end of the song you will hear a "click" sound in the middle of the word "*omanqoba.*" (The letter "*q*" represents the click.) The Zulu language actually uses three different click sounds, the letter "*c*" is a soft click; "*q*" is a harder click, almost like the sound of horses galloping one can make with the mouth; and the letter "*x*" represents a click created at the back of the cheeks. South African singer Miriam Makeba popularized the Xhosa-language "Click Song" in the late 1950s and early 1960s when she sang with Harry Belafonte in New York City. The clicks clearly represent the exotic for those of us who speak English.

When listening to the "Homeless" track we might be tempted to presume that the marriage of cultures, languages, and voices was a happy one from the beginning, because its final product works so beautifully. But in the *Graceland* video, Joseph Shabalala comments on the struggles that Ladysmith Black Mambazo had working with Paul Simon's initial ideas for the song. Simon sent his ideas to Shabalala before they met together to work out the song more fully. Shabalala recalls that he liked Simon's lyrics very much, but making the music work was far more of a challenge.

> It's a little bit difficult to blend the voices, the American voice, the African voice. The first day we were just touching, many people were trying to help us, and I just said, OK. Even the producer . . . was there, trying to teach us. That was confusing me, it was his first time to teach us: we didn't know him. We are used to working together alone, and come with something solid and good. (Shabalala in Marre 1988)

There may have been some misgivings among the group, too, because Shabalala remembers having reassured the group that Simon was a good and a polite man. Roy Halee agreed. "At the beginning it felt a little strange, [Ladysmith Black Mambazo] are tricky to record because they don't produce a lot of sound, those bass voices are very soft."

After the group returned to their hotel, they prayed. They decided that they would just give Paul Simon what they knew and not try to do what he wanted. Mambazo would give what they knew, and Paul Simon would give what he had. The plan worked, and the next day the "Homeless" musical collaboration began to take shape.

Gumboots

This track on *Graceland* is composed using the music on the cassette that Simon first listened to in 1984. The original tracks were performed by a South African band, the Boyoyo Boys, now overlaid with the wailing saxophone sounds of South African jazz performed principally by Barney Rachabane. These saxophone sounds are clear signifiers of the sounds of South African jazz, harking back to the excitement that African jazz produced for South Africans in the 1940s and 1950s—sounds that were silenced by the apartheid regime, particularly if they brought people of all races together in a single place.

Missing from the recording, but included in the *Graceland* video, are the actual sounds of gumboot dancing, the boot dance of migrant workers from southern KwaZulu Natal who worked both in the port city of Durban and on the mines in Johannesburg. I have a peculiar attachment to gumboot dancing: I learned to perform the dance in 1985, trained by a migrant worker, Blanket Mkhize, and his team. When I visited the United States in early in 1986 and told people that I gumboot danced, I would regularly be confronted with blank stares. "You mean Gumby?" people would laugh. But by 1987, *Graceland* had been released to the world, and everyone now "knew" what gumboot dancing was because of this track. Of course, few had actually heard or seen the dance, but everyone knew its name.

South African Responses to the Graceland Recording

Several musical responses to the plight of black South Africans in the mid-to-late 1980s were generated both inside and outside of South Africa by the publicity associated with *Sun City: Artists United Against Apartheid* and the *Graceland* project.

Sarafina

Out of the workshop-style theater training identified with protest theater in the 1970s and 1980s, South African playwright Mbongeni Ngema created a Broadway musical, *Sarafina! The Music of Liberation*. It tells the story of Sarafina, a woman who teaches history at a school for black South Africans in the township of Soweto. Sarafina seeks to teach history in a way that the South African government disapproves of, so she is arrested and put in prison. In the stage production, Sarafina symbolically represents Mandela—a man emasculated and feminized by his imprisonment. At the end of the production, Sarafina returns from her imprisonment as a man—the male figure of an imagined Nelson Mandela (he was still in prison at the time, and all visual representation of his face was banned in South Africa until his release in 1990). The Broadway production of *Sarafina* was subsequently produced for a popular audience in Hollywood, starring Whoopi Goldberg as Sarafina. A documentary film on the making of *Sarafina* from the perspective of its performers/co-creators was also made in the late 1980s.

There are several aural connections created between *Graceland* and *Sarafina* in the video made about the production of *Sarafina*. It opens with the South African performers standing close to one of Manhattan's famous bridges singing "Homeless." And *mbaqanga*, the popular musical style used in *Sarafina*, was introduced to the world by the *Graceland* album.

Field Recording, March 1988, AmaOti, KwaZulu Natal

This is an instance of a school choir performing at a meeting for parents of the students in March 1988. My husband, a U.S. citizen, was teaching in this informal school and had been called to an all-day parents' meeting. Inanda, the area in which the AmaOti school was located, was a hotbed of student protest against the apartheid government, school boycotts, and political instability. Partway through the performance, the choir suddenly moved from a series of religious and gospel style songs to a version of "Diamonds on the Soles of Her Shoes." I recall the sense of amazement I felt at the relative speed with which the *Graceland* album had rooted itself in this community. Even more amazing was that it had been picked up by these students who were clearly engaged with the political issues of the moment. They could have refused to sing the song because of its use of South African musicians despite the cultural boycott. Instead, they sang the song with enormous pride and satisfaction on a Sunday morning in 1988.

Soweto String Quartet (1994), "Zebra Crossing"

The title of the track referencing *Graceland* is "The Paul Simon *Graceland* Collection" which includes excerpts from four songs, "Homeless," "Diamonds on the Soles of Her Shoes," "Graceland," and "You Can Call Me Al" arranged to sound like a single piece.

The Soweto String Quartet hails from Johannesburg's largest and best-known black urban township, Soweto. It has clearly established itself in an attempt to give respectability to the traditional and contemporary music of black South Africans—to "classicize" the music. This is a recording made by Gallo (Africa) Records, the white-controlled commercial record company that is the dominant force in the South African recording industry. There is a dual signification in the title, "Zebra Crossing." On the one hand, the black and white of the zebra represent a kind of racial mixing, the zebra symbolizes African-ness, and the unity of black and white in a single space; but the Zebra Crossing also resonates with global popular culture, referencing the Beatles' "Abbey Road" symbols from three decades earlier!

Distancing the group from the cloud of controversy that hung over the release of the recording, the author of the liner notes for this recording celebrates Paul Simon's intervention in South African music history by showcasing South African music and musicians. The collaborative project is justified by the already hybridized nature of *mbaqanga* music—adding a little more to the *mbaqanga* pot where "the rich flavors of South African black music culture simmer" (Liner Notes 1994). The notes convey appreciation to Paul Simon and the *Graceland* project for opening the ears of the world to South African music, and for "stirring up" the *mbaqanga* pot once more.

David Kramer (1996), Klassic Kramer

David Kramer is a South African singer and writer of protest song and theater. Born in England, he immigrated to South Africa many years ago and now lives in Cape Town. He is well known in the Cape for his depictions of the Afrikaans poor and working class (largely white) in the Western Cape. On his CD *Klassic Kramer*, he tells a story to a live audience about the time he met Paul Simon in 1985 when Simon visited South Africa to record what became the *Grace-land* album.

The story he told in 1991 at the Dock Road Theater in Cape Town, South Africa, begins with a song he calls "Weskusklong," sung in Afrikaans that I have translated into English here.

The earth is large and the stars are small,
Only lizards in the desert.
Goats and thorns and the bitter aloe
I know the "East Coast," but it's not the same
Biscuits and biltong, I am from the West Coast.
Give me a whip, give me a stick
Give me a woman in a bright red dress.
Give me the open veld where the goats graze
You'll find me there between the stones.
Biscuits and Biltong, I am from the West Coast.

David Kramer then recounts his version of the story about when Paul Simon traveled to South Africa to lay down the tracks for the *Graceland* album. It is an important narrative for the way in which he positions himself in the relationship between the powerful American music industry, represented by Paul Simon, and South African musicians.

Kramer's story revolves around being invited to the studios in Johannesburg (seen on the Marre DVD) to witness Paul Simon and the South African musicians collaborating. (Though Kramer is himself a popular musician in South Africa, he is not asked to collaborate with Paul Simon.) He meets up with Simon at the studio, though, and suggests that Simon should come to Cape Town, a place many in South Africa consider the treasure of the country. He never thought Paul Simon would actually come, but it turns out he did.

So Kramer took Paul Simon to the Cape Point, the place where one can see both the Indian and Atlantic Oceans simultaneously, a place of great beauty and a popular tourist destination for foreign and local visitors. Kramer was standing next to Paul Simon when a busload of tourists arrived and disembarked from the bus. When the tourists saw the two men, they came rushing towards them, asking Kramer for his signature. Nobody seemed to recognize Paul Simon, though they probably knew his voice and his music. So there Kramer stood, signing autographs, while Paul Simon, the powerful international star, stood to the side. This was truly a moment of glory for the internationally lesser-known but locally popular South African musician.

That night Paul Simon and David Kramer shared songs and stories at Kramer's home. Simon sang for Kramer, and then asked Kramer to sing for him. And the song he sang was "Weskusklong." As Kramer tells the story, Paul Simon took a copy of Kramer's song back to New York with him, and a little while later he had a call from Bob Dylan asking permission to do a cover version of the song. Kramer asks Bob Dylan to send him a cassette of the cover version. And he ends his story by imitating Bob Dylan's distinctive voice singing "Weskusklong."

David Kramer's spoken narrative is remarkable for the way in which it generates ideas about how the margins and centers operate not from the perspective of global centers, but indeed, from its margins. In this narrative, the focus has shifted from the global star to the local: rather than the unknown international star, at least a star known only in voice and not in body, the tourists flock to the person they know from live performance and television commercials. (Kramer did a commercial for Volkswagen on national television.) Then of course, there is the lovely idea of a famous musician like Bob Dylan not being able to sound like anything other than his own voice, not being able to cover the music of others, even though they have been covering his songs for decades. Finally, Paul Simon, the famous musician, is unable to categorize David Kramer's music because he doesn't recognize it. The joke is on him, because it derives from the singer-songwriter tradition shaped by Paul Simon himself, just in another language. Ultimately Kramer's narrative is a discourse about shifts in the balance of power: who holds the power depends on what your perspective is.

Leeukop Prisoners' Choir (ca. 1996), "Homeless"

The recording of "Homeless" by the inmates of a Pretoria prison provides a poignant example of the way in which the words represent the real experience of not having a home for many South Africans. In this context, however, "Homeless" comes to mean something very particular: men in a high security prison, trained by two white choral directors, articulate anxiety about the possibility of having no home when they are released from prison. Once again, a close copy of the original version, but without the white voice of Paul Simon, the Leeukop Prisoners' Choir extends the *Graceland* archive deeper into South African musical history and experience.

Khayelitsha United Mambazo

Geared toward the tourist market, this is a look-alike and sound-alike group modeled on Ladysmith Black Mambazo. They were selling their compact disc at the edges of their performance space while they sang at the Victoria and Albert Waterfront, a popular tourist destination in Cape Town's harbor, in July 2002. The disc has two songs sung in *isicathamiya* style. This group has clearly identified themselves as part of the larger Mambazo musical network, hoping to sell copies of their CDs to tourists for whom the name "Mambazo" and the sounds of the group will probably ring a bell. Copies and imitations are the ways in which South Africans have learned the repertories of the global entertainment industry. These actions foster a sense of connection to the centers of power. Imitation has long been a tradition in South African performance. In the past African people copied the sounds and gestures of animals and birds to harness their power; in the nineteenth and twentieth centuries, the model shifted to recorded objects and radio programming.

Inspiration's "Homeless"

We come full-circle with this 1996 version of "Homeless" by Inspiration. Established in 1989 at the University of Pennsylvania as a group celebrating the power of black music, Inspiration focuses on music written and performed by people of African descent. And so the transatlantic identification between African peoples and its diasporas continues.

NOTES

1. South African Rob Nixon has written concisely about the sports and cultural boycott (1994:131–174) against South Africa.

2. See for example Garafalo 1992, Lipsitz 1994, Nixon 1994, Erlmann 1999, Meintjes 1990, and Hamm 1995. At the time the international press, including *Newsweek, Time,* the *Village Voice,* the *New York Times,* and other media were also deeply engaged with the controversy.

3. See Erlmann 1996 for extensive discussion of this history and its performance.

4. See Erlmann 1991 and 1996 for further explanation.

REFERENCES

Erlmann, Veit. *Music, Modernity, and the Global Imagination.* New York: Oxford University Press, 1999.

_____. *Nightsong: Performance, Power, and Practice in Black South African Performance.* Chicago: Chicago University Press, 1996.

_____. *African Stars: Studies in Black South African Performance.* Chicago: Chicago University Press, 1991.

Garafalo, Reebee. *Rockin' the Boat: Mass Music and Mass Movements.* Boston: South End Press, 1992.

Hamm, Charles. *Putting Popular Music in Its Place.* Cambridge: Cambridge University Press, 1995.

Inspiration, The. Philadelphia: University of Pennsylvania, 1996.

Kramer, David. *Klassic Kramer.* Cape Town: Blik Music, 1996.

Leeukop Prisoners' Choir: Going Home. Johannesburg: Gallo, n.d.

Lipsitz, George. *Dangerous Crossroads: Popular Music, Postmodernism, and the Poetics of Place.* New York: Verso, 1994.

Marre, Jeremy. *Graceland: Recounting the Journey of a Legendary Music Recording.* Los Angeles: Rhino Entertainment, 1998.

Meintjes, Louise. *Sound of Africa! Making Zulu Music in a South African Studio.* Durham: Duke University Press, 2003.

Nixon, Rob. *Homelands, Harlem, and Hollywood: South African Culture and the World Beyond.* New York: Routledge, 1994.

Simon, Paul. *Graceland.* New York: Warner Brothers, 1986, 1996.

_____. *Graceland: The African Concert.* New York: Warner Brothers, 1988.

Soweto String Quartet. *Zebra Crossing.* Johannesburg: BMG Records, 1994.

Chapter Three

Cape Town Jazz

There is no doubt about it, Beatrice Benjamin is the mostest, the greatest and the most appealing girl singer in the Cape, whispers Howard Lawrence. What she did to the audience at Post's show, "Just Jazz Meets the Ballet" was wow. I got it bad when she sang "I Got It Bad." Everybody else got it bad too and they kept shouting for more of that feeling. *Most promising singer for 1959. Agreed.*

This short review appeared on January 25, 1959, in *The Golden City Post*, one of South Africa's most popular newspapers targeted at a "nonwhite" audience. Sathima Bea "Beatty" Benjamin recalls that the tune referred to, Duke Ellington's "I Got It Bad and That Ain't Good," created an immediate and steadfast bond between herself and jazz pianist Abdullah Ibrahim (then known as Dollar Brand), the man she subsequently married. Benjamin and Ibrahim were each working on the Ellington tune when they first met at a jazz fundraiser in Cape Town, South Africa, in 1959. Just four years later, they met Duke Ellington and Billy Strayhorn at the Club Africana in Zurich, Switzerland. Benjamin was living in Zurich at the time and heard that Ellington was in the neighborhood. She ventured out to see if he would come and listen to Dollar Brand's Trio. Surprisingly, Ellington agreed and after a brief review of the trio's performance and Benjamin's singing, he invited these South Africans to record for Reprise Records on February 23, 1963, in Paris. Two recordings came out of that session: the first, titled *Duke Ellington Presents the Dollar Brand Trio*, was released soon after the event. The second release came much later: Benjamin launched *A*

Morning in Paris in a recital at Carnegie Hall in New York City on February 23, 1997.

Sathima Bea Benjamin and Abdullah Ibrahim are two of the most important jazz musicians to emerge from Cape Town in the twentieth century. In this chapter we will examine Cape Town's popular music and jazz scene through the eyes and ears of Sathima Bea Benjamin. Benjamin spent the first twenty-six years of her life in Cape Town, the southernmost city in South Africa. In 1962 she and Abdullah left South Africa because it became impossible for them to perform jazz. They returned to the country several times, but finally departed after the 1976 Soweto uprising. At this point they openly declared their opposition to the apartheid government. They went to live in New York City's famous Chelsea Hotel. This time they were unable to return to South Africa because the government withdrew their passports. Since the lifting of the ban on the liberation organizations and the release of Mandela from prison in 1990, both Ibrahim and Benjamin have been free to go back to their place of birth.

Benjamin was born in 1936. She was 12 when the Afrikaner Nationalists assumed power as the government in 1948; she lived through some of the most hopeful but also harshest years in South Africa. A woman of mixed race, she has a profound understanding of the consequences of apartheid legislation on people of color in South Africa. She sought to come to terms with the struggles of her life individually and of her people collectively through song performance, and in her adult life, through jazz specifically. Like many other South Africans, Benjamin left the county in the 1960s. This means that a part of Cape jazz and popular music history has to be understood beyond the geographical borders of South Africa. Benjamin provides us with a rich perspective on Cape Town's popular music and jazz performance in its postwar formations.

Cape Town Jazz in the 1950s

Cape Town is a beautiful place, with mountains, the sea, a perfect climate, exotic birds, flora and fauna, and gorgeous sunrises and sunsets. There seemed

to be music in the air, always. Is that possible, or is that just the memory I
carry? (Sathima Bea Benjamin to Lee Hildebrand, January 25, 1987)

Those who visit Cape Town, the port city in the southernmost part
of the African continent, cannot but help feel awed by the beauty of
the place. Situated along the coastline where the Indian and Atlantic Oceans meet, the city is nestled between the folds of Table
Mountain and the pounding waves of treacherous seas. Cape Town
is known both as the Cape of Storms and the Cape of Good Hope.
But it is not just visual beauty that endears Cape Town to its residents and visitors. As Benjamin wistfully remembers, when she was
growing up in the 1940s and 1950s, the streets themselves seemed
to be filled with music. She recalls that, "First you would hear the
horses coming down the street and then you'd hear [people] shouting, 'aartappels en uiwe' (potatoes and onions). They're singing the
price and everything. There was always so much music, people just
using their voices naturally. It was everywhere" (Personal communication, March 16, 1990). Benjamin's musical memories are reinforced by a newspaper article from 1936, the year she was born. The
article described some of the music of the street—"the Malay fish
hawker, with his high-pitched call, who sold his fish from baskets
yoked across his shoulders," and the "horse and cart hawker with his
characteristic fish horn" (*Cape Standard,* June 8, 1936, p. 3).

Certainly, in Cape Town in the 1940s and 1950s, the sound of
music was everywhere: on the street, in one's home, as well as on
the stage, in the movies, in the mosque or church. For young people like Sathima Bea Benjamin, even the natural world made its
own kinds of musical sounds. Cape Town is known for its powerful
southeasterly winds, winds that shape what it means to live in the
city. If you have never experienced the power of gale force winds, it
might be hard to imagine just how the wind can carry sounds that
are like music to your ears. But Benjamin has vivid memories of
such sounds, and she sings about their power in one of her compositions, "Windsong" (CD TRACK 3).

The cultural and political history of Cape Town, however, is not as
enchanting. It is woven from narratives of slavery, colonial immigration, the travels of British and American entertainers—minstrels,
classical musicians, vaudeville, and variety artists; the decimation of

indigenous peoples through warfare and disease; an ongoing interaction between Islam, Christianity, and traditional beliefs; racial and
nationalist power struggles; and the emergence of the South African
language of Afrikaans. Furthermore, South African jazz and popular music traditions and their transformation in Cape Town in the
twentieth century emerged out of this cosmopolitan and creolized
society, which began to develop in the mid-seventeenth century.

Three groups contributed to the culture: colonists (living in
Cape Town and passing through from abroad), imported slaves,
and indigenous people. The major European countries that sent
people to the Cape were Holland, Britain, Germany, France, and
Portugal, although American culture came to South Africa through
traveling musicians in the nineteenth century in particular. The
Dutch and English were the two powers who mostly fought for control of the Cape. From 1910, when South Africa declared itself as
the Union of South Africa, the struggles were fought locally between the English, the Afrikaans, and the black South African majority. In 1652, the Dutch established a refreshment station in the
Cape for sailors traveling around the African continent from Europe to the East.

A rich cultural and musical heritage came to South Africa with
the importation of slaves from West and Central Africa, but mostly
from Madagascar, India, present day Indonesia (called Batavia), and
Ceylon. One year after the Dutch came to the Cape, the first slave—
a man named Abraham—arrived from Indonesia. Slavery was out-
lawed in South Africa by the British in 1808 but not actually abolished in the Cape until 1834. Even after the abolishment of slavery,
another 5,000 "prize Negroes" were sent to the Cape between 1808
and 1856, though they were trained and used for fourteen years
and then released into domestic work or agricultural labor.

The Khoikhoi, indigenous pastoral peoples who inhabited the
Cape prior to the arrival of the Dutch, were not treated as slaves by
the colonists. They did live on European property, though, as did
the imported slaves, and intermingled with the Europeans. As a result, the cultures of the three groups became integrally entwined.
During the same period, groups of "free blacks" lived in the Cape,
that is, people of Asian and African descent who were largely either
ex-slaves or ex-convicts. They were mostly excluded from the occu-

pations of white colonists; they could not farm because they were unable to acquire credit, though some purchased their own slaves. A good percentage of these free blacks were actually Muslim (mostly of Indonesian origin), and despite initial bans on religious rituals performed by Muslims, they integrated secular musical performance into their religious rituals and played a critical role in the spread of Islamic belief in the Cape, particularly among the slaves.

It is important to recognize that 1) Cape culture has always been a Creole culture, that is, a culture that has blended the old and the new, the powerful and the less powerful, the local and the foreign; 2) sexual relations across cultural and racial groups was an integral dimension of the first European settlements in the Cape and the people now called "Cape Coloured" were some of the first inhabitants of this new culture; and 3) the archival record suggests that these slaves and their Cape Town descendants were brilliant musicians, able to hear and replicate in their singing and instrumental performances almost any musical repertories. From the outset, the place where all Cape residents met together was in the taverns.

Perhaps the most significant imported musical culture to shape Cape Town's performance life in the twentieth century, and indeed South Africa as a whole, was nineteenth-century American and English minstrelsy. In their original form, minstrel groups were actually white actors, singers, and comedians who stereotyped black performers from the southern United States. Faces were painted black, and the outfits these men wore were exaggerated, colorful, and "dandy." Songs were accompanied on violin, cello, tambourine, banjo, and "the bones." Minstrelsy in Cape Town was preceded by performances of serenaders, first spoken about in 1848 with the visit of the Celebrated Ethiopian Serenaders, who performed at the Ethiopische Club in Cape Town. An advertisement in August 1862, told of the upcoming visit of the Christy Minstrels, organized in 1842 for performances in London and New York (Martin 1999).

This is not the place to spell out the contested history of minstrelsy as it was performed in the United States or Europe. But you might wonder why minstrelsy appealed to not only people of European descent but also functioned as a model of black urban performance culture in South Africa among people called "Coloured," or those of black African descent. Despite the fact that blackface min-

---

Slave Musical Performances from the Seventeenth Century

Slaves in the Cape played a central role in providing music for European entertainment from the earliest days of Dutch occupation. In 1676, for example, a slave orchestra performed for the Governor of the Cape. Wealthy Europeans in the Cape kept slave orchestras. These musicians learned to perform without formal instruction. They played a variety of European instruments, including violin, flute, bassoon, and French horn. Their purpose was to entertain children and guests on every social occasion. They regularly played social dances like the waltz, the quadrille, and the postillion.

These same slaves also performed in their own dance houses in the countryside. Here they incorporated a range of non-European instruments, including a single-headed cylindrical drum and a three-string lute with a calabash. They danced to a wide range of traditional and European music and were influenced by the music of military bands they heard performing in Cape Town. Lower-class colonists and slave girls danced together at local "rainbow balls," though it is unclear what music they danced to.

Taverns were another social site where slaves were expected to perform. Here they mingled with sailors and lower-class Europeans. These slaves performed on violins, flutes, trumpets, oboes, harps, and ramkies. The songs typically blended Dutch and Malay language and musical values.

---

strelsy mimicked and caricatured slave performances in the United States, elements of minstrelsy were incorporated into twentieth-century black performance culture, including *isicathamiya*, gumboot dance, and perhaps most importantly, into the New Year's celebrations of so-called Coloured people who have a carnival still colloquially identified as the "Coon Carnival." Some in South Africa have tried to have the name of the festival changed because of its derogatory nature in the United States. Those who participate in the festival annually tend to "ignore the American meaning of the word and its racist connotations" (Constant-Martin 1999). For some, "Coon" is an abbreviation of the word "raccoon," and for others it refers to a large bird with white eyes.

The rhythms of the annual carnival have come to be known in jazz made by musicians from the Cape as the "Cape Town rhythm." This rhythmic pattern has become a distinctive element of the musical performances of Abdullah Ibrahim, who integrated memories of the sounds of his home environment into his compositions, particularly after leaving South Africa in 1962. Sathima Bea Benjamin also has her musicians perform this distinctive rhythmic pattern, such as in "I Only Have Eyes for You" (CD TRACK 2).

"Cape Coloured" as Racial Classification

Life was fairly easy for the descendants of Cape slaves, some of the first inhabitants of Cape Town, from 1834, when slavery was abolished, until the emergence of social Darwinism and European "scientific" theories of racial difference in the late nineteenth century. These theories were based on assumptions of racial purity, and anyone "mixed" was considered impure, lacking, and of lesser value. In South Africa, as elsewhere in the contemporary world, to be of mixed race or "Coloured" was to have been born in shame. This was true not only after the Afrikaner Nationalists came to power in 1948 but also under British governance prior to that. Under the British, for example, Cape Coloureds were removed from the Common Voters' Roll in 1936. So the response of many called Coloured was to yearn for respectability. One path to respectability, it was thought, was to master European ways.

In Cape Town during the initial years of the twentieth century, a period described by South African jazz singer Sathima Bea Benjamin as "relaxed apartheid," people of color could mix fairly freely with those of European descent. Nevertheless, Benjamin recalls that two social principles were inculcated in her as a child of mixed race: know your place and do not look for trouble. These principles were manifested in the style of dance band music the Coloured musicians played for their own community dances—music constricted by musical rules and structures. This restraint contrasted markedly with the improvised and experimental jazz that musicians like Abdullah Ibrahim, Kippie Moeketsi, Johnny Dyani, Chris McGregor, and Sathima Benjamin herself were interested in making by the late 1950s.

In the nineteenth century, in both South Africa and America, Colo[u]red referred to all people not of European descent. But by the 1950s the apartheid government had created two separate racial categories: "Coloured" applied to all those of mixed race regardless of their individual or collective histories (the term largely referred to those based in the Cape). "Bantu" referred to the majority of people living in South Africa who were dark skinned and spoke Bantu languages, which include Zulu, Xhosa, Sotho, and Tswana. Within the space of about twelve years, 1950–1962, the character of Cape Town changed for people of color. It was no longer the Mother City evoking a profound sense of place and home; it was a place of exclusion, fragmentation, transgression, and boundaries. Apartheid legislation intentionally sought to keep people of color out of white space.

The 1950 Population Registration Act (amended in 1966) defined "Coloureds" as persons not native or European, or persons married to a man or woman *classified* as Coloured. The Immorality Act (passed in 1927 and amended in 1950 to include a ban on interracial marriages) made all sexual relationships across what was called the color bar illegal. The Group Areas Act (1950) required different racial groups to live in specific areas, seeking to separate out the Coloureds from Europeans to preclude any further racial mixing in Cape Town specifically, though it had wider ramifications in the rest of the country as well. The Separate Amenities Act (1950) forced racial segregation in all public venues. The newspapers in the 1950s and early 1960s are replete with articles on the implications of apartheid legislation for Coloured people. These include forced divorces and the breakup of families because some members are classified Coloured and others European, and the problem of the "science" of race that appears to be neither scientific nor historical in the South African context. Naming Coloured identity became a means to divide, rule, and marginalize rather than to unite and empower.

Many Coloureds rejected the label and sought to "pass" for white or to identify themselves through other social categories, such as class or education, because the label Coloured never translated into a positive identification. State enforcement of these laws played a critical role in the transformation and often destruction of jazz communities.

Becoming "Cape Coloured"

Sathima Bea Benjamin's family adds a new twist to the problem of being labeled Cape Coloured, because they were not Cape Coloureds in the historical definition of the term. Half her family hailed from the remote Atlantic island of St. Helena. Benjamin's father, Edward Benjamin, and his family had immigrated to Cape Town from St. Helena when his mother, later known as Ma Benjamin, was a young girl. They arrived in boats in the Cape Town harbor and settled with other St. Helenians. Many St. Helenians kept themselves apart from others of mixed race, who were called Cape Coloured. Unlike some Cape Coloureds—working class or variably employed people who spoke Afrikaans and danced to live band music on weekends—the St. Helenians aspired to English-speaking, middle-class cosmopolitanism and respectability. Some preferred to identify themselves as British, and most were proud that their birth certificates stated of "mixed St. Helenian" rather than "Cape Coloured" descent.

But under the Population Registration Act of 1950, the St. Helenians officially became Cape Coloured. Benjamin was living with her father's mother, Ma Benjamin, on the day a government official came to the house with census forms and required the elderly woman to sign that she agreed to be classified as Cape Coloured in what was becoming an increasingly divided society. The official told Ma Benjamin that in the eyes of the government, "St. Helenian" did not exist—everybody who was not white or African would now be in the same boat. Proud of her St. Helenian roots, the elderly Ms. Benjamin could not sign. In tears, she came to her granddaughter and asked her if she would please sign the piece of paper. The young Bea was not fully aware of the politicized nature of these issues at the time. She was already a Cape Coloured in her mind, because she attended a Coloured school, lived in a neighborhood of people of mixed race, and interacted with Coloured children everyday. But she had never seen Ma cry before. She knew this must be serious, and she dutifully signed the paper. From that time onward, like those classified as white, the Benjamins were required to carry identity cards that categorized them as Coloured. But for Coloured individuals and communities throughout South Africa, that identification would have severe consequences.

The Making of a Cape Town Jazz Singer

Sathima Bea[trice] Benjamin was born to Edward Benjamin and Evelyn Henry in Johannesburg on October 17, 1936. Her father had gone to Johannesburg to find work, and though she was seven and a half months pregnant, Evelyn had boarded the train in Cape Town and headed north. Baby Sathima arrived more than a month early. "You were born like Jesus," Benjamin's mother later told her. "We had no clothes for you," so the woman who ran the boarding house where she was staying tore a sheet into long strips and wrapped the newborn baby in swaddling clothes. Disappointed that she was not a boy, Benjamin's father refused to look at her for the first two weeks. When he did finally look, he saw a similarity between his new daughter and his sister, Beattie. So the newborn was named Beatrice Benjamin, later shortened to Bea.

Little is known about Benjamin's mother's family heritage. Benjamin's grandmother, Francesca de la Cruz, was of Filipino descent and living in the diamond mining town of Kimberly when her own parents died from the influenza epidemic of 1918. Evelyn Henry was thus orphaned at a young age and sent to stay with relatives in Cape Town, where she ultimately met Edward Benjamin. The couple had two daughters, Sathima and Joan, and a son, Maurice, who died. They divorced when Benjamin was about five, and the girls went to live with their father and his new wife. The loss of their mother so early in life was traumatic and formative for these young girls. As an adult Benjamin vowed that her children would always have a mother to care for them, and for several years in exile, she began each live performance with the old African-American spiritual, "Sometimes I Feel Like a Motherless Child" (CD TRACK 1).

Bea and Joan lived with their father and his new wife until Benjamin was nine years old and it was discovered at school that the Benjamin girls were being severely beaten by their father's second wife. At this point they were sent to live with their paternal grandmother, Ma Benjamin, who had a large house in Claremont, a Cape Town suburb that was middle class but informally segregated. Though she was a strong and opinionated woman, Ma Benjamin provided the two girls with a measure of discipline, security, and a sense of their extended St. Helenian family. Benjamin later described this period of her life with Ma Benjamin to Francis Davis of the *Philadelphia Inquirer:* "I was raised by my grandmother who was very strict, very strict, very proper, very British in her ways, though she was quite dark, quite African-looking. I was a very lonely child, and music was my solace, along with daydreaming, which I indulged in constantly" (Davis 1986).

When Claremont was declared a suburb for Europeans only, as part of the Group Areas legislation, people of mixed race were required to move to Coloured areas of the city, and the Benjamins lost their house. (Decades later, after years in exile, Benjamin purchased an apartment in the historically white part of Claremont—an important step in reclaiming a place for herself in the "new" South Africa.)

From an early age, then, music was Benjamin's vehicle of escape from the harshness of everyday life. She expresses the place of music in her life in one of her own compositions:

Music
Is the spirit
  Within you
  Within you
Deep within you
Deep within you
  Deep
Within you
  Is
Music, music, music.
Find your sound
Then let it flow
Free
And
Easy
And out
Music, music, music.
  (Rasmussen 2000, 64)

The Musical City

In Sathima's childhood, there was music everywhere. It could be heard on radio, in live performances at home, or at church and school. There was always live music on the streets, live and mediated musical performances at "bob parties" (similar to rent parties in the United States), at the movies, in the live sounds of teenage Bop clubs or the dance bands of Saturday night ballroom dancing. A song first heard in a film on a Saturday afternoon could be heard repeatedly in the following week—over the air, on records, and performed live in a cover version by local bands or in talent contests held at the cinema and fundraising events organized in churches and community halls.

Music in the Home

Ma Benjamin loved British popular songs, and her house was often filled with music. At gatherings in the 1940s and 1950s, family members sang the popular songs of the 1920s and 1930s, Benjamin recalls, accompanied on the piano by her grandmother. During the week, while everyone undertook their household chores, Ma Benjamin played the tunes popular in her youth—"Ah! Sweet Mystery of Life" or "The Roses of Piccardy" on an old phonograph. On Sundays, someone in the family who could play the piano would come to the house, and everybody would sing along. On occasion, the family would gather for a more spirited celebration and dance the night away to the sounds of these old tunes streaming out of the gramophone. "They were wonderful melodies," Benjamin would recall decades later. "They played in my head" (personal communication, April 9, 1990). Benjamin archived these melodies in her memory. In 1999, she would return to Cape Town to record eleven of these songs with a Cape Town trio, but in a jazz rather than straight style of performance (eight of the songs appear on *Cape Town Love,* 1999).

Sunday was the day Benjamin and her sister Joan participated in another musical repertory: that of the Wayfarer missionaries who held Sunday School classes in Ma Benjamin's garage. Benjamin recalls the wonderful melodies of the old English hymns, "Onward Christian Soldiers," "The Church's One Foundation," and "Joy, Joy, Joy, With Joy My Heart Is Ringing." (Many of these songs were also sung at school, as part of the National Christian Education policies of the apartheid government.) All the neighborhood children attended Sunday School with Bea, Joan, and the two white missionaries from the United States. After lunch, the children joined the congregation for the eventide service. Though Ma Benjamin never attended, she insisted that the girls go regularly to church, which Benjamin did until she was about fifteen. At that time, seating arrangements were segregated at churches in Cape Town, as they were in cinemas. Whites sat in the front and Coloured church members sat further back. When Benjamin decided one day that she would sit in the forbidden zone, she was immediately informed that she should either move to the appropriate place for Coloureds or leave the building. Stunned by the cold reality of racism in the church community, Benjamin left and never returned.

Benjamin was more fortunate than many of the jazz musicians she later performed with, because for a brief period her father paid for piano and theory lessons. But when he left Cape Town to live in London for a few years, there was no money to pay for the lessons. Benjamin recalls that she preferred to express herself in songs she heard others singing rather than at the keyboard reading music. In this sense, her musical preference was more like that of her friends, most of whom taught themselves by careful listening and imitation.

Vincent Kolbe, retired librarian and devoted member of Cape Town's well-known District Six Museum, is one such self-taught musician. "As a young boy," he recalls, "I learned to play music, which many of us did, because you always had a relative or a neighbor or a friend who played in these carnivals, and there was guitars and instruments all over the place throughout the year. And these same people would play at dances and at parties in homes before hi-fi. And I learnt that way; you know someone would show you how to play the drum or how to play the bass or how to play a chord on the piano, and that was good enough for the next party" (to Michael Nixon, 1993, cited in Nixon 1996, 20).

When the gramophone wasn't playing in Ma Benjamin's home, the radio played all day long. These were the days before state control, when radio stations used to play all the music people heard in America—American and English popular music and jazz by the likes of Duke Ellington, Nat King Cole, Ella Fitzgerald, Doris Day, Joni James, and Billie Holiday. But no one in Ma Benjamin's house was ever permitted to sit down and listen. The sounds emanating from the radio provided the accompaniment for daily chores. So from the age of about ten Benjamin kept a pen and notebook hidden in her grandmother's wind-up Victrola. Whenever she heard a tune she really liked, she would quickly scribble down the lyrics. Since she could not afford to buy the sheet music or fakebooks herself, she simply listened to a song over and over until she knew it. In that way, all the styles and voices she heard over the radio became an integral dimension of her musical memories.

One of Benjamin's closest school friends is a woman named Ruth Fife. The Fife family was not St. Helenian and operated quite differently from the Benjamin household. The Fifes played the European classical repertory at home. Since Ma Benjamin refused to listen to it, the Fife home is where Benjamin heard European classical music and was first exposed to a family who were politically active—a dangerous thing to be. Once, during Benjamin's high school years, Ruth's brother, a mathematics teacher at the school, handed out leaflets protesting the celebration of the national holiday that commemorates the arrival of Jan Van Riebeek, the Dutchman who first settled in the Cape. The pamphlet decried the impact of European settlement in the Cape and the lack of acknowledgment of the integral place of people of color in that history. Because of this act of protest, and because he was involved with a woman of Indian descent, which was not allowed in the apartheid regime, he was forced into political exile in Nigeria.

Music in the Streets

In addition to the everyday music of men and women selling flowers, fish, and vegetables on the street in Cape Town, Christmas and New Year's were times of street processions and musical performances. Like many of her peers, Benjamin watched the live performances of Coloured street bands and choirs at Christmastime and

Music in the Streets: Christmas and New Year's

French jazz critic and author Denis-Constant Martin of a book on Cape Town's "Coon Carnival" provides an evocative description of the sense of excitement in Cape Town on New Year's Eve in the 1990s, when the *nagtroepe* (night troupes) start to arrive in the streets. Though Martin describes the experience in the 1990s, people who recall their childhood days typically remark on the sense of thrill and enchantment these kinds of street performances engendered in the 1940s and 1950s.

Nagtroepe, also called "Malay choirs," perform through the streets of their community. People gather with their chairs, thermos flasks, and blankets.

> At first it's like a rumor. One can hear "they're coming" whispered by hundreds of mouths. After a little while, a steady beat and a solid melody drift up from the direction of Wale Street. . . . A *voorloper,* or drum major, appears and capers wearing his peculiar high hat adorned with ostrich feathers, followed by a group of men dressed in track suits and caps and carrying sticks. They walk a sort of dancing step until they stop in front of the Star Club. All along they have been singing, and as they come nearer, the words become clearer. It's a *moppie,* a comic, upbeat song, making light of events that are a source of worry. The group, a *nagtroep,* on other occasions also called a *Hollandse* team, *sangkoor* or Malay choir, stops at the foot of the stairs leading to the Club. Its members assemble in a half-circle, with guitars, cello, and the *ghoema* drum at one end. A singer stands in the middle and starts a beautifully ornate tune in a high yet sweet voice. It is a love song, praising the faithfulness of a lovely sixteen-year old girl. The choir answers quite

over the New Year holidays. There were Malay choirs, brass bands called Christmas choirs, and minstrel groups. Benjamin recalls that she often followed the groups as they paraded through town and at times got lost in the process. There was something so magical about these processions that musicians and followers alike often experi-

---

Music in the Streets *(continued)*

> squarely and on certain sentences the fusion of the soloist's
> melody and the chords sung by the group creates a unique,
> almost magic sound. (Martin 1999, ch. 1)

The troupe is warmly received, fed, and then moves on to another street or gathering of people to perform. Simultaneously,
elsewhere in the community, groups of men, women, and children
meet in what is called a *klopskamer*—the headquarters of a "coon carnival" group. Much like the costumes of the Mummers in Philadelphia and the Mardi Gras groups in New Orleans, the costumes for
each group change every year, but were initially inspired by nineteenth-century minstrels. (The *nagtroepe* do not usually like to be associated with the "coons" because they consider them wild, lower
class, and not respectable.)

> Before leaving the *klopskamer,* members apply make-up to
> their faces. Some stick to the old minstrel pattern: black
> with white circles around the eyes and the mouth, or a vari-
> ation on it where half the face is painted black while the
> other half white. Many now prefer to use bright colors and a
> sprinkle of glitter, while others do not put on make-up at
> all . . . . Outside the stadium, the troupe gets into forma-
> tion. Two drum majors lead the way, sometimes followed by
> a *moffie,* a transvestite character. Then comes the board
> bearer, followed by the musicians, the "juveniles," and the
> rank and file kept in good marching order by "committees"
> who assist the captain. They enter the stadium and parade
> on the track. The competitions [between troupes] are
> about to begin. (Martin 1999, ch. 1)

enced the performances in trancelike states. One elderly fruit
hawker recalled, "I tell you, when we were little we would follow
[the bands and choirs] to wherever they went . . . we would try to
get near to them and walk with them. They sang up close to us . . . I
wanted to touch [them] . . . They was something, really beautiful,

Three participants in the New Year's Carnival, Bo-Kaap, Cape Town, January 1996.

they wasn't far away on radio. They was here, our choirs, singing for us" (cited in Nasson 1989, 302).

These troupes would either perform on the streets through the center of Cape Town for admiring tourists and community people, or, as was the case in the apartheid era, they were confined to Green Point Stadium, a sports arena in the center of the city. Carnival rhythms and musical terminology also crossed over into Cape Town dance band sounds and discourses. According to Nixon, "When the carnival troupes marched from the center of the city they had to walk directly uphill to Schotsche's Kloof, the band leader would cry 'Heuwel op!' (Go up the hill!)" (Nixon 1996). Vincent Kolbe explains:

> It can mean "heavy" or, musically, it means you've got to really pump now because you're going uphill now [. . .] but I know the old band leaders on the dance floor would now shout to the band, "Heuwel op!" Which means, you know, the drummer does something to the beat, you know. Or the after-beat is either sooner, or the after-beat is delayed. And that actually was reflected in the dance halls as well, in the movements. . . . And this must affect the way you create your rhythm and the way you create your melodies, you create your ac-

Marching through the streets in the center of Cape Town,
New Year's Carnival, January 1996.

companiment and you arrange your instrumentation and things like
that. (Nixon 1996)

Sound Recordings

The sound recording was the most common form of musical transmission in postwar Cape Town and the primary medium through
which jazz musicians in particular listened closely to the music from
England and America. Harold Jepthah, one of Cape Town's best-
known Charlie Parker soloists in the late 1950s, recalls that he
would use any means necessary to buy the latest 78 record of his favorite musicians. He remembers as a young boy telling his mother
that he had a toothache. She provided money for a visit to the den-
tist. Scheming Harry proceeded directly to the record store and returned home with a Coleman Hawkins record. Jimmy Adams, on
the other hand, refused to buy any recordings. He feared that if he
owned the records he would listen to them too closely and lose a
sense of his own sound and musical identity. Nevertheless, he regu-

larly borrowed the recordings purchased by Jepthah to help him shape his sense of American jazz. Vincent Kolbe explains that musicians not only played exact renditions of the music they heard in the cinema or on these records; they also drew on the album-cover images for their hair and clothing styles. If you were "Cape Town's Dizzy Gillespie," you took the Gillespie album cover to the barber and got the same haircut. Then you had the tailor duplicate the clothes you could see on the album cover.

It was not until her early twenties that Benjamin was exposed to the world of American blues and jazz through the record collection of her friend, the Swiss artist and entrepreneur Paul Meyer. Meyer lived in an elite though politically liberal coastal suburb of Camps Bay. Benjamin, now classified as Cape Coloured, was only allowed to enter it if she had a permit to work as a housemaid. To her family's chagrin, Meyer would take the young woman on the back of his motorcycle from Athlone, where Benjamin was living with her mother, to Camps Bay to hear his records. Both feared they would be arrested for breaking racial segregation laws like the Group Areas Act. But, Benjamin recalls, she was so desperate to hear this music that she was willing to take the risk.

Music on Film

For Sathima Bea Benjamin, going to the bioscope was closely tied to memories of family life with Ma Benjamin. The magical world of the cinema was the place for all to feast their eyes on the dream world made real, and their mouths on the treats they were able to buy: candy, potato chips, and *biltong* (usually dry, salted beef). "Saturday was your big day for the movies," Benjamin recalls. "That's where you would get your big dollop of American culture. I saw the musicals, the westerns. It was almost as if you had no choice. . . . We had three movie houses: one was in Lansdowne, which wasn't too far, we had to walk. In Lansdowne it was called the Broadway, and Claremont was called the Orpheum, and Wynberg was the Gaiety."

In the 1940s, when Benjamin began her regular viewing of American movies, the theater offered more than a chance to consume audio-visual images. For these young teenagers and aspiring performers, Hollywood films provided clearer models of popular performance by people of color. From the movies, Benjamin and her friends deepened their knowledge of jazz performance. *Cabin in the Sky,* starring Lena Horne as singer and Duke Ellington as band leader, and *Stormy Weather,* featuring a range of African-American jazz performers and variety entertainers, were two of the most popular movies shown in South Africa in the mid-1940s. But there were many others in which musicians like Billie Holiday, Cab Calloway, and the Ink Spots appeared. In the late 1940s through the mid-1950s, several local films on black South African performance were also produced and enthusiastically viewed by largely black and Coloured audiences.

In the increasingly monitored public environment, the movies were perhaps the only space that allowed a freedom in social (and romantic) interaction between Cape Coloureds in Cape Town in the 1940s and 1950s. There were no other contexts in which young Coloured girls were permitted to appear publicly without their parents. With its mix of reality and fictional material, the program at the theater, much like television was in the United States and Britain in the same period, kept the community in touch with the outside world. The darkness of the cinema allowed audiences to sit back and open their eyes to an otherwise inaccessible world of glamour and enchantment, or to keep them closed and to dream.

Historians Nasson and Jeppe both argue that "going to the movies" was a ritualized and often boisterous communal activity in Cape Town's "dream palaces" from the mid-1940s through the late 1950s. Vincent Kolbe, who grew up in the culturally diverse District Six, comments that in his community, Saturday night was movie night, and everyone in the family would dress for the occasion. He went with his mother and grandmother, who brought along sandwiches and a thermos of coffee. The standard program from 7:30 to 11:30 P.M. was a comic strip, the weekly serial (the forerunner of the soap opera), a western, and a love story or musical. Nasson explains:

> The local "bioscope" occupied a very special niche in the recreational life of the community, a place to which both adults and children went in order to be cocooned in the dream world of the flickering screen. Attendance was regular and habitual, as films continually widened

South African Film History

South Africa made no major contribution to the early inventions of global motion picture history, but it certainly participated in the excitement and intrigue invoked by the novelty of moving images in the late 1890s. Thomas Edison's name was held in awe by South Africans for his invention of the gramophone or "talking machine," the kinetoscope (a peep-show of moving pictures), and the kinetophone, which simultaneously transmitted moving pictures and accompanying sound. To operate the kinetophone, the viewer looked at the pictures through a slot while listening through a tube to a phonograph contained in the same box (Gutsche 1972, 10). This mechanical marvel is reported to have drawn a crowd of 2,000 people on the night it first appeared in Cape Town in January 1896. Many such mechanical novelties were introduced to the public as vaudeville or variety turns, combined with live entertainment—usually of the less respectable kind. They were generally either imported by South Africans who traveled to England and Europe and brought back the machines for commercial purposes, or they were introduced to audiences by itinerant magicians or prestidigitators. San Fransisco–born Carl Hertz was perhaps the most famous showman to visit South Africa in this period.

It was not until the late 1920s that the first "talkies" were introduced to the world at large, and to South Africa specifically. By this time, numerous permanent cinemas had been constructed throughout the country, and movie going had lost much of the social stigma that surrounded its initial introduction in seedy urban music halls. The first substantial talkie was shown in Johannesburg on July 6, 1929. A British production called *Mr. Smith Wakes Up*, it was received with great enthusiasm. *Syncopation,* first run in Johannesburg on September 13, 1929, was the first full-length talkie to appear in South Africa, and Al Jolson's *The Singing Fool* followed ten weeks later. *The Singing Fool* provided Cape Town audiences with their first taste of a feature length movie with synchronized sound in one of the earliest atmospheric theaters in the country. *Syncopation* arrived in the city on December 16, 1929.

South African Film History (continued)

Rio Rita (1930) was the film that made a lasting impression on South African audiences, many of whom had been skeptical of the future of talkies, considering the thirty-year tradition of silent film. "Produced entirely in Technicolor and combining attractive music with comic dialogue . . . *Rio Rita* captivated its audiences. People who had been to the 'bioscope' only once or twice in their lives journeyed to the Astoria [Theater] at Woodstock, Cape Town, to see it during a season of several weeks" (Gutsche 1972, 220). These early films exploited old variety and vaudeville music and comic turns, but also explored new possibilities.

In South Africa, the Disney cartoons, now animated with sound and music, suggested new levels of artistry and attraction for the public. *Snow White and the Seven Dwarves* was one of the first cartoon character films shown in the country. *The King of Jazz,* starring Paul Whiteman and his orchestra (1930) through the conventions of "trick photography"—in this case, showing Whiteman holding the entire orchestra in the palm of his hand—moved Hollywood movies onto a new level for South African audiences.

After World War II, the bioscope came to play a central role in the life of Cape Town's Coloured communities. Social historian Thelma Gutsche (1972) explains the origin of the term *bioscope* to refer to movie theaters. A certain Mrs. James, Gutsche writes, popularized the term when she traveled around South Africa in 1898 with Edison's "American Bioscope," the standard term at the time for "anything to do with moving pictures." The term was also popular in the United States for a short time. In England, people preferred to use *cinematograph,* shortened to *cinema;* and Europeans (from the Continent) used the word *kinematograph,* shortened to *kino.* Ultimately, the term *moving* or *motion pictures* was preferred in the United States because it dignified the rather vulgar entertainment milieu. As a result, *movies* was the most durable word used for motion pictures, though in South Africa *bioscope* was commonly used to refer to the cinema until the 1960s.

their audience appeal and imaginative power to transport people out of themselves, and the humdrum confines of their work and domestic lives at least once a week. . . .While [cinemas] tended to be fairly small and unpretentious in appearance, their names—the Star, the West End, the Empire, the British Bioscope—dripped with the promise of glamour or old imperial splendor. (Nasson 1989, 286–287)

Even though some theaters were segregated, and white theaters definitely more plush than those for Coloureds, these were the places where the entire community gathered. In these often crowded cinemas with their hard wooden seats, people would verbally engage with the film, passing comment on the actors, reading the subtitles out loud, sympathizing and warning film characters of impending danger. Women brought their babies, and young children came in groups to the weekly entertainment. Occasionally fights broke out in the middle of a movie between members of the audience.

In these largely working-class communities, Hollywood films provided the bulk of the entertainment: westerns, thrillers, and horror movies were the favorites for men and boys, while women preferred the musicals and "weepies," as they were called. White audiences of the time opted for British productions. Underscoring the importance of the cinema, almost everyone I have interviewed has stressed that at the time, there was no television to entertain individuals and communities or provide models of performance. (Television only came to South Africa in 1976.) It was the bioscope that promised the fantasy and magical sounds that so many Coloured people enthusiastically absorbed, and then performed live for the community in subsequent weeks.

Mediated and Live Performances Side by Side

According to a well-established tradition among Cape Town's Coloured movie audiences, live and mediated experience coexisted inside the walls of the theater. Audience members recall singing along with popular songs that accompanied "Tom and Jerry" cartoons, for example, and the words and music would appear on the screen to encourage collective participation. Many local theaters also staged elaborate live variety acts and hosted talent competitions. The Gaiety Bioscope ran an advertisement in 1936 that read:

A Gala Week

The Gaiety Bioscope will have a real Gala Week for their patrons and predict full houses. It is advisable to be early to secure seats. Chandu the Magician and the Western drama, Sharpshooter [will be the features]. . . . The Two Black Crows [clever, eccentric dancers and singers] in their tap dancing and singing will entertain in a clever interlude. . . . The Moffie [homosexual/cross-dresser] Concert Party will appear on Wednesday evening.

(*The Cape Standard,* May 26, 1936, 5–6)

The Gaiety was the theater where Benjamin first appeared in public as a singer when she was about eleven years old. Thinking back, she suggests that American and British films shaped her individually and musically on three levels. She identified with child stars of the movies and recalls that her aunt even braided her hair in the style of girl stars of the period. Film culture inculcated in her a particular notion of romance and romantic love that she could express desire for in song, and the emotional force of romantic love she witnessed in the cinema was enhanced for her by the beautiful film melodies. Many of these old tunes remain archived in Benjamin's memory and have become an integral aspect of her current performance repertory.

One Saturday afternoon, Benjamin's sister and close school friends urged her to enter the talent show held during intermission. Benjamin made them promise that if she did so, they would not tell Ma Benjamin, who would have been horrified to know that her young granddaughter was appearing on stage. Benjamin won the talent contest. The prize was eight free tickets to the movies. This was the first of many talent contests that young Sathima Benjamin would win in her teenage years, singing the popular songs of Doris Day, Joni James, and others. "Mr. Wonderful" and "Somewhere over the Rainbow" were her two signature tunes. Benjamin's close friend Ruth Fife recalls that when she heard Bea at that first talent contest, it was clear, even though she was using the words and melodies of others, Bea Benjamin already had her own distinctive style.

The content of the films made a deep impact on these talent contests. "For instance," Vincent Kolbe explains, "you had Cape Town's Perry Como, Cape Town's Louis Armstong. The moffies, the gays, always had Cape Town's Marilyn Monroe, Cape Town's Brigitte Bardot. It was all a kind of stage entertainment. Anytime a school or a church had a fundraising thing, the community would get up there and perform. You just had to" (Kolbe, personal communication, September 1996).

Social Dancing

Kolbe also noted one important mechanism for the importation of Hollywood culture into the local scene: borrowing melodies from films for local dance band performance. Kolbe and a friend were paid by one of the local bandleaders to go see the newest films as soon as they came to the local bioscope. They were instructed to memorize the words and melodies of a song sung, for example, by Nat King Cole, and then pass along this musical information to the bandleader. The next Saturday night the band would play Cole's newest song at social dances for the Coloured community, but the tunes were played "straight" to sustain the regular rhythms required of ballroom dance. It was in these live renditions by dance bands rather than in recordings that the majority of Cape Town's Coloured community heard the sounds of Hollywood and American jazz.

Vincent Kolbe recounts how he learned to play in dance bands:

> I was pushing twenty, I was in my teens. There were always churches and church youth clubs where you learnt all kinds of things like dancing and table tennis and what have you, and we have social evenings in glee clubs and there was a piano there and my friends and I had a little band.
>
> Then invariably some old-timers or some other members of the church or some ex-musicians would join us and we'd get to know them and they'd pull out their fiddles and they'd show us some things they used to do in their days. And I often wondered why they kept saying to us, "You guys play too fast. Your tempo's wrong." They insisted on this tempo. "Timing! Timing!" they'd say. And of course I

realized in later years that we were just a young, jiving, rock 'n' rolling crowd, you know, and we were more energetic. But there was this emphasis on rhythm and on good timing—a good swing. Which the older people would always complain that our timing wasn't good. They would dance more elegantly, they would dance with . . . how can I say it, it's like a delayed movement. You don't really put your foot down on the beat. Good ballroom dancers don't and good jazz musicians don't, you know. And I find that totally missing in today's disco-oriented [music]. (quoted in Nixon 1996, 21)

In order to keep up with the tastes of their clients, these dance bands had to learn a varied repertory, Nixon writes, including "Muslim songs, Jewish songs, Afrikaner songs, Portuguese songs, French songs, as they could expect to be hired by a diverse clientele. . . . Elite people would hire a local band, on the understanding that they could play carnival music. It might be a bow tie and black suit sort of occasion. These people would be very elegantly dressed. It would be all very respectable people. At the end of the evening the band would be expected to play a 'selection of music' in a 'raw and raunchy style'" (Nixon 1996, 21).

At least two kinds of jazz were performed in postwar Cape Town: swing band music for social dancing and avant garde jazz, in which improvising jazz musicians strove to master American styles while searching for a local jazz sound. But there was a great deal of crossover between the two styles: many of the musicians who played in the experimental jazz styles also performed for Saturday night dances in the community. During this period, performers were able to move between worlds with considerable ease. The two most important improvisational groups in Cape Town in the late 1950s and early 1960s were Abdullah Ibrahim's Jazz Epistles and Chris McGregor's Blue Notes (see McGregor 1996).

Though dance bands were not new to the Cape, they underwent considerable change during the postwar era. Cape Town had a long tradition of music with stringed instruments—fiddles, banjos, ukeleles—but that changed when musicians went to war and were exposed to the new craze called "jazz." As Vincent Kolbe observes, musicians went to serve in World War II with their stringed instruments and returned with brass instruments. They then adapted the traditional stringed sounds to horns, the saxophone in particular. This is where the wailing sound of the saxophone in Cape jazz developed. As a result, the sound of the Cape dance bands was transformed in the years after the World War II because, according to Vincent Kolbe, many of the musicians who played in these bands had either performed as musicians in the war efforts or been trained by those who had "gone north" to North Africa.

> In the army they learnt music, they could read music. They played in the band. They had a kind of education [that] other people didn't have. They had a kind of sophistication about them. And lots of these original bands, at least the ones I learnt from, were blokes that had actually been in the army. They were interesting to talk to, and they were very skillful and talented and . . . we learnt our music from them. [We] would play in bands where the bandleader was a Sergeant Major, you know, in the army, you know, disciplined, and he'd count. 123 or quickstep you know. And he would read. And he demanded the best out of you. . . . There was a kind of pursuit of excellence. The world we lived in was full of hope. (Kolbe, personal communication, September 1996)

Vincent Kolbe explains the importance of leisure time to the Coloured working class people in the postwar period. In his and Benjamin's parents' generation, when people lived close to their places of work, what they did in their leisure time was extremely important because it was during that time that the politically oppressed created a world of social gradations and status for themselves. Individuals joined sports clubs, a dance band, went dancing, or went to the movies. Kolbe outlines a transformation of young women through Saturday evening dances similar to that of the Cape Corps Band musicians: "So women would work a whole week in a factory, and Saturdays go to a dance with this gown, golden shoes, and a cigarette holder [as they had seen in the movies]. I mean all people, no matter what color you are or where you live, you fantasize on the weekend about being a princess for the night. And men would wear bow ties and black suits. And the music, the dancing hall, and so on" (Kolbe, personal communication, 1996).

Benjamin recalls that in her teens in the 1940s she spent every weekend dancing in local community spaces with a special dance partner. Many in the community fondly recall the dancing that occurred at neighborhood "bob parties," similar to African-American rent parties. A "bob," which equaled 10 cents, was the price you paid to enter the house of the party giver, who often had a live band or at the very least a piano player to entertain the guests. All proceeds from the party were used to pay rent or to cover household expenses. The live bands played the squares, the waltz, the foxtrot, and the samba—rhythms that shaped young Benjamin's sophisticated and relaxed sense of musical time. "I used to follow the dance bands and was always hearing the saxophone," Benjamin said, "so the melodies stayed, but I didn't always know the words. [Now] I do research [in the libraries in New York City] and I find these old things. And then it's a question of running the words over in my head and seeing what I want to do with them, but still trying to recapture, you know, those moments I felt in the dance hall, listening to the melody" (personal communication, April 9, 1990).

On Benjamin's latest compact disc, *Cape Town Love,* are at least two melodies that she remembers having danced to in Cape Town in the mid-1950s: "When Day Is Done" and "If I Should Ever Fall in Love Again." After the squares and the quadrilles, which became a little wild at times, these were the slow dances, used to calm everyone down.

Benjamin Discovers Cape Jazz

When Benjamin began her teacher training, she sang in the college choir, but despite her love for singing she was never asked to perform solos in the cantatas. One day she plucked up the courage and asked why this was so. The director told her she scooped too much with her voice. But playing around with the pitch was just a game she loved to play as she sang in the group, Benjamin recalls. Fortunately, the choir director realized how much she loved to sing in the choir, so he never excluded her from performing. Later, when she met up with Abdullah Ibrahim and started to listen seriously to recordings of African-American jazz singers and instrumentalists, she would identify her sound and playfulness most powerfully with the music of Billie Holiday. She heard in Holiday's sound an expressive quality that gave her a point of reference.

Benjamin's move into the Cape Town jazz scene began at age sixteen, when she met South African jazz musician and teacher Sam Isaacs. Benjamin remembers the first time she saw Isaacs, seven years her senior, leaning against a wall smoking a cigarette. "He looked just like a gangster!" she said. Even though the gangster image did not fit the personality of Sam Isaacs, it was one of the more prevalent movie images in the 1940s and 1950s in South Africa. A drummer, Isaacs played in a trio that played jazz in the style of George Shearing and had a gig at a skating rink for whites only. Benjamin was not allowed inside because she was Coloured, so she sat outside the rink and listened to the music through the windows. At intermission Isaacs would come and meet his new friend.

When she began teaching school at the age of eighteen, Benjamin and her sister Joan went to live with their mother in Kew Town, a Coloured housing settlement in Athlone reserved for men who had fought in World War II—a move that further encouraged Benjamin's move into jazz. Her mother, Benjamin discovered, was a self-taught ragtime pianist. When the girls came to live with her she bought a piano, and it was through the piano that mother and daughter reunited. This instrument became the center of wonderful evenings for Benjamin and the group of jazz-loving friends she began to gather around her. On occasion Benjamin, her mother, and her sister went to local hotels to sing. Self-taught, Eva Green could only play in the keys of C, F, and G, and she always played the melody of old songs like "Up a Lazy River," "Chicago," "Come Back to Sorrento," and "Ah! Sweet Mystery of Life."

When Benjamin first started to sing with other musicians in public, it was usually at a talent show, many of which were created as fundraising events for local charities and community projects. A newspaper notice mentions Benjamin's participation.

The Big Jazz Show Has All the Talent
Jazz fans were treated to some high-octane music at the Woodstock Town Hall during the week when five leading jazz groups broke

loose with a concert in aid of various Peninsula youth clubs. But if you missed the session, not to worry. All these artists have offered to play for "Post's" big jazz night in the Cape Town City Hall in a few weeks time. Every Penny Raised Goes to the Cape Mental Health Society to Start a Building Fund. All Will Be There.

(*Golden City Post*, April 30, 1958)

The talent shows were modeled on variety programs. "You would be on the same bill as local tap dancers, acrobats, it could be anything that people found entertaining," Benjamin told jazz writer Sally Placksin in 1983 (Rasmussen 2000, 13). "But there were a lot of singers, both male and female, not just in the jazz vein, but doing songs that were popular at the time." One man, Joey Gabriels, sang opera.

> When the emcees would announce Joey Gabriels, . . . they would announce, he was Cape Town's Mario Lanza or Carusso or whatever. . . . Okay, we would all be back stage and just walk on the stage and go to the microphone (which probably wasn't working or working and making squeaks) . . . and there comes Joey Gabriels. He would not come from backstage. When they announced him, he came from the back of the cinema. You know, with a big chest and everything, just so pompous and full of conceit. This was all part of the act. He'd get to the stage and walk to the middle and he would take the microphone stand and walk over to the side and put the stand down there, like I don't need this. And he'd just stand there, a gorgeous tenor, you know. It was always the same thing, people always wanted the same thing. He would just get these ovations, he was so flamboyant. (Benjamin, personal communication, October 1996)

Gabriels later changed his name to Giuseppe Gabriello when he left South Africa to study opera in Italy.

Benjamin remembers the audiences at those performances as "that wonderful community of people who loved the music, who got involved. It just naturally brought people together, it was happening in Port Elizabeth, and Cape Town. In Johannesburg, you had tons of musicians there. I mean it was so beautiful. You had such a connection" (Benjamin, personal communication, March 9,

1990). She also observes that those Cape performances were completely unmediated. There were no recordings of Cape Coloured
music to make a musician famous. People knew about her vocal
abilities by word of mouth alone. She sang all over—in hotels,
clubs, school, and jazz concerts.

> Your public, they were the critics, and they would let you know. "Oh
> no, you're singing *that!*" They would throw things at you, you know.
> You really had to be very careful because they could take you off and
> replace you with someone else who would really do something beau-
> tiful. So it was really a tough audience, but also a beautiful audience.
> Because if you sang something, and you really felt what you were do-
> ing, they would respond. You would know it. They were so warm. You
> could almost hear them breathing with you. That's the way it was. It
> was always such a rewarding experience. (Benjamin, personal com-
> munication, April 29, 1990)

Night Club Life in Cape Town

One day after returning home from teaching school, Benjamin was
busy picking out a Doris Day tune on her mother's piano and
singing along when a man named Bertie Smith came to the door
selling brooms. He told her she should become a jazz singer and
that they were organizing a jazz concert at the Glemore Town Hall
in Athlone. Smith invited her to come along and sing and promised
to introduce her to the musicians. She was to perform the song,
"Don't Blame Me." Benjamin went to that concert, where she met
up with Cape Town's community of jazz musicians, all of whom had
learned their repertory from repeated listening to jazz records.

> There were people there who could play Errol Garner's solo to every
> note that Errol Garner played. Cape Tonians are very good at imitat-
> ing. Excellent. We always had the Cape Town Jerry Lewis, the Cape
> Town Bing Crosby. I think for a while I was either Doris Day or Joni
> James, before I went into the other thing [jazz]. After that concert,
> after I sang only the one song, "Don't Blame Me," the guys said that
> they were working in the clubs. If I wanted to come and work there, I

should just turn up. And I would go. Every weekend [my sister] Joan and I, we couldn't wait to go into the town, to go to Darryl's night-club or the Navigators Den. (Sathima Bea Benjamin, interview with the author, New York City, October 4, 1996)

In the mid-to-late 1950s, there was a moment where Coloured musicians were hired in Cape Town clubs more frequently than white bands because the Coloured musicians would play for less and, apparently, were more reliable. The clubs ranged from elite dinner-dance venues to seedy strip joints. The Balailaka and the Navigators Den were two of the less respectable clubs. Jazz was per-formed more often in the white clubs than in the Coloured com-munities, where band music for dancing was the primary form of "jazz." Of course all this would change in the 1960s, when no more mixing in public places across the color bar was permitted and white clubs began to import Portuguese and Greek musicians.

Benjamin's friend Sam Isaacs recalls playing nightly in one of the clubs that had white strippers. Because the musicians were Coloured, a curtain was drawn to hide the musicians when the strip-pers began their act. Ironically, Isaacs noted, there was no curtain in rehearsals. The public face of apartheid was replete with anomalies. Even though these clubs hired Coloured musicians (a practice that would later be prohibited), the musicians spent the intermissions with the staff in the kitchen—"just like black American musicians I had read about had to do in the South," Benjamin commented in November 1986.

The Public Library

Aside from her musical performances, Benjamin spent her evenings in the Kew Town library reading about the African-American experi-ence and listening to jazz recordings as part of a Jazz Appreciation Club run by the librarian, Vincent Kolbe. According to Kolbe, Ben-jamin's friend and a jazz pianist himself, the library was the hub of social and artistic activity—a bohemian community that included several sensitive, artistic schoolteachers. It was here that Benjamin listened to sound recordings of African Americans playing jazz and read the writings that inspired the Civil Rights movement in the United States. Kolbe provided her with books by Richard Wright, Langston Hughes, W.E.B. du Bois, and others. She even found the early autobiography of Billie Holiday, *Lady Sings the Blues: The Searing Autobiography of an American Musical Legend* (1956), before the Nationalist government banned it.

Benjamin began to question her identity. By reading of the experience of a people called "Colored" in the United States, Benjamin realized that she and her people were not alone in their experiences of the harshness of racism, and that others called "Colored" were singing the same music she was.

Traveling Shows

Like most of South Africa's Coloured and black performers in the 1950s, Benjamin participated in the traveling jazz and variety shows that were common in South Africa before the state clamped down on the freedom of movement of people of color. White entrepreneurs, who talked continually of taking the troupes "overseas," organized the groups. In 1957, at the age of 20, the young Benjamin joined impresario Arthur Klugman's traveling show, *Coloured Jazz and Variety*. More variety than jazz, the Arthur Klugman show was crucial in helping to develop Benjamin's sense of improvisation, as both a musical skill and a life skill. Big ideas and equally large failures were not uncommon in these traveling shows.

In this show Benjamin met Cape saxophonist and big band arranger Jimmy Adams, a central figure in the early history of jazz band performance in Cape Town. After going as far as Zimbabwe in a bus that regularly broke down, the musicians were left stranded in Mafeking, close to the South African border. Penniless, several of the performers had to entertain local people in order to be fed and housed. Both Jimmy Adams and Benjamin have warm memories of the hospitality of the people of Mafeking at that time. The gig they organized there was extremely popular, earning them just enough money to find transportation back to Johannesburg.

Although Benjamin remembers performing with *African Jazz and Variety* when it came to Cape Town in the late 1950s, the primary

Zonk!: South African Jazz and Variety

In the 1950s a handful of films about black South African experience and culture were made in South Africa. Three in particular have recently been reissued by Villon Films in Canada: Zonk!, African Jim, and Song of Africa. Zonk! is perhaps the most interesting film because it represents the kinds of live variety show performances common in black and Coloured theaters in the period. It also provides a remarkable historical glimpse at how deeply American performance culture had embedded itself in South Africa. A review of Zonk! in the largely white Cape newspaper The Argus, in December 1944, describes it as a nationally celebrated African revue that performed in the Cape Town City Hall. It praises the show for its originality and praises the performers for their talent and versatility and for being "better than their American prototypes." It also lists excellent tap dancing, a first-rate band, and some Negro spirituals among the films "surfeit of good things."

Zonk! is typical of the kind of variety shows common in South Africa between the world wars and in the post–World War II era. Called "African" entertainment, these shows included a surprising amount of "non-African" material. The shadow of minstrelsy characterizes the show. But one has to realize that in watching performances that originate in one place and travel elsewhere, it is important not to read the same contexts and messages into the texts. Minstrelsy and its impact on black performance culture is a complex historical and political issue. As I have already suggested, the "Coon Carnival," which may seem a horrific title to those outside of its culture, is what the working-class Coloured people who perform in the New Year's festivities call their festival. We must be careful not to brush South African performance cultures with the same political paint used elsewhere but instead remain open to other readings of the images and sounds that streamed in from the outside and rooted themselves locally in new and different ways.

group she traveled with was Coloured Jazz and Variety. At the time, jazz musicians from Cape Town and Johannesburg were in close contact with each other. The community was quite small, and musicians like Dollar Brand, Hugh Masakela, and Kippie Moeketsi traveled the thousand miles between the two cities quite regularly. The traveling shows enabled musicians to work together frequently.

Many African performers launched national and international careers after performing with *African Jazz and Variety* (AJ&V). These include Miriam Makeba, Hugh Masakela, and Sonny Pillay in the United States, Gene Williams, who traveled to Britain to work with bandleader Jack Parnel, and Jeff Hujah and Gambi George in Sweden. Some, like Abigail Kubeka and Dolly Rathebe, stayed in South Africa to pursue solid careers as singers there. Following the success of AJ&V, the newly formed Union of Southern African Artists organized the now well-known Township Jazz concerts in white areas (recordings of these sessions have been reissued by Gallo Records).

The Golden City Dixies was the first performing ensemble to travel abroad. In April 1959, *Zonk! The African People's Magazine* reported on their impending trip.

> At last, after many years of having farewell concerts and publicity about going overseas, a show is really going overseas, and our congratulations and good-luck wishes go with the Golden City Dixies, a live vital coon show which has left by air for a tour of Britain and the Continent, the first entertainment group from the Union [of South Africa] to tour overseas. They will give concerts and have been booked to appear on television. . . . Corrine Harris and Elizabeth Julius, both polished performers, are the female contingent of the show. Arthur Gillies, the wizard of the keys, is on the piano. Gambi George, South Africa's king of the drums, handles the percussion; Shimmy Peter Radise, tenor sax master; Graham Tainton is show compere and other famous artists such as Jusuf Williams and Brian Isaacs go to make up a very competent group of performers. (*Zonk!* April 1959, 12)

Fundraising and musical performance were integrally connected in twentieth-century South Africa. In 1953, in an attempt to build a swimming pool in Orlando township in Johannesburg, Anglican priest Trevor Huddleston organized a concert featuring black talent in the Bantu Mens' Social Center. Many of the performers who were popular in the townships performed at that event, including

Dolly Rathebe, the Manhattan Brothers, and composer Todd Matshikiza. A few white people attended the performance. They were so taken with the quality of work, they decided to constitute an organization, called the Union of Southern African artists, that would strive to encourage and protect black performers.

In 1958, lawyer Harry Bloom heard a black choir at a Salvation Army school and was so impressed, he decided to join the handful of whites working to promote black performers in South Africa. In response to a widely reported story of a South African boxer, Ezekiel Dhlamini, who was jailed because he killed a gang leader, and in a moment of jealous anger murdered his girlfriend, Bloom wrote the story of a fallen hero and called his piece *King Kong*. Todd Matshikiza was asked to write music to accompany the story, and the first African opera, *King Kong*, was created.

This piece of musical theater was remarkable for the way in which it developed and honed the talents of young black South Africans, for the successful collaboration between idealistic black and white South Africans, and for the way in which the production showcased music and dance genres popular in South Africa at the time. These included gumboot dance, Sotho traditional dances, work songs, religious songs, pennywhistle songs, and the *kwela* and *patha patha* dance styles. Borrowing from the ideas of London's West End and Broadway, *King Kong* proudly exhibited black urban performance, first to integrated audiences at the University of the Witwatersrand, then to township audiences, and finally to South Africans more generally. The show was an extraordinary success.

King Kong opened in Johannesburg in February 1959. *Zonk!* journalist Mike Phahlane wrote a review.

The days of imitating (often poor imitations) American artists have passed. This era of show business certainly served its purpose, it spotlighted the latent talent possessed by our African artists, it also went to show that we were capable of great things, but let's face it, it was not our own—there was nothing African about our theatre. . . . Now after hard work and plenty of courage, the "King Kong" team has come up with something that is really our own, really African and above all real theater. . . . There are many bouquets to be handed out—the whole conception of the show is remarkable and what "Porgy and Bess" means to the Negro of America, "King Kong" will mean to us. Todd Matshikiza's compositions, Spike Glazer's direction of the band, Harry Bloom's scripting, Leon Gluckman's production and the cast itself all deserve the highest praise! (*Zonk!* March 1959)

The news of *King Kong*'s success traveled abroad, and in 1960, producers from England and the United States traveled to South Africa to take a hard look. Two years after it opened in South Africa, the show opened in London on February 23, 1961. The show did not translate culturally for the British audience. Much of the local color and richness had been removed so that the British would understand the production, but in the process, it seems, *King Kong* lost its allure. The Broadway proposal was disbanded, and seven weeks after it opened in London, *King Kong* ended in financial ruin. Many of the performers were stranded in England without adequate resources to return home. Some finally acquired money to leave, and others decided to stay in England.

Township Jazz in Johannesburg

Stranded in Johannesburg after the abysmal ending of the Coloured Jazz and Variety tour, and without the finances to return to Cape Town, Benjamin spent the remainder of 1957 performing with Jimmy Adams in a variety of venues in Johannesburg. They were also invited to travel to Maputo (previously Lourenco Marques) in Mozambique to perform at Christmastime. While in Johannesburg she and Adams lived in Malay Camp, a housing settlement for people of mixed race, with a group of gangsters. "We were all sleeping on the floor," Benjamin recalls. "There was like a *shebeen* [a drinking establishment like a speakeasy], people were coming in so loudly. . . . But these people loved artists and musicians, and we'd sing for them. . . . We sang at functions in Johannesburg where the gangsters walked in with axes and things, and they said, they had you singing and you couldn't stop until they told you to stop" (Benjamin, personal communication, 1996).

South African singer Miriam Makeba tells of similar experiences in her autobiography (1987). She recalled what it was like to perform at these township jazz and variety events:

> Typically on their own, the men [in the Manhattan Brothers close harmony group] sing American songs by the Ink Spots and the Mills Brothers. When we are together we sing native African tunes as well as popular songs in English. Because we are black, however, we are not permitted to record songs in the English language. Six musicians make up the band: a sax, a trumpet, straight-up bass, piano and the drummers. . . . I am to be paid five pounds per show. . . . The shows, held in concert halls in the black townships, are long. We sing for four hours, from eight in the evening until midnight. The audience sits in chairs, which are removed for dancing afterward. The musicians then play until five in the morning. . . . In South Africa there is a new dance every week. The couples like to show off before the bandstand. But they are not the only ones who are showing off. Gangsters come to the clubs. I have been warned they can be rough places. . . . Some of our shows end in riots. . . . They are like actors, these gangsters, although they do not play. In South Africa, movies are taken very seriously, and there is a movie in the cinemas now in which Richard Widmark plays a hoodlum. They call him Styles, and he dresses up in a hat, a belted jacket, and those Florsheim shoes. (Makeba with Hall 1987, 46)

(For further information on the Manhattan Brothers and other close-harmony vocal groups in Johannesburg, see Ballantine 1999.)

From Dance Bands to Jazz Performance

Jimmy Adams and Cape Town's Jazz Bands

The story of Benjamin's close friend and jazz partner Jimmy Adams illustrates how Cape musicians progressed from dance band performance to jazz. Jimmy Adams claims to have started the first Coloured jazz band in Cape Town. He had played the accordion in his father's band since the age of ten. His father, Arnie Adams, ran a Christmas band and an old-style band, both of which had operated since at least the 1930s. As a teenager, Jimmy heard the band of African jazz musician Tem Hawker of Langa—the African township near Athlone—and fell in love with his music. He told his father that this was the music he wanted to play, and, in the face of stiff opposition from his father, when he was about seventeen he "took up music" and just about lived in Langa. He walked there and back to his home in Bridgetown, also near Athlone, to take lessons with Tem Hawker. He studied saxophone and jazz theory along with three other African jazz musicians in Langa township.

Adams' work over five years preparing his band produced good results. He worked with musicians who have become some of today's most popular jazz performers: Tony Schilder was 15 or 16 when he played in Jimmy Adams' band, and Hotep Galeta (then known as Cecil Barnard) was 17. Harold Jepthah was another musician who benefited from working with Jimmy Adams. The quality of the music notwithstanding, the band found itself facing misunderstanding, and racism. Coloured socialites in the inner city were so accustomed to traditional ballroom/*langarm* dance music that Jimmy Adams' band was not well received. Says musician Eddie George, "The Coloured people were not ready for him and so his band was not popular at all. The musicians in his band all became strong musicians. . . . But there was no future for jazz in the popular dance scene. Jimmy's band stopped in about 1958/9" (Nixon 1996, 21–23).

Vincent Kolbe recalled, "Jimmy Adams was one of the only guys who could bridge the gap [between Coloured music culture and jazz and the African music world]. Jimmy Adams' was never a very popular band. He played Cole Porter, et cetera, and his smooth style was not so popular in the dance halls." (Nixon 1996, 23).

Another musician, Willis Jails, was more cautious. He said his band followed "Jimmy Adams' style . . . our music was very orchestrated, lots of saxophones, two altos and two tenors. In between dance numbers we'd push jazz very subtly. The banjo was definitely out and guitars took over . . . eventually becoming electrified. . . . Rock 'n' roll was taking off but we didn't feel threatened as long as we included it to a small degree in our repertories. We still catered for the older generation's style of music—ballroom. We just adapted a little and compromised where necessary" (cited in Gassert 1988, 34).

Benjamin's Return to Cape Town

On returning to Cape Town, Benjamin continued to teach and moonlight as a singer at night and over weekends. But moonlighting was illegal if you taught public school, so the lifestyle did not last long. On one occasion a reporter arrived to write an article on a jazz singer who was also a teacher, an unusual combination for the teaching profession.

HER NAME SPELLS J-A-Z-Z

Around Cape Town's sleepless night-spots the name of Beatrice Benjamin spells J-A-Z-Z.

It is jazz in its careful, sophisticated moods. Jazz wrapped up in glamour, jazz sung delicately, teasingly, and lovingly. For "Beaty" Benjamin as hundreds of her fans know her, has a way of using her face, her body and hands, to sing a song, thereby enriching its message.

Recently Beaty went to the Naaz—Cape Town's plushiest, jazziest, all-race nightclub. Her voice, deceptively dreary, sometimes smoky and sad, reached out to the customers as she sang: "It Could Happen to You."

Then galloping away with "Fine and Dandy," Beaty whooped it up, eyes closed, forgetfully alone, in a packed nightclub. The applause at the end was worth it, for Beaty Benjamin has just made her finest statement.

At her most original Beaty breaks up the pace of the song and its lines, never losing the beat, and achieves a wonderful personal style that taps the true sources of her power.

Beatrice teaches school by day and sings by night. She has a heart too. Once she sang for a POST charity show to help neglected mental cases.

The fact that she gets engagements in all-White clubs hasn't gone to Beaty's head. On Saturdays and Sundays you can see her, working hard at the "Ambassador's Club" rehearsing. This chocolate gal is just "Fine and Dandy!" (*Golden City Post,* August 26, 1958, 7)

The newspaper article angered the school principal, who summoned Benjamin to his office and reprimanded her for her club singing. Women who sang jazz were not to be trusted, he told her, and were of questionable moral standards. After that, the principal came into her classroom to check on her every morning. She was also reprimanded because it was illegal to have more than one form of employment if you worked for the government, as all public school teachers did.

Against the wishes of many of who knew her, Benjamin decided to leave the relative security of the teaching profession for the more adventurous but uncertain world of jazz performance. From 1959 she began performing with several ensembles and pianists, including the Harold Jepthah trio and pianist Henry February's Nat King Cole Trio (February is the pianist with whom she would recorded *Cape Town Love* in 1999) in white nightclubs in the Cape Town area. At about this time she first met and performed with Abdullah Ibrahim, known also as Dollar Brand.

Jazz at The Ambassadors

The new jazz musicians in 1950s Cape Town were a serious group. "Jazz then was such a religion," Kolbe recalls. "No one spoke money then. You sat there reverently" (cited in Nixon 1994, 22). Kolbe described to Nixon the first jazz concert in District Six, Cape Town, conducted without white musicians.

In about 1955, the University of Cape Town Rag (a student group organizing the annual opening festivities of the academic year) decided to include a jazz concert in its program. Probably an imitation of Dave Brubeck's Jazz Goes to Campus. This was at the Weizmann Hall. The white racist musicians who never really jammed, though they could read very well, [dominated] the show. They eventually formed an all white union later . . . And Harold Jepthah, who was the best of our guys, sat with his sax completely ignored.

We were so disgusted, that I approached the priest who said we could have the hall, which was free on Wednesday night. We said we'd charge 5 bob a head and whatever was taken at the door would go to the church. We had a lot of big bands, including . . . the Merry Macs and Dougie Erasmus' big band. It was such a massive success that people are still talking about it. At the wake for Dougie Erasmus (September 1995) all the guys were there and recalled that concert.

Nixon also described the lively club jazz scene that developed during the 1950s.

The new jazz scene of the 1950s found its operational base in the clubs of Woodstock, a suburb just outside of the city center, which was something of a "gray" area, i.e., not so dominated by coloured culture. There were clubs like the Naaz and the Mermaid, and the Zambezi inside the city center. The Naaz . . . would have white and black musicians playing together, such as Chris McGregor, who played with African and Coloured musicians.

Richer people came to slum in Woodstock. There were quite a few wealthy white jazz fanatics who spent heavily there. They brought their friends. They looked very casual but we knew they were rich. . . . The only previous mixing I was aware of was in the Communist Party, but that was all quite Camps Bay, really quite elite. In '50s jazz culture it was a different kind of thing. In the clubs there was mixing to the point of contravening the Immorality Act! Not only was mixed clubbing a problem for the apartheid government, but individuals' relationships were targeted for individual harassment. Maude Damons became a prominent jazz singer from District Six. She ended up in London as the cops were after her and her white lover. Hotep had an older German girlfriend and they had to leave the country. Had it been left to itself, this jazz scene could have developed into something remarkable. . . . It was an apartheid casualty. (Nixon 1994)

Though Ibrahim and Benjamin both performed in these nightclubs, the place that these two ultimately created for jazz as an art form was The Ambassadors. By this time, Ibrahim was no longer performing with local dance bands but was developing his own style of jazz performance. The Ambassadors was the space for exploring new musical (and social) possibilities. Benjamin recalled: "The guy who owned [The Ambassadors] was Dave Saunders, and he was a friend of Abdullah's. He had this lovely space in Woodstock. You had to climb these stairs. He had this space and he had a piano. And Abdullah started. We had thirteen people the first week, we used to do it only on Sunday nights. And after a couple of weeks, we couldn't contain all the people. It was just a place where you went and you sat down and listened. There was no dancing, no food, nothing" (Sathima Bea Benjamin, personal communication, April 1988).

In May 1961, one of *Drum Magazine's* reporters described the Sunday night jazz scene at The Ambassadors:

> The chairs are arranged carefully, like pews, and the congregation is as devout as any other Sunday night gathering. In the darkened corner the tall, thin guy with the tight jeans and the size 12 army boots is leading his group through an original composition. The long, bony fingers slide or thump, caress or squeeze the notes out, and the horn, the bass, and the drums, catch the message and pass it on.
>
> Dark as it is, the Dollar is gleaming tonight. This is the real stuff, the pulse beat of the jazz world in the Cape, and Dollar Brand and his group are pumping it out—though this is their night off from six days of cafe-capers with the beatnik gang.
>
> From this center of the jazz scene, which is up an iron staircase near where the Cape's trolley buses get their nightly wash and brush-up, the music world stretches far down the Peninsula, and every other month some new guy with a horn or an alto sax or a bass is coming up from the shadows to catch the ear of the people who know their music. (*Drum Magazine*, May 1961, 46)

Life changed drastically for all Coloured musicians in 1960, in the aftermath of the Sharpeville Massacre and the state of emergency declared by the government. The state clamped down on all performance that catered to mixed ensembles, audiences, or clientele. By the early 1960s it became clear to Abdullah and Sathima that it would be impossible to survive as creative artists in South Africa. Jazz performance, with all its mixing of people, had become a dangerous activity, monitored and raided by security forces. "I never thought about leaving South Africa," Benjamin says. "It just happened very quickly and very naturally because the situation got very bad. . . . And it started to get very empty. And that is when we moved. We would either have to shut up completely or we'd have to leave. And that's when we decided to leave, in 1961, because it became impossible, not only to do jazz. To do any kind of music. It became very repressive" (Benjamin, personal communication, April 1990).

Literally starving for lack of opportunities to perform, they decided to travel to Switzerland where Paul Meyer had promised to help them find work and suitable housing. Dollar Brand and Benjamin left the country after a farewell concert at The Ambassadors to raise money for their air tickets, then flew to Zurich to begin the next phase in their lives as jazz musicians a long, long way from home. Others left South Africa during the same period as well. Harold Jepthah, for example, left in the early 1960s with one of the country's most popular traveling jazz and variety troupes, The Golden City Dixies. Given the opportunity to study the European repertory at a conservatory in Sweden, Jepthah remained in northern Europe playing clarinet for a symphony orchestra in Sweden until he was able to return to South Africa in the early 1990s (interview with the author, Cape Town, December 1999).

Jazz Migrants

Sathima Bea Benjamin and Abdullah Ibrahim followed several South Africans who had left before them, including singer Miriam Makeba, trumpeter Hugh Masekela, and Ben "Satch" Masinga. It was not easy to leave Africa, Benjamin recalls. "We went to the unknown. That was so shocking. It was so rough and cold. We had to keep moving to survive. We did live in Zurich, but that was like a base and we moved out from there. And the further north we went [to Scandinavia], the further I felt away from home, and I really mean home, deep inside. But, I think, you know, the music always saved me" (Benjamin, personal communication, April 29, 1990).

Dollar and Benjamin ended up performing in a variety of clubs in Switzerland. One night, when Dollar had his band at the Club Africana, Beattie heard that Duke Ellington was in the neighborhood. She went to his performance, then went backstage to try to meet him. She was lucky that night. He suggested that she stay backstage and wait until the end of the show, which she did. Prior to meeting her, Ellington had been asked by the U.S. State Department to travel to South Africa, but he had refused when he was told he would have to perform before segregated audiences (Benjamin, personal communication, April 1997). Meeting up with these two South African jazz musicians who knew his music so intimately was clearly a fortuitous moment for Ellington as well as Benjamin and Dollar Brand. Ellington agreed to come and hear the Dollar Brand Trio. He stayed for a couple of items, and then turned to the young Benjamin.

> "And what is it that you do?" Ellington asked Benjamin. "Are you the manager?"
>
> "No," she answered. "But I sing sometimes."
>
> "Then you must sing," said Ellington with matter-of-fact insistence. "Go and sing." (Hajdu 1997)

Sathima did sing, though the recording of the session was not released immediately. She found copies of the tapes and released a CD of the session in 1997. This is the recording referred to at the start of the chapter.

The following day, Ellington, who was then both a performer and producer for Frank Sinatra at Reprise Records in Paris, met with the two South Africans in his hotel in Zurich. He arranged to meet Benjamin and the Dollar Brand Trio in Paris three days later, on the morning of February 23, 1963, in the now defunct Barclay Recording Studio in Paris. Performing with Dollar Brand were South Africans Johnny Gertz on bass and Makaya Ntshoko on drums. They played six instrumental pieces that were later released as *Duke Ellington Presents the Dollar Brand Trio*.

The other thirty tracks they recorded were never released in Ellington's lifetime. Benjamin sings on twelve tracks, accompanied on piano by Ellington, Billy Strayhorn, or Dollar Brand, and Swedish pizzicato violinist Svend Asmussen. Ellington told Benjamin that the record company thought the pieces were not "commercial" enough. Never having heard the recordings, Benjamin came to believe that they had been lost or destroyed—that is, until July 1994, when Strayhorn biographer David Hajdu played a cassette copy of the recording to her in New York City. While doing research for his book on Billy Strayhorn, Hajdu had met with Gerhard Lehner, the studio engineer who was working in Barclay Studios in Paris on February 23, 1963. Lehner had been a soldier in the German army when American soldiers captured him in Russia during World War II. Taken as prisoner of war by the Americans, he had been persuaded to work for the U.S. Armed Services Radio Service in Munich. He was subsequently hired as the chief engineer at the Barclay Studios and had been involved with the recording of many of Duke Ellington and Billy Strayhorn's musical sessions.

Lehner was particularly impressed with the recording session Strayhorn and Ellington had with the young South Africans. In fact, because he liked the sound of Benjamin's voice so much, he had illegally made a second copy of the morning's work. This was the music that Benjamin heard in her apartment in July 1994, but it would take more than two years before she was able to release twelve tracks of that historic morning in Paris on the compact disc she called *A Morning in Paris*. The twelve American jazz vocal standards on that disc include "Darn That Dream," "Solitude," "I'm Glad There Is You," and "A Nightingale Sang in Berkeley Square." The Benjamin-Ellington compact disc was launched at a live performance by Benjamin, several New York musicians, and John Blake, a Philadelphia jazz violinist. Sitting in the front row were Duke Ellington's flamboyant sister, Ruth Ellington, as well as several members of the Duke Ellington Society.

For Benjamin, Ibrahim, and a number of other South African musicians, jazz became the means of survival during more than three decades of political and cultural exile from South Africa. Specifically, it was their knowledge of American popular and jazz music, along with several fortuitous encounters with African-American jazz musicians, that enabled several South Africans to settle in England and the United States. Among others, Miriam Makeba was taken under the wing of Harry Belafonte, both Hugh Masekela and Ben "Satchmo" Masinga were guided by Louis Armstrong, and Abdullah Ibrahim and Sathima Bea Benjamin were greatly assisted by Duke Ellington.

A radio journalist once asked Abdullah Ibrahim if he heard African elements in the American jazz he listened to in Cape Town in the 1950s. Ibrahim replied that he believes jazz is "Africa based." For this jazz pianist there was an inherent connection between the sounds of jazz and the music of contemporary Africa. "For us [in Cape Town], Ellington was never an American. He was just the grand old man in the Village." Similarly, Duke Ellington is reported to have remarked upon his arrival in Dakar, Senegal, in 1966, "After writing African music for 35 years, here I am at last in Africa!"

Europe was not an easy place for these young South Africans accustomed to warm sunshine, the sounds of English and Afrikaans and the Xhosa language with its complicated "clicks," and the presence of strong, vibrant communities. Europe and its culture had always been held in such high esteem in Benjamin's home and by those South Africans labeled "European" that Benjamin had come to imagine Europe as a mystical place. But the cold reality of Europe was something quite different. The language itself sounded alien, and the people seemed cold and indifferent. Few Europeans had any idea that people of color from South Africa could be performing jazz in its sophisticated inflections. Africa, with its warm people, its slow pacing, its customary friendliness, and its color and energy, seemed a long ways away. What saved these musicians during this period was the music itself. Feeling no connection to the society around them, Benjamin, Ibrahim, and the small group of exiled South African jazz musicians in Europe sustained themselves by playing their music and engaging with communities of international students living in Europe. This was truly a diasporic community of people, in but not of Europe.

From their base in Zurich, Benjamin and Ibrahim moved around Europe, to the United States, and even returned to South Africa for the birth of both of their children, who, Benjamin insisted, must be born on African soil. The couple moved between South Africa and the northern hemisphere with relative ease until the Soweto and related uprisings in 1976. On the video *Brother with Perfect Timing,* Ibrahim tells a remarkable story about two tunes that he performed in Cape Town in 1976, prior to the June uprising. According to Abdullah Ibrahim, these were the tunes titled "Mannenberg" (named after a township in Cape Town that is parallel in significance to

Soweto in Johannesburg) and "Soweto." The saxophone solos were sung to words all over the country as anthems of anger and resistance to the apartheid regime. Just a few months after the recordings of these tunes were released, the Soweto uprising occurred. This uprising, when the South African security forces gunned down schoolchildren protesting against having to be taught in Afrikaans, was the turning point in South African history. This traumatic event finally caused Benjamin and Ibrahim to make public their support of the banned African National Congress, the organization at the forefront of the struggle against apartheid.

At Home in New York City

After about fifteen years as jazz migrants, moving between Europe, the United States, and South Africa, Benjamin and Ibrahim decided to settle in New York City. Benjamin has described her relationship to this city as a "New York embrace," powerfully shaped by the musical relationship she has had, and continues to imagine, with one of New York City's finest jazz musicians, the late great Duke Ellington.

> I remember upon arriving in New York on a hot summer's day about a week before the Newport [Jazz] Festival in 1965 that it felt wonderful to me—the energy, the flow, the sight of its many diverse peoples. I was amazed that I did not feel intimidated at all. The excitement swooped me up and it felt good to be here.
>
> We stayed with a dear friend from Nigeria in Greenwich Village for some weeks after our arrival. The same day we arrived we went to meet and hear Duke Ellington at a concert in Harlem. It was all happening so fast—at times it seemed like a dream. Duke introduced us to his dear sister—Ruth—and we were sort of handed over into her care. She helped us to get settled, found us an apartment and later, upon Duke's advice, we decided to apply for the "green card" and settle in New York City. . . .
>
> We did several East Coast performances with Ellington. One was at Wolftrap, and another at Cotillion in Baltimore. The last time I sang with Ellington was around Christmas in 1972 at St. Peter's

Church in New York. I happened to be in New York at the time. He called and said, "Come and sing 'Come Sunday' with me." That was the last time I saw him as well. I was in South Africa in 1974 when he died.

In 1977 . . . Abdullah and I settled in New York City with our two children, Tsakwe [then six years old] and Tsidi [three months old]. Now it was time for me to stop travelling, settle down, and raise my children.

I've been here ever since. (Rasmussen 2000, 71)

In 1979, with the help of Ibrahim, Benjamin established the Ekapa label, primarily for the production and distribution of her own jazz recordings. *Ekapa* means "at or from the Cape."

It occurred to me that I could make a record . . . I really didn't know anything about it. I decided to do an album of Ellington songs because I figured, well, they don't know me here. Let me do something that is familiar. I was very unsteady with my own compositions, and I was very shy about [them]. Then I did it. I went into the studio. I did it.

And then I sat there with a couple thousand LP's and I said, "What am I going to do with all this?" So I had to get the courage and say, now who are all the critics in this jazz music business? I am going to write a little note, package it, and send it to them. They can either look at it and throw it in the bin, or what, I don't know. I waited six months. I got feedback. I almost fell off my feet. It was so positive, I couldn't believe it . . . I always say I have this little record company. I'm the President, I'm the musician, I'm the messenger, I go to the post office. I do absolutely everything. (Benjamin, Marymount College, Tarrytown, NY, October 1990)

It was in New York City, so far from the community of people who first enabled Benjamin to enter the world of jazz singing, that she began to find her compositional voice. Although she had had songs waiting inside her for many years, only when she settled in the city that claims to be the center of jazz performance did she muster the courage to write them down. Once she started, new materials began to come. Profoundly shaped by the anti-apartheid movement led by the African National Congress in exile and the United Nations in New York City, Benjamin's songs became explicitly political. Although the political strand of the American jazz tradition is not well known, it roots can be traced right back to Billie Holiday's powerful rendition of the song "Strange Fruit" so many years prior. And the tradition continued with the bold performances of Abbey Lincoln. With her "Liberation Suite," Benjamin made clear her support for the struggle against apartheid.

While she was in New York City, from 1979 through 2002, Benjamin produced nine LPs or compact discs of her own performance. In addition to the explicitly political lyrics of her composition "Liberation Suite," Benjamin's recordings include a combination of her very personal interpretations of Tin Pan Alley songs, show tunes, and jazz standards, as well as several of her original compositions that speak to her own vision of jazz, Africa, and the relationship of jazz to a sense of South Africanness.

1. *Sathima Sings Ellington,* recorded in April 1979 in New York City, with musicians Onaje Allen Gumbs, Vishnu Wood, John Betsch, and Claude Latief
2. *Dedications,* recorded in January 1982 in New York City with musicians Onaje Allen Gumbs, Carlos Ward, Buster Williams, Ben Riley, and Dom Um Ramao
3. *Memories and Dreams,* recorded in October 1983 at Rudy Van Gelder Studios in Englewood Cliffs, New Jersey, with musicians Onaje Allen Gumbs, Carlos Ward, Buster Williams, and Billy Higgins
4. *Windsong,* June 1985 at Van Gelder Studios, with Kenny Barron, Buster Williams, and Billy Higgins
5. *Lovelight,* September 1987 at Van Gelder Studios with Larry Willis, Ricky Ford, Buster Williams, and Billy Higgins
6. *Southern Touch,* December 1989 at Van Gelder Studios, with Kenny Barron, Buster Williams, and Billy Higgins
7. *Cape Town Love,* March 1999 at Milestone Studios in Cape Town with Henry February on piano, Basil Moses on bass, and Vincent Pavitt on drums

8. *The Best of Sathima Bea Benjamin with Friends,* 2001, released by Enja Records.
9. *Musical Echoes,* recorded in February 2002 in Cape Town with Stephen Scott on piano, Basil Moses on bass, and Lulu Gontsala on drums (Rasmussen 2000)

On occasion, Benjamin has organized performances of her own music, sometimes touring to the West Coast, or up the East Coast, to Europe, and since 1990, even back to South Africa. Each time she performs, either live on stage or in a studio, she works with the finest jazz musicians.

The Voice of Sathima Bea Benjamin

In 2000 Sathima Bea Benjamin wrote "taking a song—remembered or new—and having the freedom to adapt it to your own unique style, vision, and understanding of it, *that* is my understanding of a jazz singer. . . . The magic, the mysticism of that wonderful city [Cape Town], I carry within my soul. I remember songs, smells, sights, people—and it's all music to me. I know my sound, my sense of rhythm and time comes from there—and so it is that I endeavor through jazz singing to give that 'sound picture' to the listener" (Rasmussen 2000, 67).

But why jazz, a controversial choice that alienated her from family and friends? "I was innately attracted to jazz," Benjamin says.

> It happened at a time when I was thinking very deeply about all of this . . . about my own identity. It happened around 1957 through the 1960s. That was a very fervent time at home, and things were happening politically. And I was at such an age when it hit me. I said, "I'm not going to take this. . . . What am I going to do? I didn't write my own music then. That's the time I drifted to Duke Ellington's music . . .
>
> All I can say is that jazz came out of a very painful experience. It started with black people being ripped away, and then innately trying to go back. . . . They were denied so many things and were repressed. So the music came out of that. And that we [South Africans] were drawn to it, it just seems natural to me . . . Okay, we weren't ripped

away from our continent, but our continent was ripped away from us. And that's why I say it's similar, but not the same. (Benjamin, New York, March 1990)

How have the jazz critics responded to Benjamin's music? Recently, Benjamin told me that Lee Jeske, Philadelphia civil rights lawyer and jazz critic for the *Philadelphia Tribune,* told her he thought her music sounded like the piano music of jazz pianist Thelonius Monk, referring in particular to Monk's recording titled *Solo Monk* (recorded in 1964–1965, re-released in 1992). In that CD, as he spins out each "song without words," he demonstrates the importance of the melody embedded in a beautifully emerging sonic tapestry of instrumental voices weaving in and out of each other. And the rhythmic complexity of ragtime piano, foregrounded on that album, certainly rings in Benjamin's musical memory as the music her own mother played. But there is more. As Jeske says of the Monk reissue, Monk is the link between past and present, between old and new. "It's a twentieth century time capsule," writes Jeske, a statement we might just as easily write about Sathima Bea Benjamin's style of song performance. It is both "complex and simple, sophisticated and naïve, dense and spare."

Jazz critics Bruce Crowther and Ed Anderson paid tribute to Benjamin's performance style: "When it comes to the moment of performance, an overriding quality comes into effect. Every song that she sings, from Victorian ballads to Ellington, the songs from the great musicals to her own musings upon life, is performed with impeccable taste. She treats each individual lyric with respect and with regard to the sentiment intended by the writer and in some cases finds therein more than perhaps the writer intended" (Rasmussen 2001, 62).

In a 1983 review of a New York recital, *New York Times* critic Jon Parales wrote:

That voice is throaty and ethereal with just a hint of smokiness. Ms. Benjamin glides into a song, turning a melody into a series of smooth arcs and gracefully tapering off the ends of phrases. She favors slow tempos and even when her arrangements used a Latin or African groove—like the ingenious version of "I Let a Song Go Out of My Heart," her vocal lines took their time. She and the trio move in and out of time while maintaining a subliminal pulse, she could make a word cry out with just a flicker of vibrato. (*New York Times,* April 3, 1983)

At about the same time in *Downbeat* (March 1982), critic Fred Bouchard wrote glowingly of her performance in the Carnegie Recital Hall:

Sathima's concert in the dim, cozy [Carnegie] recital hall was sheer autobiography in song. She began her smooth unhurried way by exhorting the music with free associative poetry: "Sing naturally, like a bird . . ." She soared through two more orienting originals, "Music" and "Africa," backed nicely by a quartet led by pianist Onaje Allen Gumbs. Her African grandmother reared her on pop ballads not jazz, so she sang oldies like "Just a Song at Twilight" and "When We Were Very Young," with tinges of Holiday tone and intensity and a beautifully relaxed phrasing all her own. Teenage nightclub days had her dust off "Embraceable You," "You Do Something To Me," and "Someone to Watch over Me" (with a fine Gumbs chorus) that she built strong as pyramids, and creamy as kefir. Sathima developed the set with more standards, capped with unique version of "Say It Isn't So" (in a Cape Town rhythm, a hair's breath from calypso, where she squeezed out languorous quarter tones) and "A Nightingale Sang in Berkeley Square," decidedly un-British with parts of phrases repeated with great warmth and feeling.

Bouchard relishes the individuality of Benjamin's style while comparing her vocal timbre to that of early blues and jazz performer Lady Day, or Billie Holiday. Benjamin pays tribute to Billie Holiday with a song titled "Lady Day" on her album *Windsong* (recorded in 1985, the tune is reissued in Rasmussen 2001). A close listening to Billie Holiday singing "Yesterdays," "Strange Fruit," or "You've Changed" (*Smithsonian* 1998, vol. 3) suggests the parallels in sound that Benjamin acknowledges, and Bouchard argues, are present in her singing. These are the limited voice as instrument relative to other jazz singers like Sarah Vaughan and Ella Fitzgerald, the importance of the words and the tone quality and intensity of the voice. Both Benjamin and Holiday claim to have considered their voices as horns (saxophones in particular) rather than just instruments for melodic singing.

Listening to Benjamin Singing

In Bouchard's words the performance he heard in 1982 was "sheer autobiography in song." I have included five musical excerpts on the Compact Disc that convey for you the autobiographical nature of Ms. Benjamin's jazz performances over the past forty years. These are excerpts of longer recordings, selected because of the way in which they tell listeners, perhaps in unexpected ways, about the life of an individual and her community, but also about the lives of these songs themselves.

To begin your listening, I suggest you play the first five excerpts on the compact disc (tracks 1–5) straight through before you read the listening guidelines. As you hear the music for the first time, imagine possible contexts of performance by reviewing the range of sources that have influenced Benjamin's development as a jazz musician. Who might be hearing the music? What are they doing while the music is performed? Is this a seated audience, a community singing along, or a dancehall? What might some of the responses to both the words and the music be? What are the original sources of these songs?

As you listen a second time, try to separate some of the layers of sound. Think about the sound interims of standard American jazz singing in the style of Ella Fitzgerald or Billie Holiday. Then ask yourself, what in this music sounds a little different, perhaps more distinctively "African"? Try to identify these sounds. You do not need a deep understanding of European music theory to talk about what you are hearing; talk about the sound in ordinary language.

The third time around you might try to characterize Sathima Bea Benjamin's jazz style. If you have the musical knowledge, identify stylistic characteristics in terms of melody, tone color, timbre, phrasing, pitch, tempo, pacing, texture—the relationship between the voices, interaction between parts, instrumentation, use of instruments in unusual ways. Try using analogy and metaphor to describe what you hear—maybe the bass line sounds to you like a howling cat. Discuss the text and its relationship to other kinds of jazz singing you might be familiar with.

Finally, to help you to identify Benjamin's style as a singer and the leader of a jazz trio, take a look at the characteristics of South African jazz described at the start of this chapter, then compare them with what you hear in her singing. In the earlier description I talked only about how South African jazz instrumentalists performed, particularly the sound and number of saxophones. Now listen for some of these same elements in Benjamin's singing. They include "scooping" instead of hitting the pitch; playing with the pitch (especially in "Windsong"); the use of smooth vocal lines with small catches at the end of some words; use of ornamentation (tied to Cape Town styles), including slides, slurs, microtonal movements, large glissandos, variations of intensity coupled with the introduction of some hoarseness, and discreet vibrato. Benjamin plays with timbre, but always in a subtle way. Like the saxophones, Benjamin occasionally growls a little, and she includes the sound of breath in her singing (Martin 2000, 41). Then listen closely to her phrasing of words and melody, to the melodic contour itself—at times quite awkward and at other times quite gentle.

As for the musical arrangement, listen for the relationship between the singing voice and the jazz instrumentalists. Listen for moments in which you can hear what Benjamin calls the "Cape Town rhythm" in drummer Billy Higgins's percussive style in "I Only Have Eyes for You." Think about the absolute equality between all voices. There is no sense of the singer up front and the instruments just accompanying; rather all four parts interweave in an equal way. Then think about the very relaxed tempo of Benjamin's performances, quite consistent with the tempos she sang in the 1950s and with the relaxed pace required for good dancing. Finally, Benjamin's singing demonstrates several traditional sounds of African-ness in the use of call and response, bending of pitch, range of vocal utterances, grunts, growls, and shrieks, and the overall soft percussive quality she draws out of the drummer in particular.

Ultimately, Sathima Bea Benjamin's musical creation and re-creation of jazz standards is complex and deep. She adheres to no prescribed formula. She makes complex musical phrases and never hits a pitch "in tune." Rather, she explores the full capacity of color and tone with every sound. The drummers all know that with Benjamin you need to bring brushes. Musicians do not accompany her in the conventional sense, but weave together a musical fabric that allows each voice to find a place and to be heard. Benjamin once suggested to me that what drew her to Duke Ellington's music was the way in which he wrote for horns; she always imagines herself as a saxophone. She has no concept of frontline musicians typical of big band jazz line-ups. Everyone in Benjamin's ensemble has an equal role in the making of the music. She creates a metaphorical community in the way in which she allows for jazz sound to emerge in performance.

Conclusion

Sathima Bea Benjamin and I both claim Cape Town, South Africa, as the city of our childhood experiences, and though it is a city that has profoundly shaped our sense of place in the world, our engagement with that city was fundamentally different. Sathima was born in the same year that my parents were; I was born in Cape Town a year after Sathima left for Europe. Though there are many places we remember in common, racial difference fundamentally informed our knowledge and understanding of the world. I grew up in a working-class suburb called Mowbray in the period after those classified Coloured had been moved from Mowbray to other parts of the city. Sathima's home, the one originally owned by her grandmother, was in a more respectable suburb, but it was on the "wrong" side of the railroad tracks, that is, the Coloured side. But ultimately even that was irrelevant, because the family lost their home under the Group Areas Act. A few years ago, Benjamin returned to Cape Town and went to find that home. She struggled to identify the exact house because, even though she knew the road well, she did not remember the exact number. And since her family had been turned away and the whites moved in, the neighborhood had been given a new, more "Chelsea" style.

There are many strange twists in the story of my scholarly relationship and personal friendship with Sathima Benjamin. It is more than a little ironic to me that Sathima, her husband, and children have spent almost all of their time in New York City living in the Chelsea Hotel. But there is more. Through quite contrasting personal decisions, Sathima and I ended up in New York City in the late 1980s, both of us a long, long way from our sense of home in the grand old Mother City of Cape Town. For Sathima, New York is a vast urban space she has come to know and love because of the memories she has etched upon its landscape. One significant portion of these memories embodies the musical relationship she had and has continued to nurture imaginatively with American jazz great, Duke Ellington. My own knowledge and love for the city has similarly been marked by the many conversations I have had with Sathima and the rare but always remarkable performances by Sathima that I have witnessed there. We have both subsequently returned to South Africa on numerous occasions, each of us pulling out our very distant recollections of a bygone era, united in our travel by our common love for jazz, particularly in its South African inflections.

REFERENCES

Anderson, John. *King of Jazz.* Hollywood, CA: MGM Studios, 1930.

Ballantine, Christopher. "Looking to the USA: The Politics of Male Close-Harmony Song and Style in South Africa During the 1940s and 1950s." *Popular Music,* 18/1 (1999): 1–17.

Cape Standard, Cape Town, South Africa. June 8, 1936.

Gassert, Richard. "Bop 'Til You Drop: An Oral Study of Popular Music Cultures in Cape Town from the Late 1940s to the Early 1960s." Unpublished Honors Essay, University of Cape Town, 1988.

Gutsche, Thelma. *The History and Social Significance of Motion Pictures in South Africa.* Cape Town: Howard Timmons, 1972.

Hajdu, David. *Lush Life: A Biography of Billy Strayhorn.* New York: Farrar, 1996.

Makeba, Miriam, with James Hall. *Makeba: My Story.* New York: New American Library, 1987.

Martin, Denis-Constant. *Coon Carnival: Cape Town, Past and Present.* Cape Town: David Philip, 1999.

Monk, Thelonius. *Solo Monk: Original Recording Remastered.* New York: Sony, 2003.

Nasson, Bill. "'She Preferred Living in a Cave with Harry the Snake-catcher': Towards an Oral History of Popular Leisure and Class Expression in District Six, Cape Town, c. 1920s–1950s." In *Holding Their Ground: Class, Locality, and Culture in 19th and 20th Century South Africa,* edited by P. Bonner et al., 286–295. Johannesburg: Witwatersrand University Press, 1989.

Nixon, Michael. The World of Jazz in Inner Cape Town, 1940–1960. *Proceedings of the Symposium on Ethnomusicology No. 14, July 1997.* Grahamstown: International Library of African Music, 19–23.

Nixon, Rob. *Homelands, Harlem, and Hollywood: South African Culture and the World Beyond.* New York: Routledge, 1994.

Rasmussen, Lars. *Sathima Bea Benjamin: Embracing Jazz.* Copenhagen: The Booktrader, 2000.

Simon, Sylvan. *Rio Rita!* Hollywood, CA: MGM Studios, 1942 [1930].

Township Jazz and Jive. Music Collection International, 1997.

Zonk! An African People's Magazine. Johannesburg.

Chapter Four

Music and Migrancy

Labor migration, the movement of black South Africans from the rural regions of South Africa into urban areas in search of work, is one of the most powerful forces shaping black South African life, music, and performance in the twentieth century. A substantial literature exists on labor migration and its musical consequences. But for our purposes we can simply note that for centuries, people from the present province of KwaZulu Natal migrated from the northern, southern, and interior parts of the province to the ever-growing cities of Durban, Johannesburg, and Kimberley. Beginning in the latter part of the nineteenth century, those who migrated to Johannesburg and Kimberly went in search of work in the mines. (Johannesburg is known in Zulu as *eGoli,* "the place or city of gold," and Kimberly, the city where the first diamonds were mined, as *eDiamane,* "the place or city of diamonds.") Others found work and housing in Durban in the harbor or as house servants or gardeners for white and, increasingly, for Asian families. The early migrants were predominantly men, though women began to enter the urban areas by the mid-twentieth century.

Three performance cultures are discussed in this chapter: *isicathamiya, maskanda,* and gumboot dance. Although I have participated as a researcher in all three musical cultures to a greater or lesser degree, I have been more deeply engaged with *maskanda* and gumboot dance. All three traditions moved during the twentieth century from being performances of largely illiterate, Zulu-speaking migrant men from KwaZulu Natal into genres of performance that are now available in the United States through world music labels and sources. This remarkable transformation of very local traditions has been accompanied by significant shifts in who performs, in the sound of *maskanda,* in what audiences have come to expect, and the standardization of all three genres.

Rhythm of Resistance

In 1979, British documentary filmmaker Jeremy Marre produced a video titled *Rhythm of Resistance* in his series *Beats of the Heart.* Shot on location in Johannesburg, it features the music and larger sociopolitical context of black South African musical production in the late 1970s, a period in which the Afrikaner Nationalist government's policy of apartheid was fully entrenched and enforced. Marre's book, also called *Beats of the Heart,* provides an expanded version of the narrative used in the video. The book gives the reader a powerful sense of the obstacles a foreign, white filmmaker faced in trying to make a movie on black South African life and music in the 1970s. First, Marre was required to have a permit from the South African government because, like all white South Africans, he was prohibited from entering black residential areas, either in the rural parts of South Africa or in the townships. Second, he was only permitted to film in white cities, and because he chose not to abide by the restrictions, the police constantly followed his vehicle and harassed him and his crew. Third, he describes the anxiety black South Africans experienced in relationship with whites, even those who live in the rural regions of KwaZulu Natal that seem, from the outside, idyllic.

In many ways *Rhythm of Resistance* is a useful audiovisual documentary source for this chapter because, though it was filmed in Johannesburg and rural KwaZulu Natal, it is quintessentially a film about music and migration. All three of the performance styles discussed in this chapter are addressed in the *Beats of the Heart* book chapter, though gumboot dance is only mentioned and then dismissed by Marre at the end, a point I return to below.

The video begins with the all-night male choir competitions of *isicathamiya* held in both Johannesburg and Durban. The next important group in the video is the singer-songwriter duo that Marre simply calls "the Johnny and Sipho group." In South Africa, Johnny and Sipho are more lovingly known as founding members of the group Juluka. They are significant not only because they represent a much larger and older tradition of Zulu guitar-accompanied singing called *maskanda,* but also for the politically transgressive performances they created in the 1980s simply by appearing on stage together, a black and a white South African.

The *Rhythm of Resistance* video focuses on the sacred dimension of the group Ladysmith Black Mambazo in its pre-*Graceland* days, performing inside a black church. Between segments on several traditional musicians, the video zooms in on the studio production of black South African KwaZulu Natal–derived popular music, *mbaqanga.* Although they are not a part of my discussion in this book, the spirited performances of the Zulu war dancers, the very lively Mahotella Queens (who continue to perform though they are all in their sixties now), and Abafana Baseqhudeni provide energetic interludes.

Should you have the opportunity to view *Rhythm of Resistance,* which I strongly urge you to do, you should bear in mind the particular "voice" or position of the filmmaker. When I first viewed the film in the mid-1980s, it seemed to me to convey a message of political urgency, a need for social and political transformation and reform in South Africa. I sympathized at the time with Marre's project. In the post-apartheid era, I watched the video again, and this time I was acutely aware of its strong political message, a message that suddenly turned the video into a historical document for me. It was clearly a document from and about the past. In the mid-1990s, as I re-viewed the video in writing this chapter, it took on another new tone, and in 2002 the director's view of black resistance politics seems to me to be quite romanticized.

Without doubt, the laws and realities of apartheid impacted all South Africans. To claim, however, that all black South African performance was resistance against white domination, that no whites (besides the white filmmakers) knew about black performance, is to present a crude image of both black and white South Africans, even for that period. If you look, for example, at www.3rdearmusic. com and find the reminiscences of white South African Dave Marks, who did the sound for numerous events involving black musicians in the 1970s and 1980s, you will realize that racial divisions were not as clear-cut as Marre claims they were. Furthermore, to convey the idea that all black South Africans are the same, with the same agenda, is to deny to millions of people with diverse experiences, education, language, and family backgrounds the individual intelligence and ability to act upon the world on their own terms. While reducing all political struggle to a single issue might assist sloganeers and political campaigners, it does not allow for a more insightful and nuanced reading of a political moment or the value and meanings of its music and dance performances.

The absence of gumboot dance footage in the video provides a case in point. At the end of his chapter on *Rhythm of Resistance*, Marre suggests that in the twentieth century "white colonizers have imposed their own cultural forms on blacks as a means of domination. And the black people of South Africa have taken up those forms and transposed them into their own rhythms of resistance. . . . Most publicized of all the tourist traps are the so-called miners' gumboot dances which we were asked to film one day. Nattily dressed miners in polished gumboots performed in a sort of circus for the avid, chattering tourists who photographed the show to take back as a 'real slice of black South African life.' It was, in fact, funded by the mining authorities" (Marre 1986, 50).

Marre closes by contrasting his unwillingness to film the "contrived event" of gumboot dancing with the "real *Ngoma* [dance] in a workers' hostel inside Johannesburg. . . . Amongst the milling, tired workers marches a procession of Zulu workers beneath the harsh glow of a setting sun. They were naked, except for loincloths, wrist and ankle decorations and the spears they brandished. . . . Every week they danced and sang their message of defiance—towards the enemy from within" (Marre 1986, 50).

Marre seems to want to keep Zulu men pre-modern and untainted by commercial interests—naked except for their loincloths rather than clothed in the Western dress and footgear worn by the gumboot dancers. And the distinction he draws between the Zulu gumboot dancer as co-opted by white rule and the defiant and implicitly free Zulu in his loincloth is flawed. Jeff Thomas, Zulu linguist and social anthropologist turned *ngoma* dancer, has argued convincingly (1988) that even the "traditional Zulu war dancers" adapted their attire to meet the criteria of white management and their dance judges. Changing traditions to meet the requirements of the judges was, after all, a strategy for winning. Certainly, the recently produced video titled *Gumboots* (2001), discussed at the end of this chapter, presents a different perspectiveon gumboot dance in contemporary South Africa and its place in twentieth-century black South African performance history. Finally, my own video footage of male union members performing gumboot dance at labor rallies in 1985 argues that gumboot dance has long been a sign of worker solidarity and obvious political consciousness.

Isicathamiya

If you have heard the song "Wimoweh" or "Mbube," which begins with the words "In the jungle, the mighty jungle, the lion sleeps tonight," then you know one of the songs that figures in the early history of *isicathamiya* in South Africa. The song was originally composed by a Zulu-speaking man, Solomon Linda, and recorded in 1939 in South Africa for Gallo Records. Ethnomusicologist Veit Erlmann has reissued that original recording. The tune itself is believed to have been adapted from a traditional wedding song. The story is that in the 1950s white South African record producers sent a version of that song along with others to the United States to showcase local talent and songwriting skills. Several folk groups covered the Zulu melody with English lyrics and new musical arrangements.

Without doubt, the melody and words of any of the many versions of "Mbube," "Wimoweh," or "In the Jungle" are part of American folk and popular culture. Of all the melodies that have come out of South Africa in the twentieth century, "Mbube" is the most recorded, re-arranged, and regularly performed the world over. Early cover versions of Solomon Linda's "Mbube" include those done by the Kingston Trio (1959), Jimmy Dorsey (1952), and the Tokens (1961); it appears on recordings for children including "Barnyard Beat" and Kid's Fun (the latter cited on allmusic.com); on a Burger King commercial; and of course, in *The Lion King* sound track for the Broadway musical and Hollywood film.

Finding Maskanda *in the United States:*
Shanachie Records' Indestructible Beat of Soweto *(43033)*

The Earthworks label in Britain has issued a four-volume compilation under the same title, but the album I refer to is the one originally released by Shanachie Records (USA).

Recorded prior to *Graceland,* this compact disc represents some of the traditions in transformation pertaining to indigenous guitar styles in South Africa. Though it claims on the liner notes that the music is all *mbaqanga*—basically the studio-produced sounds popular in black South African townships around Johannesburg and Durban (that is, largely Zulu-language, guitar-based popular bands)—this recording actually includes four popular styles: *maskanda, mbaqanga, mqashiyo,* and *isicathamiya. Mbaqanga* and *mqashiyo* are the least traditional sounding of the four, with *maskanda* and *isicathamiya* situated between rural traditions and urban styles. The most strongly *maskanda* in style are tracks 1 and 6 by Udokotela Shange Namajaha. Tracks 2, 3, 4, 7, 8, and 11 are clearly in the *mbaqanga* range, though the use of concertina hearkens back to *maskanda,* perhaps of the *isishameni* style (one of the less traditional-sounding *maskanda* styles). Track 8 is more specifically in the *mbaqanga* style used in the *Sarafina* film and musical of the 1980s discussed briefly at the end of Chapter Two. Tracks 5 and 10, performed by Mahlathini and his group, is in *mqashiyo* style. Track 9 by Nganeziyamfisa no Khambolomvaleliso presents a style somewhere between *maskanda* and *mbaqanga*—it is in the format of a *maskanda* band, with bass guitar, concertina, and drum kit. Finally, Track 12 presents Ladysmith Black Mambazo in a typical *isicathamiya* performance of the early 1980s. There are three distinctive sections to their piece. The introduction is sung standing still. Then the words *"halalala"* repeated over and over signal a new rhythm, the point at which *isicathamiya* groups begin their synchronized dance movements. The concluding part of the song is marked with a deliberate slowing in tempo and an increased sense of musical and textual closure.

"Mbube"/"Wimoweh" has recently come under public scrutiny in South Africa because of an ethical and financial controversy about who should be benefiting from the royalties it generated, a controversy that leads right to New York City. You can find out more about the legal wrangling that ensued in the 1990s by looking at the Third Ear Music website: http://www.3rdearmusic.com. You will no doubt be surprised at the number of times that one melody has been reissued in all kinds of formats, for television and radio commercials, in Hollywood film sound tracks, as children's songs, folk revival songs, and indeed, in all manner of popular guises.

The contemporary manifestation of *mbube*-style performance or *isicathamiya* is found in the weekly all-night choir competitions held from late Saturday evening through Sunday morning in the cities of Durban and Johannesburg. I was first exposed to these all-night competitions as an undergraduate student at the University of Natal in 1984. My fellow student Janet Topp Fargion and I had been asked by our teacher, Veit Erlmann, if we would like to judge one of these competitions, which were held regularly in the Glebeland hostel for male migrant workers in Umlazi, one of the townships on the fringes of Durban. Janet and I had no idea what was in store for us on that night in 1984. All we knew was that a man in a van would meet us on the steps of Memorial Tower Building at the University of Natal in Durban at 2 A.M. on a Sunday morning. When the driver arrived, Janet and I scrambled into the front seat of the little van and were taken to the performance site. We were instructed not to talk to anyone, and we were told which groups had won several times in the recent past and encouraged to let others take home the prizes.

By the time we were seated at our table, with our backs to the audience so that we could not be influenced by any of the supporters, about eight or nine groups had already registered. That seemed like a reasonable number of choirs. We did not realize at the time that nine or ten more would still arrive and expect to perform. An event that was already in full swing with the *praktisa* (rehearsal) session would clearly continue long after the sun rose on Sunday morning. Several of the supporters were napping in their seats, waiting for the actual competition to begin. We had no guidelines about what should be the winning qualities of a choir; it was presumed that because we were music students we would know.

The "Fair View Boys" team of isicathamiya *performers in a* praktisa *session at the Beatrice Street YMCA, Durban, July 1995. Take note of the women supporters in procession with the male performers.*

I still have a vivid sense of the moment the first choir began to sing. Impeccably dressed in suits, with white gloves, sparkling white shirts, shiny black shoes, and red socks, the group processed into the humble hall. Deep, rich strains of men singing Zulu words in close harmony resonated throughout the building. I recall the chill that ran up my spine, because I had never before heard a sound as powerful as the voices of those men. The leader, dressed in opposite colors to his team, led his group in a solo call and choral response. As they moved in single file down the middle of the hall between two groups of enthusiastic supporters, the men raised their legs together, and then released, their shoes brushing the concrete floor. Walking stealthily, like cats. Moving, but not stepping. In Zulu, *ukucathama* means "to walk stealthily, like a cat," and *isicathamiya* is the name of the style.

The men proceeded up the steps and onto the stage, singing in four-part harmony as they went, with the leader singing soprano, two voices on alto, a couple on tenor, and everyone else in the bass (the mixed-voice choral SATB format was sung here by men only).

Another isicathamiya *team rehearses in the* praktisa *period before the official competition. One of the female supporters publicly marks "her man" by giving him a gift while the group performs. Beatrice Street YMCA, July 1995.*

Their bodies bent, their legs moved smoothly, voices and bodies in harmony. The first part of the performance was in the old *makwaya* (choral) format: the choir sang with their bodies still, as in the old mission style. In the second part, the men begin to dance, the rhythm of their bodies in sync with the rhythm of the song. At this point, the participants' girlfriends or wives came up individually to show their support for the men they were involved with. One woman took the necklace from around her neck and placed it over the head of her lover. As she left the stage she gestured to the audience that the man was taken—not available. Another came up and put her wallet inside the pocket of one of the other performers. The group's followers applauded. (Clapping from the audience is not generalized but limited to one's own supporters.) Having completed their two songs, the choir left the stage, winding their way back through the audience to the back door as the next choir prepared to make their entrance.

In the mid-1990s I returned to *isicathamiya* competitions, not as a judge this time (white judges are no longer used for these events), but as the ethnomusicologist from the music department at the University of Natal. Since I had first heard *isicathamiya*, Bongani Mthethwa, Paulos Msimango (both now deceased), and Grammy award–winner Joseph Shabalala had formed an organization called the South African Traditional Music Association. It was instrumental in rethinking the rules of *isicathamiya* performance to eliminate the white influence that had been so pervasive when filmmaker Jerry Marre had been on site in Johannesburg in the 1970s and to reclaim *isicathamiya* as a form of traditional music. Competitions were no longer held in the Glebeland hostel but at the YMCA in Beatrice Street in the center of the city of Durban. (See CD TRACK 6 for an example of *isicathamiya* performed at this venue.)

Though the format of *isicathamiya* competitions remained the same, the YMCA competition introduced some variations on the basic theme. Between the rehearsal and the formal competition, a competition for the best-dressed man was regularly held, with the winner decided by the music judge. On occasion, a similar competition for the best-dressed women would take place. All who registered to enter the competition now paid a voluntary amount to the event's conveners, and the contribution of each group was announced as they entered the hall to perform. But the most pro-

Supporters of isicathamiya *performers take naps while they wait through the night for their teams to rehearse and compete at the Beatrice Street YMCA Hall in Durban, September 1996.*

found change to *isicathamiya* performance in the last two decades of the century was the fact that Joseph Shabalala and his Ladysmith Black Mambazo group had achieved worldwide recognition. To give back to the community that supported *isicathamiya* in South Africa, Shabalala and his group regularly conducted workshops for aspiring *isicathamiya* singers. The effect of Shabalala's workshops could be heard in the more polished tone and overall quality of performance of those groups taking part.

The leader of an *isicathamiya* group is usually its founder and composer. However, a composer among migrant workers is not someone who writes down songs in musical notation but rather someone who creates new songs in a variety of ways. Social historian and musicologist Chris Ballantine (1996) interviewed Joseph Shabalala in the 1990s about his compositional process. Shabalala composes at night, he told Ballantine, when his body is sleeping and his spirit is at work. New songs come to him in different ways, he says, but often in response to songs he has heard or things he has seen that trouble him. He strives to address the troubling situation by composing a new song. Since he does not read or write music, he either takes the song directly to his group to begin working on it in performance or tapes portions of it until the song is more complete.

Shabalala also explained to Ballantine how he came to compose in the particular style of *isicathamiya*. For a period of about six months in the early 1960s, Shabalala says, he was visited by voices in his dreams. These were the spiritual elders who were singing in a new style. Night after night, they taught him this style. It was like attending school in his sleep, he recalls. Later on, after the voices had visited for several months, Shabalala was given a kind of final examination in which spiritual elders tested his musical knowledge in his dreams. Each of the twenty-four elders asked a question of the student musician, and Shabalala achieved a perfect score. Then they asked one more question, which he struggled to answer. Ultimately, he achieved his goal of satisfying these elders. Since then Joseph Shabalala has composed hundreds of new songs and has had a group singing in the style of Ladysmith Black Mambazo for four decades.

A good performance of *isicathamiya* includes a call and response, multilayered vocal polyphony. For the most part, an *isicathamiya* song sung at a competition starts off with the group standing in a semicircle with the leader in front of the group; all are facing the judges and the audience. Although some of the earliest recordings of *isicathamiya* have piano or banjo accompaniment, because the record producers thought the instruments would appeal to the black elite, *isicathamiya* is typically performed a capella.

Ladysmith Black Mambazo in Concert

On February 15, 2003, Ladysmith Black Mambazo (LBM) were scheduled to perform at the Annenberg Center at the University of Pennsylvania in Philadelphia. It had been more than a decade since I had seen them perform live in a theater in Stamford, Connecticut. At that earlier event, just a few years after the *Graceland* recording release, their onstage performance paralleled what one might have expected of an *isicathamiya* group singing at one of the all-night competitions in Durban or Johannesburg. Their music was sung exclusively in Zulu, but their performance style was in the historical tradition of European choral styles, though there were a few differences. Each song began with bodies still, but the singers gradually began to move and, through dance movements, illustrate what the songs were about. Shabalala "conducted" his group while facing the audience rather than the group. But like more classical choirs, LBM engaged the audience minimally.

The evening at the Annenberg Center fifteen years later was a different kind of performance. It was clear that Ladysmith Black Mambazo had become accustomed to performing the same songs concert after concert, city after city, because one moment in the live performance that night strongly resembled a track on the *Ladysmith Black Mambazo Live at the Royal Albert Hall* DVD. In the Philadelphia concert, one Mambazo member remarked to the audience that because they had traveled far and wide, north, south, east, and west, they no longer had any sense of where they were. "What is the name of this place?" he asked the group. "Ah, something beginning with P." Then Shabalala proceeded to teach the audience the words of "Homeless," the most South African sounding track from the *Graceland* album. As we saw in Chapter Two, this song begins in Zulu, but the English text that comes in later is not merely a translation of what LBM sings in Zulu at the beginning. In a call and response form, Shabalala proceeded to teach the Philadelphia audience the Zulu words.

Ladysmith Black Mambazo's performance had changed in other ways as well. First, it was clear that numerous social and political issues pertaining to life for black South Africans in KwaZulu Natal weighed heavily on the minds and hearts of Shabalala and his group. A large hand-painted backdrop covering the entire stage portrayed contemporary issues, such as HIV-AIDS, crime, violence, and rape, along with the heroes of South African society, including Nelson Mandela and Archbishop Desmond Tutu. The group used the performance to educate the audience. One of Shabalala's wives had recently been murdered—Shabalala had been beside her in the car when it happened. So the group opened the performance with a song about heaven, the place they would go after they all died. They sang about the deep sense of separation from their homes and families that accompanied global travel and performance. But there were also several humorous moments in the performance, where members of Mambazo played out the tensions between the older and younger generation.

Second, the level of interaction between Shabalala and the audience had increased markedly. When I first heard LBM in Connecticut, they filed onto the stage and began to sing to the audience with Shabalala conducting. At the Annenberg Center, Shabalala and Mambazo communicated with the audiences at several levels, not just in the harmonious strands of mostly Zulu-language *isicathamiya*. The audience members laughed as Mambazo acted out a series of scenes that they could identify with in their own lives, there was less sense of distance between audience members and performers, and everyone went home to listen to the *Graceland* album's version of "Homeless" knowing now how to sing the opening lines of the song.

The third significant change occurred in the opening moments of the show. Instead of Ladysmith Black Mambazo walking onto the stage to start the performance, two Zulu *maskanda* (traditional musicians playing on European instruments, guitar and concertina) appeared on stage to perform. These two musicians from South Africa were being used to "open" for the bigger act. It struck me then that Joseph Shabalala had taken on the same role Paul Simon played in the mid-1980s. It was now Shabalala and not Simon who was using his powerful place in the global networks of the entertainment industry to showcase South African music. The difference was that it was live performance, without the intervention of high-tech music producers reshaping the act and the sound to suit the needs of a mainstream popular music audience. The *maskanda* performance came across as unmediated tradition, quite unlike the "cleaned up" sounds of Mambazo that one hears on the *Graceland* album. Joseph Shabalala was not "producing" *maskanda* performance, as Paul Simon had done at the mixing board in the recording studio in New York City by manipulating many tracks of sound recorded in South Africa. Shabalala was simply showcasing the musicians in their own traditions.

Back in South Africa it is quite striking the extent to which being musically successful overseas impacts the local environment, even among those who might appear quite cut off from the wider world. Musicians in South Africa now dream of international success in a way that is quite startling and, in my experience, less common in the United States. Even the partially literate or non-English-speaking South African carries inside him or herself images of the world "out there." This was driven home to me one day while I was studying at New York University in 1988. I received a package in the mail containing a cassette made for me by my gumboot dance teacher and his team. On the cassette, Blanket Mkhize played his Zulu guitar and sang a song he composed in which he asked me to "Open the gates of New York City for gumboot performance!" Clearly, Joseph Shabalala was opening the gates to world performance for these two opening act street musicians as Paul Simon had done for Ladysmith Black Mambazo two decades earlier, and as Blanket Mkhize hoped I would do for him in New York City.

Maskanda Migrant Performance

Older South Africans in Johannesburg and Durban might recall seeing domestic workers and gardeners strolling the neighborhoods playing guitars and singing softly to themselves on Thursday afternoon, the scheduled "afternoon off." This was the time when guitarists, collectively called *maskanda,* walked the street singing songs of migrant experience in a style that reminded them of their rural homes. Davies (1994) suggests that the *maskanda* musical style emerged either in the early decades of this century or in the late nineteenth century, when guitars were first made available in KwaZulu Natal. She cites Johnny Clegg, who dates the Portuguese introduction of the guitar into the region to about 1880. An old Zulu-English dictionary compiled in 1894 by a missionary named A. Bryant includes an entry for "guitar": *into e-shaywayo nezimTambo* ("the thing that is struck or sounded by means of strings or with a bone"). It is quite possible that rural Zulu speakers who had never heard an English or Afrikaans word for guitar used this unwieldy description. This suggests that the first encounter with the guitar by Zulu speakers in the late nineteenth century was in the rural rather than urban areas of South Africa. Those who first saw it simply described it without having a word for the object.

The word *maskanda* suggests a similar kind of encounter. *Maskanda* is a Zulu version of the Afrikaans word for musician, *musikant.* In KwaZulu Natal what Europeans called "music" was called *imusic.* All other forms of Zulu traditional performance were called *ngoma* (song-dance-drumming-healing complex). Clearly *maskanda* was associated with music made by Afrikaans-speaking people, in this case, white farmers who played their music for relaxation on the farms where Zulu men worked in the nineteenth and early twentieth centuries. The word *maskanda* then suggests three levels of musical and cultural encounter in the shaping of twentieth-century Zulu guitar performance: 1) European music, 2) translated into Afrikaans cultural practices, 3) borrowed and transformed by Zulu-speaking musicians into a musical language more consistent with their own aesthetics but played on European instruments like violin, concertina, piano accordion, and most important, the steel-string guitar.

From Musical Bow to Guitar

Although the musical bow is not played much any longer, Zulu guitarists have borrowed and transformed principles of Zulu traditional

Zulu mouth bow,
drawn by Daphne Maree

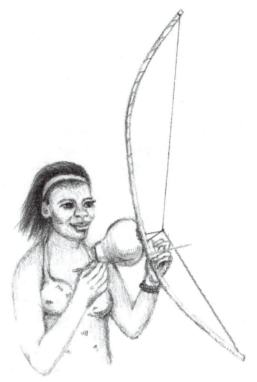

Zulu umakweyana *bow,*
drawn by Daphne Maree

musical bow performances for guitar performance (much as Thomas Mapfumo did with *mbira* music in Zimbabwe in the 1980s, and as Salif Keita and others have done with *kora* music in Senegal and the Gambia). The musical bow is a technologically simple instrument with several features that vary from one bow to the next. Like the hunting bow, all musical bows consist of a sturdy piece of branch trimmed and bent into a semi-circle, with the ends of the branch held together by a piece of wire. Some bows are braced, others are not; some use the mouth as the resonator, others a gourd; some are struck with a wooden stick; others are bowed more like a violin. The idea of the braced bow transfers into the use of a capodastra on the guitar to raise the register of sound produced while keeping the same finger positions for the chords.

Though the instrument may seem simple, the acoustical principles it is based on are more sophisticated. The pitch material for the musical bow is a single wire, string, or gut. When the wire is plucked, it creates a low-sounding tone we call, in the conventional language of acoustics, the fundamental tone. If the wire is pinched (or braced) and then struck, plucked, or bowed, it creates another fundamental tone that is higher than the fundamental of the unpinched string. The exact pitch of the fundamental depends on where exactly the string is pinched or braced. The point is that on an unbraced musical bow the player can produce two fundamental pitches by striking the string stopped or unstopped. Each time a musician creates a fundamental tone, however, he also sets in motion a series of overtones. But most people's ears are not sensitive to hearing these higher and softer pitches unless a musician or instrument has a mechanism for amplifying these sounds.

These overtones are produced in a particular order. Typically one hears the third, fourth, and fifth partials or overtones above the fundamental, and they sound two octaves above the lowest tone. This means that by setting the fundamental pitch D in motion, we can hear the third and fifth pitches above D as well: D F# and A, plus the D two octaves above the fundamental. Similarly, if the musician produces as his second fundamental tone an E, the performer can produce the E G# and B. This gives the performer a fair range of pitches for melodic use. The scale produced with two roots and three overtones with each is D E F# G# A B and D'.

Most Nguni musical bows operate using either two or three fundamental pitches or roots. These fundamentals resonate in two kinds of chambers, either a gourd attached to the frame of the bow, which is moved back and forth from the musician's body, or the performer's mouth, where the bow rests on the lips of the performer and is constantly reshaped to selectively amplify harmonics. (This process parallels the way in which we produce vowel sounds. As you say the vowel sounds, you reshape the resonating chamber—your mouth—to selectively amplify certain harmonics that result in different vowel sounds.) Quite often, three fundamentals, D E and G, are played to produce only the fifth above the fundamental tone, that is, a D and an A, and E and a B, a G, and a D. The result is a pentatonic scale—D E G A B D'—the basis of much traditional music in South Africa. From here we can see it is an easy jump to the common chords of much mainstream popular music and the harmonic progression of the Christian hymn—I IV V I, or I IV I6/4 V I, or I ii V I. Chord I is D A (without a third), chord ii is E B, chord IV is G D, I6/4 is A D, chord V is A E. All are missing the third of the chord.

The transition from the traditional root progressions of the musi-

A group of Basotho men living in the mountains of Lesotho gather together on a misty morning to listen to the sound of the lesiba *mouth bow and homemade guitar, or* ramkie, *June 1994.*

cal bow to the common chord progressions of the Christian hymn and more mainstream popular music is embodied in the traditional performances of *maskanda* guitarists, who structure their music by using two or three root progressions, the first two a whole tone apart, such as C and D, and the third root, the interval of a fifth above the C. The oscillation between the two root pitches is commonly heard in the more traditional sounds of Shembe singing discussed in Chapter Five but is also heard on the 1979 commercial recording by Johnny Clegg and Sipho Mchunu, *Universal Men.*

Track 9 of *Universal Men* demonstrates the relationship between musical bow performance and *maskanda* guitar styles, because it freezes in performance the transition between the musical bow and *maskanda* guitar playing. (An audiovisual clip of the track is also available on the *Rhythm of Resistance* DVD at the end of track 3, leading into track 4, titled "Zululand Roots.") In this example, Johnny Clegg plays a traditional mouth bow with the two fundamentals, a C and a D, created with the cane or wooden stick scraping first the lower fundamental and then the higher fundamental. Quickly one hears the overtones in the melody produced two octaves above. The

Basotho shepherds entertained by a ramkie *player, early morning in the mountains of Lesotho, June 1994. Blankets are commonly used for warmth in the winter months in this region.*

melody of the bow repeats several times until a clear rhythmic and melodic groove is established. These overtones are amplified both in the mouth and electronically in this recording.

At this point Sipho Mchunu joins in the performance on guitar, sounding out three interweaving and contrapuntal melodies, a bass line, a line in the middle that keeps the rhythm steady, and the melody. Mchunu sings the words of the song using the same melody Clegg introduced on the bow and also sounds out the melody in the upper register of the guitar. Clegg and Mchunu start to sing in call and response between the two voices, with their melodic phrases overlapping each other. Sipho sings in a higher range than does Clegg, but both voices seem to blend in with the tone color of the stick scraping against the gut of the bow.

It is clear that there are eight pulses per measure, grouped into two beats of four pulses each. But this does not induce the same 4/4 feel one might have listening to marching band music, for example. Rather, the strong and weak beats, or the stressed and unstressed beats, continually pull against each other. The tempo is steady, and the melody Mchunu produces on the guitar repeats in numerous cycles through the course of the performance. About two-thirds of the way into the piece, Clegg improvises in the higher ranges of the mouth bow, producing a whistle-like sound with the overtones. The pitches he uses include C D E G and A, a pentatonic scale that fluctuates between the C root and the D root. Clegg and Mchunu harmonize their melodic lines in intervals of parallel fourths and thirds.

Listening to the combined performance of Clegg on mouth bow and Mchunu on *maskanda* guitar in this example helps one understand the transition from mouth bow to guitar in Zulu *maskanda* performance. Clegg starts the performance on the mouth bow, the instrument that preceded Zulu music on guitar. Mchunu enters playing the same music but on guitar. The traditional musical principles of the musical bow then seamlessly transfer onto the guitar. The same song and its accompaniment can be performed on either instrument. Here the historical relationship between the two instruments is clearly illustrated.

Maskanda *Technique*

Gumboot dance teacher Blanket Mkhize observes that the guitar is like a band—it can play all the parts. It can produce rhythm, melody, and harmony, and can sound like an entire choir of voices. The guitar is also relatively inexpensive and easy to buy. Because of the central importance of the guitarist in *maskanda,* it is usually the guitarist who is the composer and leader of a group. The capacity to play up to three separate melodic lines on the guitar while rapidly declaiming self-praise is a skill admired in *maskanda* performance.

Guitars used in *maskanda* have six steel strings, which produce a more percussive timbre than do strings made of nylon. The guitar is played with plectrums, which are called *ikati* because they resemble a cat walking on the floor.

In *maskanda* performance there are two styles of guitar playing: *ukuvamba,* strumming chords percussively in the tradition of township *marabi* from the 1920s and 1930s, and *ukupika,* finger-picking styles from north of South Africa. Typically, *ukupika* is the more desired style, because it usually demonstrates greater skill and complexity on the part of the performer and is thought to adhere to the laws of the Zulu, *umthetho womZulu*. There are numerous kinds of "chuning," that is, ways in which the strings of the guitar are tuned in terms of both register (how high or low the overall sound is) and pitches used. Some styles, such as *isiZulu* from northern KwaZulu Natal, use only five of the six strings, while those of *umzansi* from the southern coastal area use all six in performance. A typical tuning draws on the Western system but starts on the D rather than the E above middle C. So the common pitches tuned to in *maskanda* guitar are (from the D above middle C descending down two octaves) D B G D A E. This pitch pattern suggests a structure based on intervals rather than absolute pitch—usually a *maskanda* tunes his or her instrument to match the register of the singing voice. In other words, the starting pitch is relative while the intervals between pitches remain constant.

Many *maskanda* guitarists learned musical technique by first playing on a homemade guitar or violin. According to Nollene Davies (1994), a boy would start off on an instrument with one or two strings—a "toy instrument." The one-stringed instrument was called *udloko, ubhek'indlela,* or *ikopi*. If the boy proved to be talented, he would gradually add to the number of strings and the complexity of his musical performance. It was usually when a man began "courting" that he would finally purchase a guitar to woo his lover. Although these musicians are usually self-taught, a more experienced player will often guide the novice in learning the basic principles, even if these sessions are not regarded as formal lessons. The young student is taught the tuning of the instrument, various styles of *maskanda* music, and compositional techniques.

As with the leader of an *isicathamiya* group, the *maskanda* must be a skilled composer who can create original songs and lyrics, including the three kinds of texts produced in a good *maskanda* rendition: the choral part, the narrative part, and the self-praises. Davies tells the story of one *maskanda* who said that he did not care about politics, but because his audiences wanted to hear what he had to say about such things, he composed songs that addressed political matters. The *maskanda* has a powerful pulpit, as audience members are painfully aware. One audience member warned Davis that anyone

---

African Guitar Styles

Ethnomusicologist Gerhard Kubik's video *African Guitar* shows the finger-picking style of guitarists filmed and recorded by Kubik over almost two decades (1966–1983). The video has a detailed set of liner notes, telling of the lives of musicians and of their style of guitar performance. It is a wonderful audio-visual document on African guitar styles generally, and it also suggests the kinds of musical exchanges that might have taken place between black South Africans and other Africans who migrated into the country from the north in search of work. *Graceland* guitarist Ray Phiri traces his gentler style of guitar playing to the influence of his father, a migrant worker and musician who came to South Africa from Malawi in central Africa.

---

who knows a *maskanda* should guard his actions because the *maskanda* might write a song to shame that individual in public.

Although the principles of *maskanda* musical performance are integrally linked to Zulu tradition, the social position of these traditional urban musicians was often contested. There is a Zulu saying about *maskanda* performers: *isiginci asak'umuzi* (a guitar doesn't build a homestead). The guitar was viewed negatively because it was associated with the values of *isidolopho,* "the urban or township life," and the concertina was thought to be the "instrument of Satan." There were several reasons for this perception among rural people. *Maskanda* used to wander from homestead to homestead in the rural areas, which created the impression that they were vagabonds. They smoked wild hemp or marijuana, locally called *isangu.* Furthermore, the *maskanda* was thought to be popular with young women and to use his musical and verbal skills to lure them away from their homes and good living. Finally, they were usually migrant workers and away for a long time. When they returned to their rural homes, they brought new instruments, sounds, and ideas to the more traditionally minded communities. And if a *maskanda* successfully recorded his music in the studios in town, his success was likely to lure him away from his rural home forever.

Maskanda: *Tradition in Transformation*

In August 1993, just after a large gathering of ethnomusicologists at the South African Symposium on Ethnomusicology at the University of Natal in Durban, the music department hosted another of its annual *maskanda* competitions for migrant worker performers. My colleague Bongani Mthethwa initiated this competition in 1988 out of his and Joseph Shabalala's growing concern for the demise of traditional music in KwaZulu Natal. While Shabalala dreamed about starting a music school for traditional performance, Mthethwa decided that a competition organized by the University of Natal, with its attendant prestige as an educational institution, would help rejuvenate passion for the intricacies and beauty of *maskanda* performance in the region. Initially the competition was quite small, but within a few years the first rounds of the competition were held in six separate regions, with the final showdown on the university campus. By this stage, the competition was funded by National Sorghum Breweries, a locally owned brewer of traditional sorghum beer, also known as *iJuba*.

The final round of the 1993 Maskanda Competition was held in the Sports Hall at the University of Natal in Durban. The audience, judges, and emcee were seated on the spectator stands around the central performance space. Six microphones were set up to accommodate singers and instrumentalists in larger groups. The emcee for the competition was the ever-popular "Bodloza" Nzimande, local radio personality from Radio Zulu (now *Ukhozi Radio*); the primary judge was *maskanda* expert Sipho Mchunu, who performs with Johnny Clegg as part of Juluka.

There were three broad categories of *maskanda* competition: for guitarists as soloists or leaders of *maskanda* groups; for musical bow players; and for those who played the jaws harp, the accordion or concertina, violin, and the mouth organ, or homemade versions of these instruments. While there were not separate categories for men and women, women tended to play the musical bow, mouth organ, and jaws harp, and men the concertinas, violins, accordions, and guitars. Because of the large number of participants in the competition, each individual/group entry was allowed to perform only two songs. Typically, a song would begin, and once the judges were satisfied that they had heard enough, the emcee cut the musician off, and the second song began. In this context, musicians rarely completed an entire song/story performance before being told to stop.

The body is central to effective *maskanda* performance. Unlike *isicathamiya* and gumboot dance performances, however, there were no guidelines or rules about what *maskanda* competitors should wear. At this event, there was a wide range of costumes, from the humble to extremely elaborate. Some were quite traditional—using animal skins and ankle rattles; others were more familiar, with small modifications, such as trousers with Zulu traditional designs sewn into the pockets or around the edges. These *maskanda* used a range of materials in creating the densely layered costumes: animal skins, beads, rattles, layers of pleated fabrics, plenty of elaborate and colorful trim on trousers, skirts, and shirts. The instruments themselves were often decorated with rich colors, textures, and designs embodying the character and spirit of the performer.

The more ambitious groups in the competition typically included a troupe of *ngoma* dancers performing on the side of the stage. Attired in animal skins—from deer, to goats, and sheep—they kicked their legs up and dropped them hard onto the floor, their legs reinforcing the rhythms created by the guitarist and his rhythm section.

Several individuals and groups incorporated a humorous element in their performances. Either they sang songs that made the audience laugh, or they included one or two performers in the front of the group who gestured and danced in ways that elicited much laughter from the audience. One group had a young man breakdancing on the floor, while a second performer gestured in comical ways. Laughter makes for a memorable performance, and with so many competing to win, it was important to leave a strong impression on the judges.

The 1993 competition was the last held at the University of Natal, and 1994 was the final year of the event. In the space of just six years, the competition had served its purpose. *Maskanda* had reasserted its popular presence on radio and national television; it had even become a force in the dissemination of South African music abroad. But at the same time, the competition had contributed to the growing commercialization and standardization of *maskanda* musical performance in KwaZulu Natal.

Guitarist John Bengu began the commercialization of *maskanda* in the 1950s and began recording in the 1960s. In the process he changed his name to Phuzushukela (Sugar Drinker), formed a *maskanda* band with bass guitar, drums, electric guitar, *ngoma* dancers, and backup singers. He was so successful in the 1960s that he helped create the 1970s performance category called "Zulu-Trad" on the radio and in the local recording industry. This kind of performance became standard recording and radio fare, with numerous bands playing a *maskanda/mbaqanga* mix of music on Radio Zulu and other stations. As *maskanda* became more of a mediated than live sound, Sipho Mchunu recalls that women listeners often chose the recorded version, with its booming volumes, over the softer voices of live performance. The mediation of *maskanda* began to transform traditional notions of masculinity and courtship between young men and women in rural areas of KwaZulu Natal. To appeal to women, musicians now needed a recording contract, and they preferred *maskanda* music loud, and accompanied on bass drums.

The standardization of *maskanda* through competition occurred because of the privileging of one or two regional guitar styles over others: *isiZulu* from northern KwaZulu Natal (including the region you see in *Rhythm of Resistance,* where Sipho Mchunu grew up) and *Umzansi* (the style developed in the coastal region south of the city of Durban). To win an award at the *maskanda* competition, the musician had to display technical virtuosity and be a showman. He or she also had to compose his own words and music, words that would speak to the experiences of the audiences and were about current events, some political, others more social. The song was divided into three sections: the *intela* or improvised introductory instrumental section; the chorus part, where the musician's voice sang in harmony with the guitar voices; the narrative part, where the *maskanda* told his story; and the *izibongo* part, where the musician sang his own praises as a musician. A musician who could do these praises while accompanying himself on the guitar was considered an outstanding *maskanda*. (This musical structure is further discussed in the section on Thami Vilakazi and can be heard on the Vilakazi tracks of the accompanying CD.)

The guitarist personalized his instrument by decorating it, painting it, and putting stickers on it so that it expressed something of his own character and place of origin. Each guitar part had two or three voices that intertwined with the melody sung by the *maskanda*. The middle voices had to keep a steady beat, the beat that implied certain dance steps to the musician and his audience. The thumb played the lower voices of the guitar, called *amadoda* (the men). The upper voices, which represented young girls *(amantombazane)*, usually copied the melody of the singer, both while he sang and in the instrumental interludes. Ultimately the guitar and the voice had to sound in sync with each other, without any sense of conflict between the parts, and each of the voices of the guitar had to be so clear that they could separately communicate their musical messages to the audience.

The contexts of performance have also begun to shift in the last two decades. Earlier, in the rural areas, a *maskanda* wandered from one homestead to the next. Today, in the urban areas, musicians may play when requested by their immediate community, but more frequently they seek out a deal to be recorded and mass mediated. As a result, record producers play a pivotal role in reshaping *maskanda* performance to suit the perceived tastes of the listening public. Thus the extremely fluid *maskanda* tradition is constantly manipulated to reflect on and critique the social reality of audiences in the rural and urban environments of KwaZulu Natal.

More recently the texts have been adapted to cohere with the contemporary issues surrounding love. *Maskanda* now sing about women who love men but who also break community taboos, carry venereal diseases, drink excessively, and smoke. More recently, mass-mediated *maskanda* musicians like Vusi Ximba and Phuzekhemisi and Kethani have become popular because of their biting social and political satire. One of the most profound changes to the urban *maskanda* practices in the 1990s, however, was the way in which women musicians began to assert themselves as guitarists and recording artists. The musical bow was traditionally the instrument of women in the rural areas of KwaZulu Natal, and when migrant men began to play guitars, they drew heavily on the musical practices of rural women in the cities. More recently, however, several women have reclaimed a musical space for their own compositions and performances. Three of the best-known artists are Tu Nokwe, Busi Mhlongo, and Five Roses, a woman mouth organ player who won the *maskanda* competition at the University of Natal in 1992.

Maskanda *Guitarist Thami Vilakazi*

When I first interviewed *maskanda* guitarist Thami Vilakazi in 1994 he was a migrant worker, often unemployed, who lived in Cato Crest, Durban. He learned to play the *maskanda* guitar style while he was growing up in Eshowe, in northern KwaZulu Natal. As a young boy in Zululand, Vilakazi made his first *igogogo* (guitar) from an oil can and a plank, using fishing line for the strings. He played alone but learned the sounds and style of *maskanda* performance by following young men in his district who went off to court young women with their songs and guitar sounds. (This was the primary activity of a Zulu guitarist, who would progress onto the concertina once he was married.) Vilakazi recalled that he would hide away so that the courting couple could not see him and listen as the man played for his lover (personal communication, June 1995). He would then go home and work out the tuning system for the guitar, and gradually he began to compose his own songs.

Vilakazi's community has acknowledged his special talent as a guitarist and songwriter with the name they have given him: Chakide. The name derives from the Zulu root form *chaka,* which means "to blurt out a secret, publish openly a secret affair; betray a person's identity; give away; tell on; report" (Doke et al. 1990, 108). *Chakide* also refers to a mongoose or weasel, and Chakijana is the proper name for a cunning little mythical being in Zulu folklore (Doke et al. 1990, 108). Vilakazi explains that like the Zulu trick-ster, the subject of many folktales, he is called Chakide because he is "clever, very, very clever" (personal communication, 1994). He portrays the image of Chakide in the section of self-praises he in-serts into the majority of his compositions. Thus Vilakazi brings to the urban space a strategy for self-definition that draws on a belief system far removed from the everyday struggles of life in the city. Similarly, he gives textual form to these experiences in a perfor-mance that uses traditional Zulu musical principles to groove on the instrument of the city, the instrument of the devil: the guitar. These sounds performed by the Zulu *maskanda* underpin the creation and reenactment of the urban stories, myths, and legends.

The twenty songs of Thami Vilakazi that I have recorded draw on his experience as a migrant worker in the city of Durban in the early 1980s. From his experience as a restaurant cook, a painter, a gardener, and an unemployed worker living in one of the squatter settlements in Durban, Vilakazi constructs in performance a vision of the urban environment that contrasts sharply with his "home" in Zululand. To construct his vision of urban life, he walks through the city. The physical act of walking, combined with thinking, is his method of composition.

> I am not talking to anybody. I am just thinking, just thinking. And touching here and touching this side [of the guitar], then you get what you like. If you get what you like, you have to think now again, what [are] you going to say with your mouth? That means composition. Sometimes, if I walk, I am thinking, I am thinking, I am always singing. I am singing, singing, singing. If I get something I can sing about, then I take it . . . It's easy. No problem. If you are thinking, you must get what you want. (personal communication, December 1996)

Each of the pieces Vilakazi performs is an original composition. Through the total musical package of text, guitar sound, and song structure, he articulates his own moral and geographical vision of the urban experience—a vision that exists in tension with his vision and memory of the rural Zululand of his childhood.

What does he sing about? He remembers the stories that people have told him, and these become the substance of his performance. When the song is complete, he takes it to the person who told him the story and sings it for him or her. People are almost always happy that he composed a song about them, Vilakazi says (personal communication, December 1994).

Most of Vilakazi's songs consist of three kinds of verbal texts that differ in content, presentation, and audience addressed, each framed by instrumental sections. Vilakazi himself assumes a different performance persona in each. The performance begins with an introduction called *intela, izihlabo,* or *isawundi,* in which the tuning is tested and skillfully executed melodies are presented. The introduction is followed by an instrumental section consisting of several interweaving lines, a sung section that is fairly repetitive in text and sound, the self-praises, and sometimes an additional narrative (the song section is often repeated), and finally, an instrumental conclusion with a gradual fading out of sound. There is some flexibility in the ordering of the verbal sections, so Chakide's praises may be heard more than once, or the song section might return, possibly with the lines of text presented in a new sequence.

Although the practice of praise singing or praise naming is not new, it has generally focused on praising others rather than self-commendation. The self-praises of a *maskanda* might be understood as a specifically spatial practice, de Certeau (1988) argues, a strategy for delimiting one's own place and for inscribing the individual into the moral and cultural topography of strangers that characterizes the urban environment. It is through his self-praises that Thami is able to articulate the superiority of his performance when compared with that of other *maskanda* guitarists, and it is through these words that he becomes known and remembered in his community.

The contents of Thami's self-praises illustrate the mongoose/weasel image of *chakide*. Although the details may vary from one context to the next, the central ideas become the "signature tune" in each of his performances. Every repetition creates continuity from one song to the next within a single performance, and from performance to performance. (CD TRACK 13 has one version.)

Nango uChakide uphume kanje	There is Chakide going the other way
Bethi bamkakile	When they surrounded him
Obaphosel'uhlamvu	He threw them a grain
Bathi baylunqaka	When they tried to catch it
Bathaphun'isithingi senkhukhu	They soiled their hands with chicken shit
UChakide waphuma kanje.	Chakide went the other way.

This text suggests a scene in which the weasel or mongoose (*chakide*) is stealing chickens. In an attempt to catch him out or trick him, they surround him. But he tricks them by throwing some grain at them. Instead of catching hold of the weasel, however, the person grasps in his hands nothing but chicken shit. The weasel disappears around the corner. His wit and guile can clearly not be matched by anybody around him.

Vilakazi's representation of himself as *chakide,* the clever one, refers to both his guitar skills and the manner in which he creates his texts. As Chakide (the man transformed into animal/musician), the quick-witted, sharp, guileful guitarist and storyteller is able to beat any who dare challenge him. Such a transformation of self through performance is crucial if Vilakazi is to be the metaphorical *chakide*—the reporter, the teller of people's secrets and affairs. The attribution embodies a particular tension between Chakide and his community, for in telling others' tales, regardless of the artistic expertise with which he does so, he risks community retribution. The potential conflict is conveyed in another section of his self-praises (CD TRACK 12):

Usehleli phezulu-ke manje	Now he is right on top
UChakide ukhanda kulendoda	Chakide is on top of this man's head
Ilibele ukuvimba ubala	He tries in vain to stop [Chakide]
Abangani bayo	[The man's] friends
Bayayibuza ukuthi	Are asking
Ubani lapho wemfowethu	"Who is that there, my brother?"
Hayi!	"Hey!"
Kululekani nina	"You relax
Khohlwani yimina	and forget about me.
Khon'uChakide la.	It is Chakide here."

Vilakazi explains this section in the context of competition between musicians:

You see, I say to other maskanda, I say, "You are not very good for playing, you maskanda. So, if you want to come to me and hear what, how I am playing here, you can't see me. Even if I am in front of you, you can't see. . . . No, no, you can't see me. You are looking at me, you ask other people, you ask other people, "Where is this Thami?" You can't see me because now I look like a chakide.

And what else? Even if you sit like that, I can stay on your head. You ask "Where is Chakide?" The people they are going to tell you, "There is the chakide, on your head." You say, "No, it's not Chakide, it's my hair. My hair is very big." The people say, "Oh, you are very stupid man. There's the chakide." You say, "No, it's not Chakide, it's my hair." (personal communication, February 1995)

In the context of Vilakazi's performance the trickster is praised for his adeptness at guitar playing, though his relationship to his community is considered with some ambivalence in terms of the stories that he sings about. Such ambiguity is embodied in the uncertainty in his friends' identification of him as either hair or *chakide*.

In the sung sections of his performance, Vilakazi criticizes the morals of the members of the urban community in which he stays. This is the "poetic license" that Vail and White (1991) suggest is a central aesthetic principle in southern African performance. However, the subjects of Vilakazi's songs are not those distant from daily life, such as government officials or religious leaders, but the people with whom he interacts on a daily basis. In Vilakazi's view, their moral fiber is inferior to that of the people of his home in Zululand, to whom he appears to address his critique. The songs are simple in text and structure. They usually consist of four or five lines that are repeated several times.

Akuyiwo naw'amanga kulelizwe	There are so many lies in this world (9x)
Kukhona abathi sebazi	There are some who say that
uNkulunkulu emafini	They know God in the clouds
Kukhona abathi sebebuya	There are some who say they have come
KuNkulunkulu emafini	From God in the clouds
Akuyiwo naw'amanga kulelizwe	There are so many lies in this world
Ngikhonz'idlozi	"I honor the ancestors
Mina Baba ngixolele (3x)	Father, forgive me." (3x)
Tathi sembato sakho	"Take your church attire
Sihambe sontweni (3x)	We are going to church." (3x)
Ngikhonz'idlozi	"I honor the ancestors
Mina Baba ngixolele	Father, forgive me."

Akuyiwo naw'amanga kulelizwe   There are so many lies in this
world.

Vilakazi's song texts are remarkable for their embedded conflicts. In this song, there is a contest over belief systems—Christianity versus Zulu traditional religious practice (the ancestors); implicit in the text is a generational difference—Vilakazi addresses his "father" and asks forgiveness for the perceived discrepancy; there is also a dissonance over domains of truth and deception, of what people say versus how they act. Each of these contradictions is framed by Vilakazi's urgent desire for truth: "There are so many lies in this world." With the repetition of sections of this song at the end of the performance, Vilakazi sings that line no less than sixteen times!

Both the self-praising and the narratives woven into Vilakazi's performances are delivered in the style of the conventional *imbongi*—somewhere between sung and spoken poetry (Rycroft 1984). The delivery is rapid, with minimal repetition of complete lines or blocks of text. The crucial difference between the performed style of an *imbongi* and the *maskanda* is the musician's guitar accompaniment to his praises and the narrative style of the *maskanda's* performed texts. In Vilakazi's performances, there is seldom a clear distinction in sound or delivery between his self-praises and the story that he inserts into individual songs. Nevertheless, the narratives vary with each new song while the core of his self-praises changes only in detail.

In the narratives, where he exposes the untruths and deceptions that he senses characterize his urban environment, Vilakazi articulates the moral disconnection he senses between rural and urban spaces. He suggests, for example, that the *sangoma* (traditional healer) is not a real healer but someone interested only in the money. He sings of a man who steals everything he sees, of young men and women who transgress traditional moral boundaries by sitting and kissing in the park in front of young children, of the impossibility of marriage, of a young woman who ran off with all his money.

The following narrative is taken from a song addressed to his father (CD TRACK 13):

Akenithulenini phela kenginixoxele	Be quiet while I tell you a story
Ngitholiphepha lapha incwadi	I received a paper, a short letter
Libhalwe usisi obath'ufunummendo	From a sister seeking marriage
Ngisukenaye lomuntu la eThekweni	I left Durban with this person
Ngimuse ekhaya afik'agilimkhuba	I took her home, only for her to break taboos
Aqomabafana lababelusa izinkomo	She fell in love with the herdboys
Ngitheng'isidwaba	I bought her the skirt for marriage
Athi isidwaba siyamusinda	She said "The skirt is heavy."
Ngeke asifake	She won't wear it
Usekhohliwe ukuthi ifun'umendo	She has forgotten that she seeks marriage
Ucabang'ukweqa manje ashon'eGoli	She is now thinking of running off to Jo'burg
Thenengakeqi nje wabanjwa ubaba	Before she could do so, my father caught her
Eshuk'igudu la emva kwendlu	Rolling a joint behind the house
Ngenhla Wakhuz'ibhadi ubab'ebon'imikhuba	My father was appalled at the behavior a spectacle
Abizumama ukuba azombukisa	He called my mother to see for herself
Kuthe kunjalo-ke washaya wachitha	She ran away immediately
Umakhoti wami lona esebhek'eGoli	My bride, to Johannesburg
Uma ngithi ngiyabuza ukuthi	When I asked her,
Kwenzenjani	"What is wrong?"
Ahleke kancane nje athi gwegwegwe	She just laughs a little, gwegwegwe
Unginika malini njengoba wangithat'eThekweni	"What do you give me for taking me from Durban
Wathi uyongithengel'inyama	Saying you are going to buy me meat
Kanti uyongidlis'imfino	But giving me only greens."
Awukahle phela khoti ukutheth'	"Hold on a little, my bride, lower your voice
ekhaya	at home.
Ubab'uzothini ngoba usafika emzini	What will father say? You are new in the family."
Anginamsebenzi mina, ngizobuyel' ekhaya.	"I don't care, I will go back home."

Yeyeni webantu kanti eThekweni	Oh my, my, such are the
kunjani.	people of Durban.

Vilakazi closes his song addressed to his "father" in Zululand with a rueful lament over the kinds of people he knows in the city of Durban. In conversation, Vilakazi insisted that, even though he sings in the first person, the song is not about himself. It is a story about the experiences of one of his friends from Eshowe, which he then transformed into song performance. Vilakazi suggests that the conclusion to be drawn is that you cannot marry "a woman of loose morals."

The distaste that Vilakazi articulates toward lax moral practices in the urban areas is contrasted in his self-praises, where Vilakazi constructs for himself the role of a teller of the truth through the sounds of his guitar and the words of his songs and stories. In the song "*Akuyiwo naw'amanga kulelizwe*" ("There are so many lies in this world") cited above, Vilakazi adds to his self-praises a conversation he has with a brother, the chief from Eshowe, in which he tells him that this Chakide is the same Vilakazi that he knows.

Kuseyiyo leyondoda wethu	It's the same man, brother
Hlala phanzi uthule uthi du	Sit down and be quiet
Uzwekahle intambo	And listen carefully to the strings
Ngizibambe zonke wethu	I am holding all of them
Angikulobhi	I am not cheating you
Yathula inkosi	The chief Mkhathini is quiet
UMkhathini lapha phezulu eNgogo	Up there at Ngogo
Awunikeze umfowethu uMashokani	Please pour my brother Mashokani
Injongo ibeyinye isiqatha	A tin of the brew [skokiaan]
Athi ukushaya kancane khona	So he can drink a little and
Ezozwa ukuthi ngenzejani la.	Hear what I do here.
Hop!	Hop!
Ngikhathele!	I am so fed up!

At another moment in his self-praising, Chakide tells us that we must watch the various voices in his guitar strings so that none of them falls down. He monitors individual guitar voices carefully, in a manner that parallels his moral surveillance. Chakide can tell others' secrets because he presents himself as the bearer of moral right, of cultural truth.

Gumboot Dance

After the 1976 Soweto uprising, schools were in chaos. So a local community organizer decided to create a community center for black youth. She raised funds to build a structure where she taught a group of young men traditional and contemporary dance—the cha cha, gumboot dance, traditional Zulu dance, and a host of others. Ultimately, this group went on to busk on the streets of Johannesburg and perform in a community arts festival. After their director, Zenzi Mbuli, transformed their busking into a theatrical production, they became known around South Africa. British film director Wayne Harrison, from Back Row Productions in London, traveled to South Africa and decided to film the production. *Gumboots: An Explosion of Spirit and Song* (2000) is a commercially produced video of their show.

The video is divided into two sections. The first shows the production that has traveled internationally to festivals and music theater stages in Europe, the United States, and Asia. Here gumboot dance as a cultural practice of migrant workers has been transformed into a stage production about being gold miners in South Africa in the twentieth century. It is a moving production that combines narrative, gumboot dance, drumming, and singing. The performers use a mix of English and Zulu, and the instrumental accompaniment has been worked into a musical language palatable to an international audience.

The second section of the video is a 53-minute commentary on the performance. It provides insider perspectives on gold mining, language use, and the creation of the *Gumboots* production itself. Rare and old footage of the early days of labor migration and migrants in the gold mines as well as old dance performances are interwoven with the documentary narrative. Excerpts from the stage performance are also inserted into the documentary as the narrator explains the larger meaning or history of a specific sequence. In addition to what it tells us about gumboot dance, this documentary provides a lens through which we can see how local performance is remade for a transnational audience. In the spirit of the documentary portion of the gumboots video, I have inserted segments of information from the video into my own ethnographic and historical narrative on gumboot dance as I learned about it from my teacher Blanket Mkhize over a period of almost two decades.

Entering the World of Gumboot Dance

My entry into the world of gumboot dance came quite unexpectedly in 1984, when Blanket Mkhize invited me and my fellow ethnomusicology student Janet Topp Fargion to learn to gumboot dance. For our initial meeting we were instructed to travel to the same place that *isicathamiya* competitions were held, the Glebeland migrant worker hostels. Neither Janet nor I spoke any Zulu at the time, and Mkhize and his fellow dancers spoke almost no English. Initially we agreed to meet on Saturdays and Sundays at the Glebeland hostel community hall for lessons, although Mkhize had asked us to come every day for long periods of time, which was more in line with how migrant workers themselves taught each other and rehearsed their routines. But we couldn't afford the cost in time and expense of traveling to and from Umlazi so frequently. Furthermore, the townships were dangerous for both black and white South Africans, because migrant worker hostels only housed men. Women stayed out of the townships, not only out of fear but also because it was illegal to enter without special permits. We were also meeting Mkhize at the migrant worker hostels, large barracks for single men. No women were allowed to live in these buildings, so the few women there tended to be either family members on brief visits or prostitutes.

We met in the Glebeland hostel for several weeks, but ultimately our lessons became more complicated to negotiate. In 1985 the apartheid government declared at least two states of emergency, clamping down on what it called "political unrest" by putting a curfew on travel in black residential areas and increasing security force surveillance, particularly in a township like Umlazi, because of the migrant worker hostels at the entrance to the township. These were the sites of politically motivated violence and killings in the 1980s and early 1990s. Mkhize became concerned for our safety at the hostel, so we agreed to rehearse at the University of Natal. This meant that Janet and I had to pick up and drop off the gumboot dancers every time we met.

The classes consisted of a couple of dancers simply going through their dance routines at speed, over and over, and expecting us to pick up the moves somehow. It was hard. Slowly we began to work out a way that might work better for us. It was clear that Janet and I needed to have the steps broken down into smaller units, even though the dancers themselves had learned them in much larger segments. At one point we asked Mkhize if he would mind if we videotaped the moves so that we could learn them at home. He agreed.

Our first public performance with the team of Blanket Mkhize was at the University of Natal's Music and Dance Jamboree held at the South African Music Educator's Conference in August 1985. We performed alongside a variety of musical groups, including an *isicathamiya* ensemble from Umlazi. The audiences were amazed that women—white women, at that—could do the dance. Although Janet and I both left South Africa at the end of 1985 to study abroad, we were able to perform together with Blanket's team at several other events later in the year. I maintained contact with Mkhize over the years, and when I returned to South Africa in the early 1990s, we reestablished our performing relationship. I danced with Mkhize several times until I again left South Africa in September 1996.

On January 6, 1996, when both Janet and I were back in the country, Blanket threw a party at his homestead in the southern part of the province of KwaZulu Natal. Blanket told his chief that he and his neighbors would be welcoming to his homestead the two white women he had taught to gumboot dance in Durban in 1985. As with all traditional Zulu celebrations, an animal (a sheep, in this case) was slaughtered and its meat shared with the community and guests, *utshwala* (traditional sorghum beer) was brewed beforehand, and competitive song and dance took place.

Two teams of dancers prepared to perform. Mkhize's sons and their friends, who lived in Jolivet (near Ixopo) in the interior part

Blanket Mkhize (guitarist on right) and his 1985 team,
including Janet Topp Fargion (on left) and Carol Muller (to the right),
perform at a school function in KwaZulu Natal.

of southern KwaZulu Natal, the area known as Umzansi (below the
Tugela River), had been rehearsing their own gumboot dance
team, and a second team arrived in a mini-bus taxi from Creighton,
the Bhaca area in southern KwaZulu Natal. Most of the members of
that team were migrant workers employed by the parastatal company called Spoornet, formerly the state-controlled South African
Railways. The Railways had been active sponsors of gumboot dance
until the mid-1980s, when political violence disrupted urban life in
South Africa, destroying much of the vibrancy of the black urban
culture that existed.

As is typical of gumboot dance, the team of dancers from Bulwer
was heralded by a guitarist and concertina player playing a cyclical
riff that moved between the tonic, subdominant, and dominant
chords. The leader of the team walked ahead of the dance team,
who moved into the performance space with a stylized walk, their
arms outstretched at the sides of their bodies. Occasionally, the
dancers punctuated this movement by hitting their boots together
at the ankles in a quick rhythmic pattern. They circled around the
open space in the homestead, and then moved into a stationary

Blanket Mkhize (guitar) and his sons gumboot dance at a community celebration in rural KwaZulu Natal, September 1996.

straight-line formation, with the leader and musicians standing apart from the rest of the team.

The leader was dressed slightly differently from the others, but all had on the traditional black Wellington boots, baseball caps, black trousers tied at the knee with a white handkerchief, and "cowboy" shirts. One or two of the dancers had tied pieces of wire with bottle tops strung on them around the lower part of their boots, to create the sound of rattles.

The dancers claim that the bottle top rattles remind them of the history of gumboot dancers' experiences in the mines. The sounds, they say, resonate with the sound of chains around the ankles of miners in the early years of mining history, a claim that corresponds to reports that prisoners were often supplied as cheap labor to the mines and may well have been chained together. However, since the ankle rattles in traditional Zulu dance were made from dried pea pods, it may be that the natural materials from rural environments were simply replaced with new materials available in the urban context.

Blanket Mkhize had a different version of ankle rattles. These rattles, called *amakhehlezi* or *amaspeaker,* were round shoe polish tins with small stones inside. The lid of the tin had been pierced with

Blanket Mkhize (guitarist on right side) plays for his team who arrive to perform at the community celebration in rural KwaZulu Natal, September 1996.

multiple holes to make it look like a speaker. The speakers were attached to large strands of rubber that were pulled over the boot and placed at the ankle. Mkhize told us that it was an honor to wear these speakers because only those who had mastered the movements were allowed to put them on.

While the dancers waited for the leader's call, they marked time with a quick marching movement in place. The leader paced up and down in front of the team, checking the attire and making sure that everyone was standing in the correct position. The stronger dancers usually stand at the outer ends of the line, with the weaker ones in the middle. "Lef-light" called the leader, and the team responded with a quick hitting of the boots together as they continued to march on the spot. He began to call out a series of commands more aggressively. The team of dancers responded with precision and power. "Attention!" "Attention!" "Two-Attention!" "Nasisalutho!" ("Salutho" is one of the first dance sequences performed on *Gumboots*, the video.) The leader continued to randomly shout out a series of commands. Each of these called for a fixed pattern of steps that had been composed by individual dancers and learned by team members over time in many rehearsals.

The gumboot style of dance draws on a variety of sources: Bhaca tradition; the various missionary heritages, such as that of the German missionaries; dances of sailors who visited the port city of Durban, such as Russian folk dance; the popular social dances that accompanied jazz music in the 1930s and 1940s, such as the jitterbug; and most clearly, tap dance, as performed by the visiting minstrel groups of the nineteenth century and popularized through films of Fred Astaire and Gene Kelley in the mid-twentieth century. The aesthetic of gumboot performance also embodies the regimentation of military marching and the discipline required of mine laborers working underground. The dancers are expected to respond quickly, without hesitation, regardless of what the leader commands. Precision of movement—starting and ending on the same beat—is crucial to effective and powerful performance.

The community of people that had gathered at Blanket's homestead that day stood in a circle around the dancers. Those watching the gumboot dancing hardly noticed the dust kicked up by the fast-moving footwork, boot slapping, and thumping on the ground as the group performance intensified. Women ululated and danced in front of the dancers, men whistled, and everybody cheered at the sharpness and discipline of this team of dancers in peak condition. The leader paced back and forth across the line of dancers, occasionally blowing on his police whistle to keep his team alert and responsive. "*Abelungu!*" (White People—Watch Out!) "*Amaphoyisa!*" (Police!) "*GwazamaZulu!*" (Stab the Zulu!) "*Germiston!*" (name of a mining town) "*Jowanisberg!*" (Johannesburg!).

Sometime in the middle of the collective performance of *amadoubles,* the leader called for singles. These are highly competitive solo performances by individual team members where each dancer demonstrates his improvisatory skills. It is in these singles that the links with the tap dancing of Hollywood film stars such as Fred Astaire and Gene Kelley are particularly evident. With each new improvised sequence, the power of the performance increases.

There are several moments in the *Gumboots* video performance where singles are danced. (See especially the item "I'm too sexy for my body" where the man performs his manliness displaying his improvisational skills in gumboot dance.) Such display reminds us of the *isoka* qualities of the *maskanda*—the physical and musical display of attributes of a man that would make him a good lover. After all, successfully courting a young woman was the goal of being a skilled singer and Zulu guitarist.

Selected members of the community began to throw small coins at the performers, to communicate to the dancers and the rest of the onlookers which of the soloists they favored. The more coins thrown, the better the spectacle. The practice of throwing money has a long tradition in black performance culture. Coplan (1985, 76) describes the auctioneering and bidding on performance that characterized shebeen culture in the slumyards of South African cities in the 1930s and 1940s. Similarly, Hugh Tracey describes these practices in urban townships in the 1940s: "In many concerts, members of the audience show their appreciation by showering pennies upon the stage, or by walking up and putting silver in a saucer. The 'Turn' will oblige just so long as the pennies fall. It is an infallible indication of the degree of popularity" (1948, xi).

Finally, the leader called "*Shiyalekhaya.*" All the dancers re-formed the straight line to "leave behind at home," as the leader had instructed. They danced a few more patterns, and finally the performance ended, as freshly slaughtered and grilled meat was passed around to all in attendance.

Although the dancers did not mention it that day, their party coincided with the centenary of gumboot dance performance, which had emerged a century earlier among Bhaca migrant workers from KwaZulu Natal as a black, predominantly male genre. Beginning in the late 1980s, these men migrated, sometimes on foot and often by train, to and from both the gold mines in Johannesburg and harbor and railway work in the port city of Durban. Gumboot straddles the rural and urban spaces within which migrant workers from southern KwaZulu Natal have operated for the past 100 years. Though there are traditional characteristics embedded in the performance, as the video *Gumboots* demonstrates so powerfully, the gold mines in and around the city of Johannesburg were the environment most critical to the development of gumboot style. For most Bhaca migrants to eGoli, the City of Gold, work and leisure were continually controlled by structures of authority and surveillance in the form of mine bosses, managers, and police. Gumboot dance was forged out of migrant worker experience: it is a style that reflects on that experience, commenting with humor and at times with biting satire on its brutality.

This genre embodies what Hannerz (1994) calls the "global ecumene"—the simultaneous presence in a single performance of ancestral beliefs and dance style, Hollywood cowboy and tap dance films, nineteenth-century Anglo-American minstrel performance, industrial labor relations, European folk music, mission Christianity, and ethnic tensions. In this sense, gumboot dance is neither essentially African nor Western, neither Christian nor ancestral, neither traditional nor modern. Much like its migrant practitioners, who are neither fully urban nor fully rural, gumboot dance has long existed in the interstices of South African society.

Early History of Gumboot Dance

Several elements of gumboot dance are characteristic of precolonial Nguni musical practices: the call-and-response interaction between dance leader and the rest of the team; the competitive element, both between dance teams and within the teams; the importance of audience/community support during the performance; the comical element in performance, drawn from both traditional and minstrel performance; and the manner in which gumboot dance engages with and is constituted from the substance of everyday life and experience.

What clearly distinguishes gumboot dance from earlier rural dances is the use of footgear for its performance. The differences in footgear and style distinguish two different kinds of gumboot dance performance. The first, *igumboots* dance, is deeply connected to the heavy stamping of the traditional dance of Zulu men. It is also clearly associated with the working class—with those who labored in the mines, in the Durban harbor, and perhaps even on white farms. The second is more directly connected to the civilizing project of the mission station. It is the lighter style, one more clearly tied to light stepping or tapping—what Mkhize's dancers call the style for girls. This is *isicathulo,* the style developed with shoes and performed by the likes of Reuben Caluza (see Erlmann 1992) and other members of the mission-educated elite of KwaZulu Natal.

Pre-colonial dance forms were generally performed barefoot. The Zulu name given to gumboot dance—*isicathulo*—provides the first indication of innovation. Initially, the word referred to the leather shoes worn by warriors who had to travel long distances. In the nineteenth century, it also began to refer to shoes and rubber Wellington boots, both of which were crucial apparel when an African came into contact with Europeans and Americans on mission stations and farms and, later, in the urban areas. In all cases, *isicathulo* constituted signs of contact with the Western or non-African world. The root of the word *cathama* means to walk softly, quietly, and stealthily. It has been incorporated into two kinds of black performance culture in South Africa: *isicathamiya* and *isicathulo*. The first is the style of music and dance performance recently made famous by Joseph Shabalala and Ladysmith Black Mambazo. In this context it means to walk softly like a cat. The second refers to the opposite, gumboot dance, which is characterized by loud aggressive stamping of boots and hand clapping.

The earliest evidence of the new dance styles that emerged with the introduction of shoes and boots appeared at the mission stations. Several terms associated with gumboot dancing point to the Western influence on its development: *thamba, boloha, isicathulo,* and *umqhumqhumbelo* (Cockrell 1987, 422). The first, *thamba* (discussed below), refers to dancing in a straight line with uniform movement controlled by a conductor who usually plays a concertina. Such movement is typical of gumboot dance performance as we learned it from Blanket Mkhize. *Boloha* is possibly an Afrikaans or Xhosa derivative of the word "polka." It is defined as a boot dance (and cross-referenced with *isicathulo*), a rough concert, or an all night carnival party. *Isicathulo* means shoe, boot, or sandal; it also refers to a boot dance performed by young boys since the first contact with Europeans. *Umqhumqhumbelo* is perhaps the most intriguing in terms of the development of gumboot dance. It is defined as "a modern rhythmic dance adopted by certain Christian natives, in which dancing is both individual and in groups" (Cockrell 1987, 422). *Umqhumqhumbelo* is also related to the word *umqhuqho*. This translates into the onomatopoeic sound of the trotting of a horse and the clopping of its heels. A reference to the sound of horses ties in with the word used in competitions to indicate poor performance: *ihashi* or horse.

According to Jonney Hadebe, one of the dancers on Mkhize's team, *ihashi* is what is called out when a team in competition makes two or more mistakes and is disqualified from the competition.

In addition to the linguistic evidence pointing to the missions as the points of origin for gumboot dance, Hugh Tracey (1952, 7) suggests that the origins of the dance itself are to be found in step dances developed in a mission station where traditional Nguni dancing was banned. Several Catholic missions are located in the Bhaca region, which suggests the impact of mission culture on local Bhaca communities from the nineteenth century. In the documentary *Gumboots,* the theater expert suggests that the German missionaries forbade traditional dance and replaced it with their own folk dancing. However, the film footage from earlier in the century also shows Russian sailors who visited the city of Durban and demonstrated their dancing to local workers in the harbor.

The following primary source material suggests that mission culture had an additional influence on the shape of gumboot dance because of its stress upon marching and musical drills, elements common to the older style of gumboot dance that we learned from Blanket Mkhize in the 1980s.

MUSICAL DRILL, 1st Exercise.
Marking Time
    When the children have marched to their places they should be made to "Mark Time!" This is done by alternately raising the left foot and knee and setting it on the ground again, then raising the right foot and knee and setting it on the ground again, always stepping in the same place and keeping time to the music.
    The children should be instructed to place their feet on the ground very softly each time, not to stamp, and not to move from their places. This marking time should be done with the hands in the attitude of "Attention," but, to prevent any tendency to swing the arms about, they may be folded behind the back, or with the right had grasping the left arm behind the back, and vice versa.
    (Mariannhill Monastery, Catholic Mission Archives)

It is clear from Hugh Tracey's photographic essay *African Dances of the Witwatersrand Gold Mines* (1952) as well as the archival film footage on the *Gumboots* video that the mines were central sites in the shaping of gumboot dance style. (Mkhize's father participated in the dance at the mines.) Tracey locates the next development of the genre in the Durban harbor, where migrant workers were issued gumboots when they began to handle chemical fertilizers. Performing outside at both mining and municipal compounds (where migrants were housed) would have required more sound, so boots would have become preferable to the shoes of the mission station.

The Influence of the Minstrel Show

The other cultural force that shaped gumboot dance was the minstrel show, performed in Durban by American and English troupes beginning in the nineteenth century. Jonney Hadebe, one of the members of Blanket Mkhize's team, explains the early history of gumboot dance in a program note written for the South African Railway's gumboot dancers:

> In 1896, subsequent to watching white men tap dancing and clapping their hands, the amaBaca decided to make a dance of their own. They called it the gumboots dance. The dance was a rhythmically performed act of dancing, clapping hands and slapping the calves—the calf muscles being protected by the rubber gumboots.
>
> In the year 1896, the group consisted of eight members in all, six dancers and two playing musical instruments. In those days, the soles of the gumboots were cut off and the dancers wore shoes.
>
> With the passage of time, the group became more sophisticated in their dancing performances. They started playing a guitar, concertina, violin and a piano accordion all at the same time. The group presently consists of from twelve to twenty persons. After performing all over the country, where they did their duty towards the younger generation, the group changed their base from Johannesburg to Durban.
>
> The amaBacas dance in the SATS [South African Transport Services] tournament and have danced in Johannesburg, Bloemfontein and Durban. I have been a gumboots dancer for the past twenty-three years. (Jonney Hadebe ca. 1978)

Both Cockrell (1987) and Erlmann (1991) provide evidence for the tours of mostly white minstrels from America (such as the famous Christy Minstrels) and England who entertained South Africans with the painted black faces in the nineteenth century, although the African-American troupe of Orpheus McAdoo also visited South Africa several times in the 1890s. Cockrell highlights the outstanding features of the minstrel show, many of which became central to the shaping not only of *isicathamiya* performance (as embodied in Joseph Shabalala and Ladysmith Black Mambazo) but also of *isicathulo* and gumboots dance.

> Perhaps the most striking feature of a typical [American] minstrel show was the makeup used by the performers. In the early years all the entertainers were whites in blackface, who wore additional makeup to exaggerate their lips and eyes. Their dress was of two sorts: shabby, ragged, and grotesque to depict southern rural slaves, or fanciful and dandified—replete with tails, white ties, and white gloves, all in excruciatingly bad taste. . . . The troupe was arrayed in a semicircle. The interlocutor was usually named Mr. Johnson and sat in the center. He served as the butt of jokes that streamed forth from the end men, typically called after the instruments they played: Mr. Bones and Mr. Tambo. Other minstrels formed the chorus and played banjos, guitars, fiddles, concertinas, triangles, or other instruments. The entertainment took the form of derisive mimicking of the black man. (Cockrell 1987, 419)

Several of these elements transferred into gumboot dance performance: the exaggerated makeup (still used by black school children in Durban in the mid-1980s, often to make their audiences laugh at the exaggerated images); the shabby dress for the leader (as the dance leader, Mkhize typically wore such attire) and dandy dress for the chorus (smart attire for the team could make or break the group in competition); the leader in the center (Mkhize typically paced up and down in front of the group); satire and humor in the performance (Mkhize frequently deliberately fell over in performance to make the audience laugh); and finally, musical accompaniment in the form of guitar, violin, and concertina.

Hadebe's narrative of gumboot dance links its early history to these minstrel performances in several ways. The first is with his reference to "white men tap dancing and clapping their hands." It is quite feasible that the amaBhaca saw minstrel shows by white black-faced minstrels in the year 1896. It is not clear, however, if it is tap dancing or simply the complex footwork of minstrel performance that impacted upon these men in that year. It seems more likely that Hadebe is recalling two distinct processes in the development of gumboot dance style: what was recounted to him by older gumboot dancers with regard to minstrel performances in the 1890s and what he may have seen himself in mining compounds in Johannesburg in the 1950s—films of tap dancing by Fred Astaire and Gene Kelley. Tap dancing is also reported to have been extremely popular at the Bantu Men's Social Center in Johannesburg in the 1930s (Phillips ca. 1938, 297). This would have been the more sophisticated gumboot dancing that Hadebe subsequently discusses.

Hadebe's description of the early troupe as a group of eight with six dancers and two instrumentalists also points to the influence of the minstrel shows. Cockrell (1987, 420) quotes an article called "Kafir Christy Minstrels" from the local Durban newspaper, *The Natal Mercury,* that describes a black minstrel troupe: "A novelty this Christmas, is a troupe of eight genuine natives, *bones and all,* complete who really get through their songs very well" (my emphasis).

The two instruments mentioned may well have been the bones and *tambo.* Cockrell suggests that the bones played by white minstrels were similar to indigenous instruments played by black South Africans in the early twentieth century. In the handwritten manuscript of the first English-Zulu dictionary, compiled by missionary A. Bryant in 1894, the entry for *tambo* (guitar) reads as follows: *into e-shaywayo e-nezimTambo* (the thing that is struck or sounded by means of strings or with a bone). *Tambo* clearly refers to both strings and bones. Perhaps the reason the bones of the minstrel show are replaced with the guitar in gumboot dance performance is that the guitar is viewed as a percussive instrument as well as a melodic and harmonic one. In contrast, the concertina is simply translated by Bryant as *inkositini.*

Mining Culture and Gumboot Performance

No one needs to be reminded that mining is hard labor. But perhaps we do need to be reminded, as social historian Dunbar Moodie observes, that mining is a particular kind of hard labor. As a form of production, he writes, mining is hard labor undertaken under conditions of extreme discomfort, exacerbated by tension stemming from the need to watch constantly for signs of potential hazard. "Whenever you go down into a shaft," says a Sotho miner quoted by Moodie, "you are not sure that you will come out alive. You don't want to think about it. . . . Death is so real you keep on praying and thanking God each time you come out alive" (Moodie 1983, 180).

The *Gumboots* video shows mine experience as the narrative into which gumboot sequences are inserted and reshaped. Similarly, the peculiarities of mine experience, or "mine culture," have been indelibly imprinted into popular consciousness through the very substance of the older style of gumboot dance performance. Although gumboot dance has clear precedents in the radical shifts away from pre-colonial performance cultures as they were repressed by the mission and re-modeled on nineteenth-century Euro-American popular culture, I argue that it was the experience of migrant labor in the gold mines of South Africa that most powerfully shaped the distinctive features of what is now called gumboot dance. Gumboot dance engages and comments on the exigencies of every day experience in mine culture. Perhaps the most revealing source of information on the development of the dance style and on the mine culture itself is the dance as practiced by the older dancers and transmitted to their sons in KwaZulu Natal.

Men who entered into the culture of the mines in South Africa walked into an environment quite alien from their prior rural experience. This was particularly true for those who went underground. One captures a glimpse of the differences, of the harshness of this culture, from the documentary section of the *Gumboots* video. Two miners explained it to Moodie: "One man told me that when he goes to work underground he is not a full person. Another said: 'When I am underground I do not think of anything else except coming out of the mine'" (cited in Moodie 1983, 183).

The mine culture worldwide is characterized by emotions of both pride in the courage to go underground and fear of doing so. The ambivalence the miners feel about mine labor is articulated in the *Gumboots* video where the miner begs the owners not to shut down the mine because he has a family to support. Without the mine, he has no hope of subsistence, yet the mine is a dangerous place. In South Africa, this ambivalence was intensified, because South African mining culture differed in two ways from that in other parts of the world: first, racially structured authoritarianism defined the local culture and second, labor migration for mine employment involved only the men, not their families. As we are told in the "Joburg" segment of the *Gumboots* video, a man's family remained a thousand miles away, and he might see them only once in a period of six to eighteen months. He ate, slept, and worked within the confines of the mine and the compound—the cramped, sometimes prison-like buildings where miners lived year round.

The mine compounds were highly controlled residential dormitories in which workers resided for the length of their contract. They were convenient and efficient for mine owners: "The compounds were located close to mineshafts, making rapid and efficient mobilization of labor for work possible. Furthermore, they provided a fit workforce, absenteeism would easily be policed, and strikes could be broken with a minimum of effort" (James 1999, 3). But for the miners, life in the compound was difficult. They were crowded into rooms that might house from sixteen to eighty men at a time, and there was little possibility of private space or time—even during their time off from work.

Nevertheless, the men found means to relieve the stress of their jobs inside the compound, through both officially sanctioned activities and those they organized themselves. The official channels were films shown in compounds and competitions in sport and traditional dance organized by the Chamber of Mines from at least the 1940s. This was one of the spaces in which Bhaca migrants from southern KwaZulu Natal gumboot danced, certainly in the 1940s (James 1999, 3) and, according to oral history, much earlier. The unofficial activities, which the *Gumboots* video alluded to, included alcohol, drugs, and sex, either in the compounds or in nearby urban townships, such as Sophiatown and Vrededorp.

Miners Underground

Hugh Tracey (1952) provides visual documentation of a wide range of dances performed by migrant workers at the gold mines in the Johannesburg area in the early decades of this century, including the gumboot dance of the Bhacas. Though several of the teams of dancers in Tracey's book are wearing shoes, the Bhaca are the only ones wearing the boots that typify mine labor. This dance attire suggests the close relationship between the content of the dance and mine experience, which is articulated in contemporary gumboot performance. I argue that the tensions associated with the underground experience of Bhaca miners provide the material for the formation of a worker-style dance performance. More than simply reflecting mine experience, it constitutes a satire on labor discipline and interaction as shaped by the experiences of mining and living in a compound. This is manifest at several levels.

Early groups of miners were organized into gangs or teams of workers, each with a black "boss-boy" who was answerable to the white miner. The boss-boy's relationship with the white boss frequently conflicted with his loyalties to his black subordinates, fostering considerable tension between teams, the boss-boys, and white management. This gang structure of early mining operations is reflected in the outstanding feature of gumboot dance performance: the team.

The nature of the relationship between ordinary workers and the boss-boy is embodied in the call-and-response interaction between the dance team leader and the team. In the dance structure, however, the boss-boy (dance leader) holds total control. Whenever he calls and whatever he requires, his team has to respond with rigor and precision. He often blows on a police whistle to keep his team in tow—a standard of discipline and teamwork that was also important in the mines. In the mines, Moodie points out, any worker who did not cooperate put his own life and that of his teammates on the line: "According to an observer who worked underground, black miners 'are keen that every one of them should do a perfect job . . . else they all face the risk of danger from falling rocks. They try hard to prevent or minimize accidents at work places by giving advice and helping one another.' Despite ethnic tensions in the compound, black underground workers in South Africa 'regard themselves as members of their work team first and foremost and do not appear to have any interest in ethnic composition'" (Moodie 1983, 180–181).

Because of the danger intrinsic to underground mine labor and the racially loaded authority structure, the interaction between supervisor and workers was authoritarian. Immediate response to commands was demanded on at least two levels: between the boss-boy and his team and between black laborers and white superiors. This style of interaction was entrenched in the racially constituted labor relations of South African mines from the earliest days and is indelibly imprinted in gumboot dance performance itself.

As the *Gumboots* documentary video corroborates, the linguistic manifestation of this unequal pattern of communication became known as *fanakalo. Fanakalo,* which means "do it like this," is defined as a "pidgin language used and sometimes taught as lingua franca on the mines." It was embodied in a series of booklets issued by the Chamber of Mines from the 1920s through the 1970s under various titles, such as the 1920 *Miner's Companion in Zulu,* for the use of Miners on the Witwatersrand Gold Mines (issued by the Prevention of Accidents Committee), the *1938 Miner's Companion in English, Afrikaans, Sesotho and Mine Kaffir,* and the 1970s version of *The Miner's Dictionary in English, Afrikaans and Fanakalo.* The preface to the most recent version, *The Miners Dictionary,* explains that the language originated with Indian workers in KwaZulu Natal in the nineteenth century. They developed the language while trying to learn English and Zulu simultaneously. The Chamber of Mines explains that it is a language that developed between black and white miners for effective communication in a context of linguistic diversity.

Fanakalo has been generally regarded with contempt by black South Africans, who view it not only as the defilement of languages such as Zulu and Xhosa but also as a language of subservience. *Fankalo* consists of a set of instructions issued by the white miner to the black laborers. The majority of words in the dictionary are commands with exclamation marks. Examples of the *fanakalo* for miners include:

Qala!   Begin!
Bulala!   Destroy!

Penduka!   Go Back!

Suka!   Go Away!

Pas Op!   Look Out! ("Pas op" was also the name given to
the supervisor, presumably because that was all
he ever said to the miners.)

This dictionary, compiled by white miners and their boss-boys, had a specific goal: to give workers enough language to keep them safe in an extremely dangerous situation but not enough to enable them to talk back to their supervisors. It also set the precedent for race relations in South Africa for many decades. The only common language for some black and white South Africans continues to be one symbolized by *fanakalo*, that of master and servant.

The pattern of interaction established by *fanakalo* constitutes the core of gumboot dance performance, which does not simply reflect the timeworn tradition of a respectful call and response. Rather, it is deeply loaded with mine labor tensions and frequently caught up in racist patterns of social relationships. These commands became the titles of specific dance sequences: *Bulala!* (Destroy, Murder!), *Dayinja!* (Danger!), *Attention!* (Attention!), *Gobek!* (Go back!), *GwazamaZulu!* (Stab the Zulu!). Just as a team member underground in the mines never knew what command would be issued next, a gumboot dancer cannot predict which dance sequence the leader will order next. He has to be ready at all times to obey the command or he will put his team at the risk of loss—of life when underground, or of losing the dance competition.

Miners in the Compounds

A constant feature of a miner's life in the compound was the continuous presence of police, both mine police around the compounds and state police monitoring the movement of black South Africans in the urban areas. Mining police enforced particular modes of behavior among migrants by frequent patrolling and checks for drugs and alcohol in the compounds. Jonney Hadebe, one of the dancers on Blanket Mkhize's team, attributed the two names of a single dance routine, *AmaPhoyisa!* and *AmaBlekjek!,* to

Gumboot team of Steven Shelembe competes against the team brought by Blanket Mkhize to celebrate the visit of researchers Janet Topp Fargion and Carol Muller, Creighton KwaZulu Natal, January 1995.

the presence of both kinds of police in Johannesburg. The commands represented the warnings miners issued to each other when the police were coming. Dancer and team leader Steven Shelembe commented that another routine, *Isihamba nodali* ("to go with your darling"), was the way around police harassment. If a man walked alone in the urban areas, the police would often harass or arrest him. If he walked along with a woman, the couple would be warned but seldom arrested.

A less stringent type of worker control in the compounds took the form of films that were regularly shown in the compounds, both to educate largely illiterate workers and to keep them busy in their time off. Phillips (1938) provides a list of some of the films shown in the compounds in the 1930s, which included both Hollywood-style entertainment as well as educational materials developed by the Chamber of Mines. Considering the lists of films starring Charlie Chaplin, Fred Astaire, and Gene Kelley, as well as Jonney Hadebe's account of the early history of gumboot dance, some music historians have suggested that later gumboot dance style may have been modeled on the humor and the tap dance steps in these films (see Muller and Topp 1985 for specific examples of the links). Certainly, the cowboy movies powerfully influenced the kinds of attire worn by dancers—such as the handkerchiefs tied around their legs, the cowboy shirts, and the Stetson hats typical of movies in the 1950s and later.

A third connection between gumboot dance performance and the mining compounds was the institutionalization of competitive dance between mining teams by the Reef Consolidated Mines in the 1940s. As the *Gumboots* documentary suggests, it has been reported that dance competitions at the mines were open to the public earlier in the century. In 1943, this mine dancing was institutionalized as a tourist activity with the construction of a semicircular stadium or amphitheater at one of the mine compounds. The money set aside for dance attire and the criteria by which teams were judged (usually by white adjudicators) profoundly shaped the emergence of gumboot dance as a genre peculiar to mining experience.

A final though less obvious link between miners and the compounds is embodied in the commands *Skhula numtwana!* ("The child is still growing!"), *Shiyalekhaya!* ("Abandoned at home!"), and *Germiston!* (Germiston is the name of a mining town where Hadebe first worked, and he composed the Germiston sequence in memory of that experience). Each of these commands refers to the rural home (a homestead or *fum*—farm) a miner leaves behind and sometimes never returns to when he goes off to find work in the urban areas.

Maskanda *Musical Accompaniment*

Though gumboot dance performance almost certainly originated with Bhaca migrants from southern KwaZulu Natal, the musical accompaniment is more clearly associated with Zulu *maskanda*. Nevertheless, the particular style of Zulu guitar that accompanies gumboot dance is an older one from the Umzansi region that is distinct from *isishameni* and *isizulu*. Furthermore, the *isicathulo* style of gumboot dance in Inanda, north of Durban, for example, does not use guitar accompaniment, while the *igumboots* dance from southern KwaZulu Natal does. The instrumentation is typically guitar,

Collage of Thoughts on Performing Race and Gender in Gumboot Dance

Carol Muller

gumboot dance
the boot performance of zulu-speaking male migrant workers in
south africa
believed to be the creative form of amabhaca men
who migrated from southern kwazulu natal to *egoli*, the place of
gold
the witwatersrand
where black men went to mine gold and diamonds for de beers
and anglo american corporation
black men, white diamonds, yellow gold, white capital

gumboot dance
forged from the fear of going underground
lef-lite
(performed right-left)
right (2, 3, 4)
right (2, 3, 4)
attention!
attention!
Two-attention!
kaps! (2, 3, 4)
off! (2, 3, 4)
kaps! (2, 3, 4)
off! (2, 3, 4)

gumboot dance
call and response resignifies as
fanakalo!
literally do it like this!
white miners' pidgin for commanding multilingual black miners
nasisalutho! dayinja!

(continues)

Collage of Thoughts on Gumboot Dance (*continued*)

gumboot dance
the dance of amabhaca men
despised by other black men
amabhaca
bucket people
who clean toilets in the middle of the night
gwazamazulu!
watch out for the zulus who stab

gumboot dance
black male bodies in cowboy shirts
shirts with tassels cover the backs of white cowboys in movies from
hollywood
white cowboys from hollywood control black workers in
johannesburg

gumboot dance
black men tap with heavy boots
black men tap like white men from hollywood
white men from hollywood tap like black men from harlem
fancy footwork of black men from harlem looks like fancy footwork
of black men from africa
fancy footwork of black men from harlem looks like fancy footwork
of white irish cloggers (or germans or russians)

gumboot dance
in the 1870s
black men saw white men from england and america
make their faces look black like theirs
white men called christy minstrels
on stage performing in south africa in the 1890s
with faces painted black with white around the eyes and lips
ragged shirts and full of laughter
the "kaffir christy minstrels"
took the stage
in durban

Collage of Thoughts on Gumboot Dance (continued)

gumboot dance
1959
king kong the african musical opera with gumboot dancers
miriam makeba and dorothy masuka
black women with black boots on stage
perform for black and white audiences
though never together

gumboot dance
1960s
wait a minim
white African music specialist andrew tracey
Spreading the message of african music
dancing in black boots for white liberal audiences
in johannesburg, durban, london, and new york
an eerie sense of 20th century minstrelsy?

gumboot dance
1987
white woman in white wedding dress
hitched up with black belt
white hosed legs inside black boots
gumboot dancer?

gumboot dancer
march 1985
white woman invited to learn to gumboot dance
by a black man named blanket
abhaca man living between creighton and durban, kwazulu natal
south africa
a migrant now for almost thirty years
blanket

black male gumboot dancer
works for defy
defy

(continues)

Collage of Thoughts on Gumboot Dance *(continued)*

in addition to political rhetoric
is blanket's place of work
defy corporation
assembles electrical appliances, washing machines, stoves,
dishwashers
blanket offered the white woman learning to gumboot dance
a good deal on a stove
blanket's home has no electricity
white woman with a stove, ok
but white woman to gumboot dance?
white english speaking woman at university living in a house with a
defy stove
to perform
black male migrant worker dance from the gold mines of
johannesburg?

gumboot dance
abelungu! white people! (watch out!)
black leader with his team
team with musicians
musicians play white man's guitar and concertina
with black man's chuning
black man's chuning from black woman's musical bow and white
man's mandolin

gumboot dance
learned by all in zulu migrant worker hostels in black townships
white women don't go to black townships
nice black women and nice white women don't go to male migrant
worker hostels
basopha! watch out!
1985 declaration of state of emergency
townships manned by white south african defense force
white women breaking the law going into the townships
stopped by white soldiers
amaphoyisa! amablekjek!

Collage of Thoughts on Gumboot Dance (*continued*)

---

gumboot dance
durban, south africa, 1996
gumboot dance for reconstruction and development
london england 1996
the state president nelson mandela's award gumboot dancers
perform in the music village
winston salem usa 1997
white woman gumboot dancer sees african-american steppin'
surmises some global connection
tappin' steppin' cloggin'

gumboot dancing

---

concertina and/or piano accordion, and occasionally violin, though each of these instruments is re-tuned to suit a more traditional Zulu ear. The style of playing for gumboot accompaniment is *ukuvamba* (percussive chord strumming) rather than the finger picking *ukupika*.

According to Jonney Hadebe, there are two styles of tuning—the *isiflench* (French in F) and the *isimondolini* (in C). The French tuning is used if there is only a single guitar accompanying the dance, and mandolin if there are other instruments. The *isimondolini* is a style of Zulu guitar developed around 1940; it is the transitional style between traditional bow playing and urban sounds of *mbaqanga*. *Isimondolini* is similar to another style called double *ifesi* (double first string). It tends to stress the upper range of pitches; to accommodate the higher range Blanket would use a capodastro (or bridge) to raise the pitch. The tuning is as follows: from the top (that is, from the thumb position of the right hand or the lowest pitch) E A G D D G, or C F E♭ B♭ B♭ E♭. Hadebe explained that *isimondolini* is a C and D together, that is, in these two examples, a mixture of G and A or E♭ and F together. The strings are divided into two sets, with the thinnest strings in the middle to protect them from breaking under the pressure of the aggressive strumming. Jonney describes the arrangement of strings: "There are the small strings, the one in the middle, and the two basses; so to make it half and half." His description shows how traditional bow music has been adapted on the guitar, the two fundamentals a whole tone apart and the interval of a fifth above each fundamental form the basis for Zulu guitar chuning.

IsiMondolini Chuning

5 E♭
4 B♭
1 B♭
3 E♭
2 F
2 C

The *maskanda* re-tunes the concertina by opening up the inside and making the necessary adjustments. The concertina plays a harmonic ostinato on a four-chord riff in 32-pulse cycle, typical of the early *marabi* style (as is the three-chord *ukuvamba* cycle). The concertina player may improvise melodically at will and frequently does so, shifting register and chord inversions. The violinist improvises melodically, filling in the pitches of the vamping chords (CD TRACKS 8–10).

The Aesthetics of Gumboot Performance

The history of gumboot dance outlined above suggests multiple influences on the formation of this dance style. Each of these—pre-colonial performance, minstrel shows, mission culture, industrial labor, and migrant experience—has contributed to the development of a gumboot dance aesthetic, that is, a sense of what makes for good and powerful performance. According to this aesthetic, the best gumboot dance

- engages with everyday realities, and it does so in a humorous and frequently satirical manner;
- includes performers that are highly skilled, both as individuals (soloists) and as a team;

- is deeply competitive, which is evident in the performances of both individuals and the group as a whole;
- is performed by a team that is together and "tight," and there is "power" in the resonant sound of their boots.

Jonney Hadebe describes the competitive dimension of gumboot dance, a dimension also common to other migrant genres, *maskanda* and *isicathamiya,* in particular.

> [Competitions] have changed. Now we go for money. Before, they were winning cups, and the compound manager was giving them food and beer. Now we want money. . . . A team is supposed to be 12 [men] including the leader. Not the musicians, that means 14. . . . The best team [has] the leader [who] must shout nicely, and the players must know what they are doing. Then the uniform must be very nice, very smart. The steps must [be done] as one. They must all be the same. . . . When you play it wrong, we call it *ihashi* (horse). When a team plays wrong, the people just hit their boots and tell [the others] to come out [stop performing]. The whole team must come out because they are doing it wrong. Then the other team goes in and if they do it wrong, we do *ihashi,* and they must come out. When all the teams have gone, we can start again. If you do one *ihashi,* you [lose] one point, if you do two, you lose two points. . . . If you've done one *ihashi* then you are better than a team which has done two. (Muller and Topp 1985)

When Janet and I learned to dance in 1985, Blanket Mkhize encouraged us not to watch the fast footwork so much as to hear its rhythms. He urged us to "fight" the boots, that is, to hit them hard, and the sounds of the boots were reinforced with the timbral qualities of the rattles or "speakers." Once a dance team achieves precision sounding together, the leader will pay attention to the details of performance, like whether you should be using the left or right arm. In contrast with the tightness of the sound, the body is expected to be flexible, creating a sense of fluid, relaxed motion.

Perhaps the definitive feature of this collective experience, however, is the manner in which this dance performance is shaped by a series of commands. Each member of the team looks and sounds the same in collective performance. It is only in the solos, which occur in the middle of the performance, that individuality is catered to. It is at this point that an individual man emerges from the anonymity of the team or the gang and is valued for his skill in improvisation—his capacity to take the patterns he knows and to transform them into a strategy for self-expression.

Contemporary Gumboot Performance

Unlike contemporary *isicathamiya*, which is strongly supported by the South African Traditional Music Association, gumboot dance had no centralized models or organizational structure until the creation of the theater production *Gumboots*. The rampant violence that began in the late 1980s continued to plague communities in KwaZulu Natal through the mid-1990s, effectively silencing cultural production such as gumboot dance performance. Community venues were often burned down or came under attack; schools stopped holding end-of-year celebrations where gumboot dance normally would have been performed; and the national sponsor, Spoornet, halted its involvement with gumboot dance in the late 1980s because of political violence between team members who represented opposing political groups.

The old spaces of performance disappeared, but gradually new pockets of gumboot dance performance began to emerge in the late 1990s in schools and dance companies. Gumboot dance is currently performed by a diversity of school and university students, and by labor unions and other worker groups. Since 1990, it has been featured in television commercials, by local performing arts groups, and at cultural events. In each of these new contexts, it is being imaginatively recreated to coalesce with the particular vision and daily experiences of each group of performers.

Blanket Mkhize and Steven Shelembe, Jonney Hadebe's brother-in-law and a leader of the Creighton gumboot team, have three goals for gumboot dance: to pass on the dance skills to the next generation (Blanket's sons are all superb performers); to boost their sons' chances of catching the eye of industry managers, who would then be more likely to hire them over some of the thousands of unemployed men desperate for work; and finally, to keep party politics out of gumboot dance performance. Currently anyone may join their team as long as they have no political affiliation. In their experience, party politics divides rather than unites its adherents. Gumboot dance is now viewed within the broader aims of programs for social uplift: it must keep young people busy so they do not become involved with drugs, alcohol, or criminal activity.

The Local Goes Global

What does it mean for a South African genre of performance to be part of a global ecumene, a global community? How could these partially literate, frequently non-English-speaking migrant workers really articulate a relationship to the wider world through gumboot dance performance?

In the late 1950s, gumboot dancing was featured in a range of African stage productions. *King Kong: An African Musical Opera* traveled to England in 1961. In 1962 Leon Gluckman, an English theater director; Andrew Tracey, now director of the International Library of African Music; and a group of other white English-speaking South Africans produced a show titled *Wait a Minim!*, which featured gumboot dancing. *Wait a Minim!* traveled to London in 1964, where it played for two years, went on to the Golden Theater in New York for a year, and then proceeded into other parts of the United States, Australia, and New Zealand. *King Kong* was revived in 1979 with gumboot dancing in its opening scenes, but the show was not well received in South Africa. Finally, *Graceland,* Paul Simon's collaborative musical project with South Africans features one track titled "Gumboots." The basic riff in the drums, bass, and guitar parts could be used to accompany contemporary gumboot dance.

Without doubt, in the twenty-first century, the production that has engendered the most interest in gumboot dance is the staged production represented in the video *Gumboots.* If you are able to view this video, I urge you to consider the way in which gumboot dance as a genre of music and dance from South Africa is reconstituted both by South Africans and those from abroad to meet a global audience and to make the show commercially viable—that is, to translate culturally for those who can neither speak Zulu nor perform the complex steps that make up the dance. Our musical and entertainment worlds are filled with world music and dance collaborative performance. Few projects, however, provide the kind of step-by-step discussion that the *Gumboots* project does on how the cultural form of unemployed young men was transformed into a worldwide music and dance phenomenon through their creativity and their openness to working together across national, cultural, language, and geographical distances. Note, too, the differences in the reception of gumboot dancing in 2002 versus 1986, and between the *Gumboots* collaboration and commodities produced and that of the controversial *Graceland* project. Lastly, ask yourselves just which dimensions in the music and dance in *Gumboots,* or indeed in the *Graceland* project, might be considered local and which are global. Is gumboots a universal music and dance language? Can audiences around the world really understand gumboots? What, if any, are the limits of thinking about music and dance as a universal language?

REFERENCES

Ballantine, Christopher. "Looking to the USA: The Politics of Male Close-Harmony Song and Style in South Africa During the 1940s and 1950s." *Popular Music,* 18/1 (1999): 1–17.

Cockrell, Dale. "Of Gospel Hymns, Minstrel Shows, and Jubilee Singers: Toward Some Black South African Musics." *American Music,* 5/4 (1987): 417–432.

Coplan, David. *In Township Tonight! South Africa's Black City Music and Theatre.* New York: Longmans, 1985.

Davies, Nollene. "The Guitar in Zulu Maskanda Tradition." *World of Music,* 36/2 (1994): 118–137.

De Certeau, Michel. *The Practice of Everyday Life.* Translated by Steven Randall. Los Angeles: University of California Press, 1988 [1984].

Doke, C. M., et al. *Zulu-English, English-Zulu Dictionary.* Johannesburg: University of the Witwatersrand Press, 1990.

Erlmann, Veit. *African Stars: Studies in Black South African Performance.* Chicago: Chicago University Press, 1991.

Hadebe, Jonney. Program notes for South African Railways Gumboot Dance performance. ND.

Hannerz, Ulf. "Sophiatown: The View from Afar." In *Readings in African Popular Culture,* edited by Karen Barber, 164–170. Bloomington: Indiana University Press, 1997.

Indestructible Beat of Soweto. Newton, NJ: Shanachie Records, 1987.

Kubik, Gerhard. *African Guitar: Solo Finger-Style Guitar Music, Composers and Performers.* Cambridge, MA: Rounder Records (U.S. distributors), 1995.

Marre, Jeremy. *Rhythm of Resistance: The Black Music of South Africa.* Newton, NJ: Shanachie Records, 1988.

Moodie, Dunbar. "Mine Culture and Miner's Identity on the South African Gold Mines." In *Town and Countryside in the Transvaal: Capitalist Penetration and Popular Response,* edited by Belinda Bozzoli, 176–197. Johannesburg: Ravan Press, 1983.

Muller, Carol, and Janet Topp Fargion. "Gumboots, Migrants, and Fred Astaire: South African Worker Dance and Musical Style." *African Music,* vol. 714 (1999): 88–109.

Philips, Ray. *The Bantu in the City: A Study of Cultural Adjustment on the Witwatersrand.* London: Faber and Faber, 1938.

Powell, Aubrey. *Gumboots! An Explosion of Spirit and Song.* Chatsworth, CA: Image Entertainment, 2000.

Rycroft, David. "Stylistic Evidence in Zulu Song." In *Essays on Music and History in Africa,* edited by K. P. Wachsmann, 213–241. Evanston, IN: Northwestern University Press, 1971.

Thomas, Jeff. *Ingoma Dancers and Their Response to Town: A Study of Ingoma Dance Troupes among Zulu Migrant Workers in Durban.* Unpublished MA Thesis, University of Natal, Durban, 1988.

Tracey, Hugh. *African Dances of the Witwatersrand Gold Mines.* Johannesburg: African Music Society, 1952.

Vail, Leroy, and Landeg White. "Plantation Protest: The History of a Mozambican Song." In *Readings in African Popular Culture,* edited by Karen Barber, 54–62. Bloomington: Indiana University Press, 1997.

Chapter Five

The Hymns
of the Nazaretha

The residents of Durban represent all of the world's major religions and a plethora of local spiritual communities. I remember so clearly one Sunday morning in Durban in July 1995, when I had taken a group of overseas visitors to the all-night *isicathamiya* choir competition held in the Beatrice Street YMCA hall. At sunrise, while the competition was in full swing, we left the building and ventured down to the ocean. Though July is mid-winter in South Africa, even at this time of day we found a surprising array of people at the waterfront: Indian fishermen, usually Hindus or Christians; white surfers who may connect to a 1970s charismatic Christian group called the Invisible Church; men and women out jogging who participate in the more conventional Christian, Muslim, or Jewish practices, or perhaps belong to such independent churches as the more evangelical Christian Olive Tree or the modern, global, Hindu-derived Sai Baba communities. A busload of visitors from Johannesburg who traveled for the weekend to participate in a regional *makwaya* (choral) competition by singing the religious works of Handel or Bach had come to the beach to fill bottles with seawater to take home with them and use for ritual purification.

A handful of men and women stood on the soft sand at the edge of the water, clothed in long robes of blue, yellow, green, or pure white. All of these Zulu-speakers were engaged in the practice of baptism by immersion in the powerful waters of the Indian Ocean. Those in robes of deep blues, yellows, and greens were Zionists; those in white gowns or *imiNazaretha* came from *ibandla lama-*

Zionist followers baptized in the Indian Ocean,
early Sunday morning, July 1995, Durban, South Africa.

Nazaretha, the Church of the Nazarites/Nazaretha—followers of the charismatic prophet Isaiah Shembe and his descendants.

On that Sunday in July 1995, we ate breakfast at one of the outdoor restaurants on the beach, then rode by car to Ebuhleni, the headquarters of *ibandla lamaNazaretha,* to spend the day witnessing the final ritual events of the July Festival. These included celebrating the dead at the Shembe cemetery, a daily morning service, baptisms in the nearby river, group proposals of marriage and marriage ceremonies, and the sacred dance festival called *umgido.*

The focus of this chapter is the sacred song and dance repertory of *ibandla lamaNazaretha.* Founded by Isaiah Shembe in about 1911, *ibandla lamaNazaretha* began as a small community, predominantly of women and girls who had been miraculously healed, physically and emotionally, by the spiritual powers of this charismatic prophet. In the early twenty-first century, Shembe's community includes congregations dispersed throughout South Africa and the countries on its borders—Swaziland, Zimbabwe, and Botswana. It claims a rapidly growing membership numbering about one million. Though there are many remarkable dimensions to *ibandla lamaNazaretha,* we focus here on the repertory of spiritual songs composed by Isaiah Shembe and his son Johannes Galilee between 1913 and 1940. These songs were written down and later published in an official hymnal called *IziHlabelelo ZamaNazaretha* (1940). The songs themselves are performed in at least four contexts: in congregational worship (*inkhonzo*), to accompany sacred dance in church festivals (*umgido*), in less formal gatherings of church members and families, and in more gospel-music-style settings such as televised performances, on cassettes, and in world music festivals.

Music and dance occupy a central place in Nazarite belief. A new style of sacred singing and dancing were given to Isaiah Shembe as part of his calling by the ancestors to preach to and heal Zulu traditionalists, and Shembe's authority as a spiritual leader was reinforced by his musical gift. This repertory of religious song is unusual for its time in South African history because it is not merely translations of Christian mission hymns, but rather newly composed poetic forms and texts. The words have spoken directly to the experiences of millions of black South Africans through the course of the twentieth century. Isaiah Shembe also insisted on dance as an integral dimension of collective ritual practice from as early as the 1920s. This was a radical move because in the early twentieth century, Christian missionaries had forbidden all forms of dance in religious ritual. *Ibandla lamaNazaretha* was one of the first religious communities to reinstate dance.

In this chapter, I examine the hymn repertory, its composition, performance, commodification, translation, and transformation. This discussion focuses on the musical examples on the accompanying compact disc, drawn from my own field recordings, and related materials on commercially available recordings.

Finding *Ibandla lamaNazaretha*

When I went to Ebuhleni, the Shembe headquarters, in 1991 to do field work for my dissertation, my field assistant, church member Samukelisiwe Nthini, advised me to purchase and wear *imiNazaretha*, the white prayer gown. This naturally led to the assumption that I, too, was a believer, and members often asked me how I knew about *ibandla lamaNazaretha*. Did Shembe appear to me in a dream? Although I was to have a few dreams of Shembe after I began working in the community, it was not a dream but an academic connection that opened up the world of Shembe to me.

Although I grew up in KwaZulu Natal, I had not heard of *ibandla lamaNazaretha* until I joined a class on Contextual Theology at

Mvangeli Magubane (in green evangelist gown) stands in front of the administrative office where members purchase the hymnal and maps of the holy mountain of Nhlangakaze (both seen behind), as well as marriage and baptismal certificates. Ebuhleni, September 1996.

Union Seminary in New York City in the fall of 1989. There I learned about the work of religious studies professor Pippin Oosthuizen, who had long been studying *ibandla lamaNazaretha* and other indigenous or independent church communities. In fact, Oosthuizen had written a controversial book that examined the Shembe hymn texts as the source of Nazarite theology (1967). I was looking for a religious community in which women were a central part, and one that had its own song repertory.

I traveled to South Africa in December 1989 and made contact with Professor Oosthuizen, who invited me to go to the Nazarites' holy mountain, Nhlangakaze ("the big or great reed"), with him and a team of white filmmakers. We were to prepare for the trip by bringing along a thermos of coffee and sandwiches, because no cooking was allowed on the Sabbath. For our feet we brought a couple of pairs of thick socks. Nobody was permitted to wear shoes on the sacred site, even for the walk up the mountain, though white people were allowed to wear socks because their feet were considered soft from wearing shoes.

Nazarite members typically spend time during January on the holy mountain. Some come for the entire month, others for a weekend, or even a single day. While we and some members arrived in

"The Arc of the Covenant" heads the procession of members on the annual pilgrimage to the Holy Mountain of Nhlangakaze (January 1992).

motor vehicles, a large group of followers had walked to the mountain from the Shembe headquarters at Ebuhleni over a period of three days at the beginning of January.

A single path runs up the side of the mountain. Lining the path are tents in which people sell goods required for the time on Nhlangakaze. These include perishable and nonperishable food items, dance attire, Zulu language Bibles, the Shembe hymnbook, photographs of important moments in the life of the church and of the Shembe leadership, prayer gowns, and materials for constructing shelter. All members are required to ascend the mountain when they arrive. Typically, they do so in groups, all wearing the white *imi-Nazaretha* and singing softly as they go. The singing is slow, performed in a call-and-response format. The year I walked the pilgrimage we sang Hymn 173, *"Livuliwe lelisango"* (open the gates) all the way. Nobody hurries, pushes, or shouts. One or two of the male leaders guide the members as they climb the rocky crags. Periodically, the group stops to kneel and pray, or to place flowers at particular spots along the way. About halfway up, an *imbongi* (praise singer) calls out the praises of Shembe.

Extract of "The Praises of Isaiah Shembe"

Composed by Imbongi Azariah Mthiyane (excerpts)
Recorded in Zulu and translated by Liz Gunner and Mafika Gwala (1991, 66–79)

He is awesome, He is awesome, Our Beautiful Kneeler-and-they-be-
     satisfied of Ekuphakameni
One who overflows with compassion, helper of those in danger.
Broad-shouldered one, never tired of bearing our sins.
Opener of the roads heading for home,
Plume disappearing over there on the mountain, Spring that refreshes
     the righteous
Hands that radiate like the sun,
Bateleur Eagle, hovering above our own place at Ekuphakameni,
Scatterer of the fog and there is light,
Restrainer of the multitudes—you would not leave them on their
     journey to Hell.
Peacemaker with the bulls instead of leaving them to kill each other.

It takes at least a half-hour to reach the top of the mountain, a decidedly otherworldly place. This is where Isaiah Shembe received his calling in a dream to preach to and heal Zulu traditionalists. At the top of the mountain is a large plateau. When we arrived we were amazed to hear what sounded like the musical strains of an organ. A heavy, damp mist covered the area so our vision was limited, but as we moved closer, we could see my colleague Bongani Mthethwa seated at the organ, sounding out the melody and chords of one of the Shembe hymns. The instrument was powered with two large car batteries, its sound amplified by several mounted speakers. Some members were milling around, others were seated in front of the organ according to age, gender, and marital status. Church elders called *abavangeli* ("evangelists") sat on prayer mats on the ground with small baskets in front of them for collecting offerings made to Shembe. A young woman sat on the rock paging through the hymnal. I moved to an outcrop of rock nearby to absorb this dreamlike spectacle around me.

The next day, a Sunday, we returned to the mountaintop for *umgido*, the festival of sacred song and dance celebrated by *ibandla lamaNazaretha*. Below we could hear the young girls preparing to open the festival; they were blowing on the indigenous trumpets peculiar to *ibandla lamaNazaretha* and beating the large bass drums. An occasional bugle melody sounded out amid the powerful, though slow and deliberate, strands of singing that drifted up from the place where the young girls stood in long lines, ready to make the final ascent, this time to the rhythms of *isihlabelelo samaNazaretha,* a Nazaretha hymn. They would be followed by the men in animal skins and the young boys in either tartan skirts, rugby socks, black boots, and a white cotton headband or in black skirts, rugby socks, black boots, white shirts and pith helmets. Then came the married women in dense layers of traditional and newly imagined dance regalia.

Each group of dancers sings its own hymn from the Shembe hymnal—though everything is sung from memory while the dance is taking place—accompanied with handclapping, dance rhythms, woodblocks, trumpets, bugles, and drums. Because several groups of dancers are spread along the mountaintop, the overall sense is of a wave of musical sounds, one part blurring into another. It is hard for the outsider to pick out specific words or melodies sung by individual groups. I recall being overwhelmed by a deep sense of calm.

These two experiences—the congregational service on the Sabbath and the sacred dance on the Sunday—made a deep impression on me that weekend in January 1990. I left knowing that field research with *ibandla lamaNazaretha* would be quite different from anything I had ever done before. It would not be easy—at the time I spoke little Zulu and there was not much English among Shembe followers—but it would open up new understandings of what it meant to be South African in the late twentieth century. I would gain deeper insights into the impact of mission Christianity on the peoples of KwaZulu Natal from the mid-nineteenth century, and the response of these people, not only as victims of the colonial encounter but also as people who wished to reshape their own music and beliefs on their own terms. About a year later, I returned to South Africa to begin my research with the followers of a third leader, Amos Shembe (younger son of Isaiah and brother of second leader, Johannes Galilee) at Ebuhleni, the current headquarters of the Nazarite religious community previously housed at Ekuphakameni.

Mission Culture

The history of Protestant mission work in South Africa dates to 1737, when Georg Schmidt, a Moravian, opened a mission in the Cape, then returned to the Netherlands in 1742. There followed a fifty-year hiatus in mission work. In 1792, three Moravian missionaries started a new mission in the Cape, building on a nucleus formed around Schmidt's cook, Magdalena, who had continued to teach reading and writing to small groups of converts after Schmidt's departure.

In the following years, missionaries arrived from England, the Netherlands, Scotland, France, and the United States; by the late 1820s, there was a veritable army of Protestant missionaries in the Cape and the interior. Early missions failed, in part, because the Bible and hymns were not available in local languages. The new missionaries turned their attention to producing such translations, creating written forms of vernacular languages, compiling dictionaries, and translating the Bible and the hymnbook.

Throughout Africa, these missionaries established missionary villages—missionary-controlled communities of African people, which had in common the goals of evangelizing, educating, and civilizing Africans. "Civilizing" amounted to little more than Europeanizing Africans. Replacing traditional music and dance with the European hymn in four-part harmony was a central dimension of the civilizing mission in this period.

Though the number who converted to mission Christianity in the eighteenth and nineteenth centuries was relatively small, the impact of the mission village and its enterprises should not be underestimated. When African converts and their families left the mission villages, they often took a portion of the culture with them, in the form of a vernacular translation of one of the books of the Bible or a hymnal, and quite quickly a new Christian village headed by a local leader would emerge close by.

In southern African mission work, singing was the most effective method of attracting the attention of those targeted for conversion. Reports from the mission field suggest it was the hymn, more than the sermon, that attracted potential converts. So an important strategy for African mission evangelists was to enter a kraal or homestead in song. With the strands of melody they easily attracted a crowd to whom they would proceed to teach the words and tune. Soon people all over a village would begin to hum and whistle phrases of the hymns.

This did not necessarily mean that everyone understood the meaning of the words, even if they were translated into the vernacular, because quite often the translations were poor. Missionaries failed to recognize that a single word in a tonal language like Zulu or Xhosa might have several contradictory meanings depending on how it was articulated, and the images and metaphors embedded in hymn poetry were quite alien to local experience and poetics. For example, the style of rhyming line endings common to the Protestant hymn was completely foreign to local poetic practices, though it was a common strategy used in translation, transforming workable hymn texts in a European language into hideous strains in the vernacular.

Nevertheless, the singing voice poured forth its sweetness to the African ear. Few foreign missionaries grasped the importance, however, of translating more than just the words of their hymns into the vernacular. Christianity has flourished in South Africa in places like *ibandla lamaNazaretha,* the Zionist churches, and the women's *manyanos* ("prayer unions"), where it has rooted itself in local forms. Song, dance, drumming, and a sense of rhythm have been key elements in such transplantation. For the most part, the conduits of this process have been African leaders rather than their European mission counterparts. Put simply, translations of the mission hymn demonstrated a lack of sensitivity to the linguistic and cultural dimensions of African song performance—a failure to understand the value of song and the place of the human voice and oral transmission in indigenous belief systems. Oral transmission is not merely a conduit of words, but the vehicle of a set of cultural practices quite alien to the world of literacy.

The emphasis on orally transmitted messages, on the power of human utterance over readable texts, was key to the success of revivalist styles of prayer, preaching, and hymn singing among largely uneducated African women. (Gaitskell 1990). From the 1880s European and American missionary wives in South Africa began organizing weekly afternoon and monthly all-night gatherings for African women. Historian Deborah Gaitskell describes these as "un-structured times of shared testimony, the exposition of biblical verses, and extemporary prayer." The thousands of black South African women who were members of these organizations were regularly involved in preaching, praying, and caring for the sick and needy. The appeal of praying and preaching in the all-night meeting was clearly connected to the lively oral traditions in which African women had been nurtured from birth. In the *manyano*, women extemporized on their own beliefs and experiences. They knew the Bible and hymns—not through reading but through hearing and memorizing what they had been taught by others. Speaking from the heart was highly valued in these religious organizations.

In a manner similar to the nineteenth-century women's *manyano*, contemporary African Zionist worship draws on indigenous modes of singing, dancing, and drumming in re-Africanizing Christianity for largely nonliterate or partially literate members. Two anthropologists have written about Zionist singing in South Africa. Research by James Kiernan examines ways in which Zionist songs structure ritual enactment among Zulu-speaking Zionists. John Blacking worked with Venda Zionists in Soweto and the more rural areas of the Northern Province in the 1950s and 1960s.

A handful of African mission converts, of varying relationships to the nineteenth-century mission villages in the Cape, are significant for the hymns they composed in the vernacular. By far the most important is Xhosa-speaking prophet, poet, composer, orator, and dancer Ntsikana Gaba, who died in 1821. Trained as a traditional warrior and royal councilor, Ntsikana had a visionary experience in which what he called a "thing" inside, the voice of *Nyengana* (that is, the teachings of the early Dutch missionary Van Der Kemp), was calling him to selectively reject aspects of Xhosa tradition, such as polygamy and smearing the body with ochre, and to selectively incorporate aspects of mission Christianity into his own brand of African spirituality. The Xhosa-speaking prophet rejected the culturally specific elements of European Christianity but accepted the tenets of biblical Christianity. He refused to accept baptism, though he remained with Eastern Cape mission villages and encouraged his rather small group of followers to stay close to these institutions and not return to traditional ways after his death.

This first Xhosa prophet has a clear place in South African religious and musical history because four of the hymns he composed have survived in oral tradition among Xhosa-speaking converts. One of these, "*Ulo Tixo Mkulu*" ("Thou Great God") was published in a Xhosa hymnal in 1876. The most famous of the four, however, is Ntsikana's "Bell," the chant that Ntsikana recited at dawn each day, to call his followers to prayer. The melodies of these hymns, while arranged in the mission structure of four parts (soprano, alto, tenor, bass, or SATB), use the parallel movement of voices derived from Xhosa practices. Ntsikana's hymns also have distinctively Xhosa-sounding melodies. All this suggests that they incorporated elements of both mission and Xhosa musical cultures. Because of this blending, and indeed, of the importance of Ntsikana in Xhosa history as a religious leader who Africanized mission Christianity for his followers, these hymns occupy a central place in Xhosa religious practice, and indeed, in South African music history. A century later, Isaiah Shembe would follow the lead of Ntsikana by re-Africanizing mission Christianity and its ritual practices for Zulu-speaking peoples.

In addition to Ntsikana, a handful of other African Christians wrote spiritual songs that were published by the mission presses. All these new compositions in the published versions were written in the traditional SATB format of the European mission hymn. The first ordained Presbyterian African minister, Tiyo Soga (1829–1871) and his successor, Gqoba, composed hymns for the more European-style congregation. Many of these songs have become an integral part of the *Xhosa Methodist Hymnal*. Soga's son John Henderson Soga was a composer who also wrote two books on black South African history. Xhosa convert John Knox Bokwe composed his own hymns, several of which were published by the Lovedale mission press, perhaps the most important mission institution and press in southern Africa. Nehemiah Tile, founder of the Tembu Church in 1884, also composed hymns for his followers. And John Dube, African National Congress founder and contemporary of Isaiah Shembe, was also a composer, though he was better known for his secular works. With the exception of Tile, however, each of these men remained in close contact with the colonial mission.

African Religious Independentism

Many of the missions' early converts had connections to the tribal elite. As a result, traditional culture was intertwined with Christian tenets; the countryside was presented as good and wholesome and the city as destabilizing. The conversion experience was, however, not without its discomforts. Christian convert James Matiwane testified in 1881: "We have given up Native dancing, and attend tea meetings, and the like. We have no social gatherings except weddings and such like. The boys and girls have no games; the boys do play at marbles sometimes" (Hughes 1990, 205). Isaiah Shembe would address these concerns.

In the latter part of the nineteenth century the discovery of gold and diamonds in the area around what is now Johannesburg resulted in the imposition by the colonial government of rigid poll and hut taxation, as well as a harsh system of labor migration. These developments—combined with the racism and colonial attitudes in mission churches and the society at large, the persistence of African spiritual beliefs and of the place of the ancestors in the Christianity practiced by converts, the contested place of polygamy in mission

Young Shembe boys playing the Shembe bugles at a wedding celebration in Kwa Mashu, Durban, ca. October 1991.

theology, and the central place of health and healing in African spirituality—ignited a significant movement towards religious independence among African Christians. With the translation of the Bible into the principal South African languages of North and South Sotho, Zulu, and Xhosa, African prophets could move away from the control of the mission. Historians of religion have identified two main streams of African religious independentism in this period: Ethiopianism and Zionism.

Ethiopianism

The exact historical roots of the term "Ethiopianism" as applied to African independent churches in the late nineteenth century are not certain. "Ethiopia" was long used by Europeans to refer to any part of black Africa; it is mentioned on several occasions in the Bible. For Ethiopian Christians, Ethiopia was itself the relocation of Zion. Ethiopianism constituted an early form of African/Black consciousness in South Africa.

In 1892 Mangena Mokone, a black South African minister in the Wesleyan Church, resigned from that institution over the issue of racial segregation. He formed a new church he called the Ethiopian Church, marking a decisive moment in South African mission history. While others had seceded prior to Mokone, his move was a truly enduring one, and it sparked similar moves among African Christians elsewhere, always in protest against mission control and racial discrimination. A short time after forming his church, Mokone fostered an alliance between his community and the African Methodist Episcopal (AME) Church in the United States, the first independent African church in America, though he did not achieve the independence from the U.S. church that he desired for his community.

Ethiopianism signaled for black South Africans that mission Christianity did not require complete Europeanization; one might convert to Biblical Christianity without losing one's cultural identity. The early nineteenth-century figure of Ntsikana was a key symbol of the Ethiopianist movement in South Africa. Many Ethiopianists joined together in 1909 to form the Ntsikana Memorial Association, a cultural, rather than religious, organization that con-

Text of "Nkosi Sikelel'iAfrika"

(prior to becoming part of South Africa's national anthem in the 1990s)
Taken from http://www.worship.co.za/sa/nkosi.asp

Zulu

Nkosi sikelel 'iAfrika,	Lord bless Africa
Maluphakanyisw'udumo lwayo;	May her horn be raised;
Yizwa imithandazo yethu,	Hear our prayer, Lord
Nkosi sikelela	Lord bless us
Thina lusapho lwayo.	Us your children.

CHORUS:

Woza moya,	Come, spirit
(Sikelela, Nkosi sikelela)	(Bless us, Lord, bless us)
Woza Moya oyiNgcwele;	Come Holy Spirit;
Usisikelele, thina lusapho lakhe.	Lord bless us, we your children.

Sotho

Morena boloka Sechaba se heso,	Lord we ask you to protect our nation
U felise lintwa le matsoenyeho	Intervene and end all conflict
U se boloke (2x)	Protect us
Sechaba sa heso (2x).	Protect our nation.

stituted a starting point for the formation of what later became the African National Congress. Out of this movement came the Enoch Sontonga composition, "Nkosi Sikelel'iAfrika" ("God Bless Africa"), adopted as the anthem of the African National Congress in 1925 and now a central part of the South African national anthem.

Zionism

Zionism provided an alternative model of secession, with its roots more clearly located in mission history. A small group of Protestants in South Africa began to connect through the name "Zion," and all identified with faith healing, baptism in a metaphorical Jordan River or the ocean, and with the Pentecostal gift of speaking in tongues. Zionism's beginnings might be traced to an Afrikaner, P. L. le Roux, who worked as a missionary among the Zulu. Le Roux named his chapel the "Zions Kerk" ("Church of Zion") because they sang Zions Liedere ("Hymns of Zion") inspired by the Moravians. Zionism resonated powerfully with African traditional beliefs, so much so that it was easy to forget its European links once it broke away from its center. Zionist hymn singing takes the mission hymn and re-Africanizes its performance practice.

Isaiah Shembe's religious belief and practice has been variously defined as Ethiopianist, because the texts and performance of his hymns reflect African experience and musical values; as Zionist, because of his healing and other charismatic practices; and as prophetic. He does not fit neatly into any of these categories. Tshabalala (1983), for example, argues for his strong ties to the Wesleyan mission; in my reading of Ranger's accounts of Protestant missions in Zimbabwe (1994), I see elements from all of the missions in Shembe's community. Without doubt, *ibandla lamaNazaretha* was, and remains, an eclectic form of religious community, one derived from Zulu traditional belief but also denying many of its tenets. *Ibandla lamaNazaretha* is a religious grouping that took the texts of mission Christianity but rejected the messengers and the cultural baggage they brought from faraway places.

Zulu Zionists

Accompanied with drumming, reinforcing the rhythmic over melodic quality, Zulu Zionist singing regularly flows from song to handclapping to body swaying and even to dance, writes anthropologist James Kiernan (1990). Each Zionist community has its own repertory of hymns, though many are drawn from the American Board Mission hymnal and are supplemented with Wesleyan and Episcopal items. The value of hymn singing in Zionist communities is to be found in the ways in which these songs are used in church services. Hymn singing is never planned into the structure of a Zionist service beforehand. Instead, hymns are spontaneously inserted. Kiernan identifies four such moments or uses. First, they provide a structure for the meeting—hymns begin and end a gathering and create continuity in a meeting as members move from one item to the next. Second, hymns operate as signature tunes—people begin their contributions to a service by intoning their favorite hymn. Third, hymns are interpolated into a service to forge an opening, if a speaker goes on too long or is tedious. Finally, hymns accompany faith healing.

Venda Zionists

John Blacking's perspective is a contrasting view on Zionist hymn singing based on his work amongst the Venda in the 1950s and 1960s. Blacking's central argument about Venda Zionism is that while Zionists have often been viewed by social scientists as apolitical and cut off from political engagement in South Africa, their worship signifies politically, not in the words as much as in the style of song performance (Blacking 1998). Venda Zionists use both the Psalms and European hymns translated into the vernacular, but their performance practices are quite distinct. Hymns adhere to a verse-refrain format modeled on the European hymn, while the Psalms operate in a more traditional call-and-response frame with drumming accompaniment. Zionists, Blacking observes, did not sing hymns in the European way; nor were the Psalms sung in a traditional manner. Hymns were sung slowly, allowing individuals to "catch" the Holy Spirit and explore the musical materials in a creative way, while the Psalms were sung at a livelier tempo.

Blacking summarizes the essential characteristics of Venda Zionist singing as follows: it is sung in call-and-response format, typically in a slow tempo but occasionally increasing speed and incorporating handclapping; the general pitch of a melody rises in a song; melodies are ornamented, slurred, and varied to increase emotional intensity; a thick harmonic texture is created with voices singing in parallel, and making distinctive tonal shifts; and finally while call and response is the overall form, pieces of a verse can be presented in overlapping, hocket-like phrases; there are no pauses or rests—the stream of sound is thick and constant. Although the start of a hymn might be hesitant as members tune in to its text and tune, once everyone is singing, individuals are free to "let go" with a variety of pitch treatments, including glissandi, ornamentation, slurs, and so forth. Increased emotional intensity is reflected in a faster tempo of performance as a hymn performance progresses (Blacking 1998).

There are significant overlaps in performance practice between what Blacking describes here and the singing of *izihlabelelo zama-Nazaretha*. The crucial difference, however, is that the songs of Shembe combine the poetry of the Psalms with the influence of Wesleyan hymnody in particular to create a single repertory of song. Blacking's argument that it is the style of performance and not the words of the songs that articulate an Africanist worldview, and thus a political sensibility, works for Venda Zionists. But for followers of Shembe the hymns articulate a political consciousness in both word and performance practice.

Isaiah Shembe's Early Life

Born in Bergville, KwaZulu Natal, in about 1870, Isaiah Shembe moved with his father to the Harrismith region of the Free State, South Africa. There, both worked on the farm of a European named Coenraad Grabe. While working on that farm, Shembe recalled hearing the "voice of God" for the first time. According to Shembe, Grabe never exposed him to the Bible as such, although the Grabe family prayed daily, usually in the morning and the evening, and Grabe himself talked in Afrikaans with Shembe about the "Word of God." It was in this period of his life that the young Shembe began to pray alone. Though he did not know how to pray, the words just came to him, he says, accompanied by the feeling that something was twisting in his chest (Papini 1999, 261–265). This is the first of several moments in which Isaiah Shembe's spiritual calling is marked on the physical body.

Isaiah Shembe had no formal schooling but learned to read and write later in life, a skill he claims he acquired by divine intervention. (However, his son, Galilee, testified that his father learned some reading and writing skills from a fellow migrant worker in Johannesburg.) Shembe had numerous dreams in which he was instructed to undertake a series of actions, some of which ran contrary to African traditional ways. For example, after marrying polygamously, he obeyed the voice that told him such union was unclean and should be abandoned.

Shembe was once struck by lightning, an event which might have killed him, but instead left a scar on his left hip. As with Ntsikana, who had a similar experience, this event created a parallel moment of spiritual empowerment to that of the New Testament figure Saul of Tarsus, who became the apostle Paul. Shembe worked for a period of time with the Wesleyans and was baptized by the African Baptists on July 22, 1906.

The young Isaiah Shembe lived through some of the most tumultuous times for Zulu-speaking people in the late nineteenth and early twentieth century. This included the Anglo-Zulu War of 1879, the annexation of Zululand by the British, the ruthless crushing of the Bambatha Rebellion by the British in 1906, the movement of South Africans away from British control in 1910, and the passage of the Land Act in 1913, which took land from black South Africans for white purposes. At the time, the region was also riddled with disease and drought, and it had been powerfully transformed by the discovery of gold and diamonds in South Africa from the late 1870s, an event that thrust South Africa into an industrial revolution and rapid modernization. This process forced many black South Africans into what became one of the harshest structures of migrant labor worldwide, a system that had severe ramifications for people in the South African countryside, many of whom became followers of Shembe. After the Bambatha Rebellion (also known as the Zulu Rebellion), Isaiah is reported to have sworn to "revive the bones" of those killed. One member recalls that after being burned by lightning, Shembe was instructed by Jehovah to go to the East, that is, to KwaZulu Natal: "There are my suffering people. Go and liberate them from their slavery. These people have naked/bare hips. When you will come to them, tell them that they should worship me, their God, the *Mvelingqangi* of their forefathers and the God of their fathers, and that they should take the vow of the Nazarites . . ." (Hexham and Oosthuizen 1996, 1–21).

Deeply disturbed by the fragmented position of his people in

KwaZulu Natal, Isaiah Shembe was called by the voice of God to go to a mountain called Nhlangakaze in KwaZulu Natal. There are several versions of this founding moment of *ibandla lamaNazaretha*. All accounts agree that while on the mountain, Isaiah Shembe had a vision in which he saw heaven itself. One version suggests that in this vision there were men wearing skins and singing songs without notation.

Shembe follower Ms. Cinikile Mazibuko told me the story, saying that the songs Shembe heard these old men singing were songs without notes; they were the songs of friends (in other words, not of mission origin), and they were sung by men dressed in what would become Nazarite men's dance attire: the skins of wild animals. The version recounted by the late church activist Petros M. Dhlomo corroborates Ms. Mazibuko's account. Take note of the appeal to the senses of smell, sight, hearing—the stress upon the human body as the mediating vessel of spiritual experience in this excerpt:

After all these events, he heard a joyful sound of beautiful singing; a mighty clamor arose from the East and came with an awe-inspiring light to him. Shembe rejoiced in his heart, the trees and the rocks shouted for joy, and the grass joined in their cries of happiness. Then Shembe was convinced in his heart: "There comes the real bridegroom, for whom I have been waiting here on the mountain Nhlangakaze."

Then Jehovah appeared; he was surrounded by the heavenly hosts and by the saints, who were clad in white robes and had bound golden belts over their chests. Shembe smelled a sweet scent, which made even his bones and the roots of his hair rejoice. It was like a large crowd of people. When they appeared, the grass stubbles shouted: "Holy!" Then the one who had called him from his home country came to him riding on white clouds, which came from the north; [streaks of] lightning flashed over him, crossing one another, and he heard a mighty thundering in the sky. (Hexham and Oosthuizen 1996, 80)

All the accounts concur that in this twelve-day sojourn on the mountain Shembe was instructed to preach and to baptize all people. On the last day Jehovah made a covenant for people of African descent in the region: Heaven became a space in which African peoples and their cultures were fully incorporated.

Isaiah Shembe's Mission and the Founding of Ekuphakameni

Isaiah Shembe began a mission of travel, moving along the coast-line of KwaZulu Natal and the Eastern Cape and eventually into what was Zululand, the area north of the Tugela River north of Durban. In his traveling mode, the prophet's method of drawing people to his community was similar to that of the Christian missionaries described by Ranger above. Scholar of African literature Liz Gunner explains:

> While traveling and evangelizing, Shembe and his little group of young men and women would, on approaching a homestead, begin by beating the large round drum used by many Zionists, and they would sing the hymns that Shembe himself had composed. Often the girls would lead the group in, dancing the steps which Isaiah had taught them or which they had devised themselves. Often Shembe would visit the homestead of a chief or headman and hope to extend his influence if he were able to convert a figure of authority. If he did obtain the nucleus of a following he would sometimes leave a woman in charge, a deaconess (*umkhokheli*), and visit again or send an evangelist. Shembe in some ways was able to adapt and use elements of Zulu dance and spectacle to give his own followers a distinctive way of "dancing to the Lord" which could be seen and felt as representing a new, centered expression of African Christianity. He created visual symbols and expressive forms of dance and song that were distinct from the old forms yet related to them, and retained their symbolic power as cultural expressions. (Gunner 1991, 100–101)

Initially, Shembe encouraged his converts and those he healed to return to mission churches, but the churches were not receptive to his sentiments. In either 1911 or 1915–1916, Shembe acquired thirty-eight acres of land in the Inanda Native and Mission Reserve in the hills of Ohlange. Members' memories of that period suggest that there was very little food, and the initial houses were so small

Unmarried female followers of Shembe gather for the service that precedes the ritual cleansing of the graves of Shembe members by virgin girls, July 1991, Ekuphakameni, KwaZulu Natal.

there was only space for Shembe's women followers and none of their possessions. By the time of his death in 1935, Shembe had purchased close to forty pieces of land, all with the financial resources of his followers, which they had given to Shembe for his power to heal and perform the miraculous. Although Shembe originally had no plan to create a settled community, he was encouraged to do so by the growing group of followers he had healed. Shembe named the settlement Ekuphakameni ("the elevated place, the place of spiritual upliftment, heaven").

Ekuphakameni became a kind of mission village, though it borrowed ideas from the layout of the Zulu royal residence, with separate living quarters for men, women, young girls, and young boys. A school, store, and several sacred buildings were constructed on the site. Space was allocated for both the cultivation of gardens and women's traditional production, including basket and mat weaving. Shembe charged a small rental for anyone wishing to live within the boundaries of his village; all had to abide by a strict code of conduct while there (Roberts 1936).

As was the case with most mission villages, the large majority of his early followers were women. Several years after establishing this village, a colonial official estimated that there were about 400 followers at Ekuphakameni, 90 percent of whom were women and young girls. There was a significant group of single women, left destitute by the dire conditions in KwaZulu Natal, who had no real survival alternatives other than joining Shembe's community. Part of the appeal of the community was the kind of self-sufficiency it required of women; part was the stress on ritual performances and sacred dance, with participants all outfitted in festival attire.

Shembe used Ekuphakameni as the headquarters of his community, though as his following grew, he purchased numerous tracts of land and established small temples throughout KwaZulu Natal, the Eastern Cape, what is now Gauteng (the Johannesburg-Pretoria area), Swaziland, and Zimbabwe. He sanctified the landscape with biblical names for his communities—Thesalonika, Judia, Betlehema, Nazareth, Eden, Galilee, and Jordan. Other communities—Bekemesiah, Gospel, eLinde—were named to memorialize Nazarite spiritual history. None of these names appear on official maps; they are known only to those who are members or otherwise connected to *ibandla lamaNazaretha*.

The Bible in *Ibandla lamaNazaretha*

The Bible, rather than mission Christianity, was Shembe's source of knowledge about Christianity. The Wesleyans probably introduced him to the Zulu-language Bible. Since he was not raised in the mission culture, he would have read the text without the cultural baggage and theological traditions of the European institutions.

Shembe's reading was rather literal, particularly in terms of Old Testament law, which became central to the theological foundation of *ibandla lamaNazaretha:* Sabbath (Saturday) worship is central. Members are required to remove their shoes when on Nazarite ground and to abstain from eating pork and leavened bread, and from having sexual relations. He also noted that the Old Testament vindicated pre-colonial African practices, including polygamy, pastoralism, and animal husbandry, and he recognized how the suffer-

Shembe boys make an offering to their leader, Ebuhleni, July 1991.

ing of the Israelites paralleled the struggles of African peoples against colonial rule and dispossession. For Shembe, the Old Testament authorized pre-colonial African practices, and the New Testament, with its stories of miraculous and dreamlike events, provided models for managing the magic of modernity, embodied in new forms of technology and the mastery of these technologies by Europeans.

Shembe utilized the power he gained from his deep knowledge of the Bible—he could reportedly cite biblical references by chapter and verse to confound and ambush angry missionaries with the tools of their own power. One such story goes as follows:

> On another day he was accused by the pastors (or mission churches) in court. Shembe asked the magistrate to enquire from his accusers whether they would agree that the case be judged according to the Bible. They agreed to this request.
>
> 1.2 Then Shembe asked the pastors through the mouth of the magistrate whether they had studied the Bible. This question of Shembe made them very angry. But in the end they agreed that they had studied the Bible. Shembe asked them to read John 4:37–38. When this passage was read, Shembe explained: "We Shembe people

Shembe girls' procession with umbrellas to the temple, Paradis, in their jafeta *attire.*
September 1991, Ebuhleni, KwaZulu Natal.

follow this way. We enter the work which has been started by others in order to perfect it." The magistrate said: "Go out, Shembe, and preach: but do not enter their place." (Hexham and Oosthuizen 1996, 170)

Other stories are told of similar cases brought against Shembe by jealous missionaries, but each time the judge clears Shembe, ordering him not to enter the territory of the missions. In one account, a white man was sent to kill Shembe for his conflicting interests with the goals of the mission, but the man was overcome by the spiritual power of the Zulu-speaking prophet and let him go.

These narratives suggest that there was a clear contest between followers of Shembe and the missions over the terms of spiritual power in the region. Hundreds of narratives exist in the Nazarite archive about Shembe's power to heal, to provide in times of destitution, and to effect miraculous transformations in all kinds of otherwise impossible situations. Particularly in the earlier history of *ibandla lamaNazaretha*, these narratives are paralleled with the models of action members read about in the Zulu Bible. Shembe's power is thereby authorized and legitimated using the measures of mission Christianity. For example:

1.4 Very early in the morning Shembe sent Miss Mntungwa and
Emmah Dlamini to the great river Umzimkulu, which is close to this
temple, and in which there is a large and fearfully deep pool; I have
not seen it with my own eyes, but I have heard about it. I like to tell
this story because it reminds me [of] the other one, when Peter
wanted to meet Jesus on the sea, when he walked on the water but
did not sink down. (Elias Khawula in Hexham and Oosthuizen 1996,
Vol. 2, 44, my emphasis)

IziHlabelelo ZamaNazaretha

Ngohlabelela ngenthokozo	I shall sing with joy
Emzini oyincwele;	In the holy place;
Bajubule abahlangabezi bani	My heavenly escorts will be jubilant
Ngokungena kwami.	With my entrance.
(Hlab. 124/2)	(Hymn 124/2)

Sitshele ngezwi lakho	Tell us about your word/voice
Nalo masilizwe;	Let us all hear it;
Lingene enhliziyiweni zethu	May it penetrate our hearts
Lisithokozise.	And delight us.
(Hlab. 54/1)	(Hymn 54/1)

In Zulu, the word *izwi* translates as both word and voice. This is significant because it speaks of the priority given to the human voice
in both pre-colonial Zulu belief and its continuity in Nazarite theology. While Shembe displayed deep knowledge of the Bible, it is
clear that the word as voice supersedes the mission priority of the
word as written. This is amply demonstrated in *IziHlabelelo Zama-
Nazaretha,* the repertory of hymns he composed. The Zulu word
isihlabelelo may be translated in several ways. The noun *isihlabelelo*
may refer to a "hymn" though the more conventional translation
references the Psalms of David found in the Old Testament; it may
mean the repertory of songs that mothers compose for their children, which are sung at significant moments in the life of a child,
such as puberty and marriage. At a more abstract level, the Psalms
convey the strongest sense of the individual voice in the Bible, the

voice of praise and struggle, of anguish and jubilation. It is quite different from most other Old Testament books, which provide spiritual histories and accounts of the battles of the Israelites collectively rather than individually.

To more fully illustrate Nazarite beliefs about the place and power of song in the lives of *ibandla lamaNazaretha,* I have selected three types of narratives told in the community. While the focus of the narratives is not song itself, but the extraordinary power of Shembe, song is used as a vehicle of spiritual power and transformation. It emerges from the mouth of Shembe, and of birds, and even the stars because ultimately Nazarite song invokes ancestral presence. The verb *hlabelela* refers to the singing of birds (that is, high-pitched sounds), or of people in chorus or recitation (Doke et al. 1990). Birds suggest ancestral presence, because in their capacity to fly they mediate between those in heaven and those on the earth. A similar case can be made for sacred dance, as discussed at the end of this chapter.

The first type of narrative tells of Isaiah Shembe's ability to raise the dead to life. Liz Gunner (1990) collected two such stories. The first is excerpted from a sermon preached by a woman named Ma Ciya.

When the child had been wrapped around, he said, "I will bear it again. I will give birth to it a second time. He counted the months, just as it is for a woman who is pregnant. He said the first month, and then the second. He counted the months speaking, murmuring, singing the hymn (No. 71), which says:

My Lord you loved me
Before the mountains were firm
In ancient times you anointed me
I am the beginning of your journey.

When he had finished counting the ninth month, he opened his larynx. He said, "Today I am giving birth to that child anew. The child began to cry and it cried like the young of a sheep. As it was crying like that Shembe said, "Hey, the child of a human doesn't cry like that!" He said, "Cry like the child of a human." (Gunner 1990)

Married women dance toward Shembe with great joy, Ebuhleni, August 1991.

The second version is an excerpt from a sermon preached by Shembe himself on December 21, 1929: "On the fifth night as the mother sleeps, stars appear shining round the child. A voice says, 'Where is that child's death?' Another voice answers, 'It has been drunk by his mother.' The stars sing, they shine on the top of his head and a great star shines with particular brightness. The stars then become birds, they fly around him, bring him back to life, and then these heavenly beings disappear" (Gunner 1990).

Nazarites also recall Shembe's power as a healer. Soweto member, Ms. Mazibuko, told of how Shembe healed her own mother from a series of miscarriages. Shembe's promise to give Mazibuko's mother children was embodied in the birdsong that her father heard while he prayed for the safe birth of his child. Mazibuko recalled:

> So my father says when he was praying under those trees, he used to hear the watucal, the snake. Not the snake. Now, the bird. It was singing. When my father prays the bird says, "Twiree, twiree, twiree." When my father stops praying, the bird stops. Everyday when my father prays. Now my mother was pregnant. When my mother went to

Ama 14 women march to the beat of the drum to make an offering to Shembe, Ebuhleni, August 1991.

hospital, my father went to pray again under the tree, calling Shembe. "Now my wife is in hospital. [S]he is going to have the baby. I pray you please to be with my wife. That she must deliver that child, give birth to it right away. I don't want the child to die anymore." Then the bird was singing there with my father. After my mother got the baby, when my father went to pray, the bird was no more there. It was finished now because now it means that Shembe is send[ing] the bird there to be with my father. (Muller 1999, 102)

Finally, there are stories told in *ibandla lamaNazaretha* of the overwhelming power of Shembe's own singing voice. In 1918, he was traveling towards the mountain of Nhlangakazi. He stopped along the way to stay in the homestead of the family of a young boy, Ephraim Fulela. Fulela recalls the experiences as follows:

I went to my mother and asked: "Who is this man there in the hut?" She said, "Shembe." There I saw him for the first time. At 1:00 P.M. a man came out and called for a prayer meeting. All went out for the devotions to the place outside the village where the chief used to hear court cases . . . the entire family of the chief went there.

One of Shembe's companions read the liturgy from the book. Then Shembe rose and started to sing, not having said a word. His singing swept all the people away from the year; only the [two] men remained there. [The people] escaped into the forest. Shembe pointed with his hand to them and all those who had escaped fell down. Then he proceeded with the service.

When he was speaking, a haze emanated from his mouth and shed light on the whole Nyuswa country, it was brighter than the sun. When he had ended his talk, this light returned to him, and only the sun was shining over the country. I thought that all people must have seen this light, but it was seen by me alone. At that time I was too young to join this church. (Hexham and Oosthuizen 1996, Vol. 2, 84)

There are numerous such reports of Shembe's use of song in a range of situations. For the Nazarites, as for the Zionists, the singing voice summons spiritual power for healing, for raising the dead, in baptism, when in conflict with mission communities, in dreams predicting death, for dancing, to cast out demons, to elicit spiritual power in battles to purchase land, and to reinforce Old Testament law, especially regarding the Sabbath. Song in dream spaces signaled the presence of heavenly beings dressed in white robes, and it offered protection, much as the white robes worn daily by Nazarite members are believed to guard the body against danger.

Composing *IziHlabelelo*

While Shembe's hymn repertory has a direct historical connection to the hymn as defined by the European and American mission in KwaZulu Natal, the way in which song composition is described is quite different from the contemporary European practice. European composition is based on writing; in Shembe's narrative, the body is the site of creation. Prior to composing his own songs, Shembe relied on the hymn repertory of the Wesleyans for ritual purposes. Wesleyan hymnody is recognized as being the inspiration for several hymns in the Nazarite repertory.

The first Nazarite spiritual song, or hymn, came to Isaiah in 1910, when he arrived in KwaZulu Natal. He received the second hymn in 1913, on the holy mountain of Nhlangakaze. It was not until 1920, however, that he began to compose Nazarite hymns prolifically. Shembe began having compositional song visions once he was more settled at Ekuphakameni; he composed the bulk of his songs between 1920 and 1935, the year he died. Shembe gave three more hymns to women after his death. The remaining hymns were composed by Galilee between 1936 and 1976, the year he died.

The human voice as the compositional vessel, rather than writing, is privileged in Shembe's compositional process. According to Galilee Shembe, Isaiah Shembe received many of his spiritual songs while walking along paths in KwaZulu Natal, and frequently they came to him in visions. Sundkler records Galilee's recollections of how his father composed (or received) new songs.

> [Isaiah] would hear a woman's voice, often a girl's voice singing new and unexpected words. He could not see her, but as he woke up from a dream or walked along the path in Zululand, meditating, he heard that small voice, that clear voice, which gave him a new hymn. He had to write down the new words, while humming and singing the tune, which was born with the words. With Is[aiah] Shembe it was the rhythm that moved in him even while he was sleeping; it was the rhythm that first came to the surface and had to be caught and written down. This rhythm expressed itself in two or three words to be sung to the accompaniment of the beat of drums, and the feet of the dancing faithful. He found the chorus, and he built the hymn on this foundation. Waking up from his sleep, he still carried within him the rhythm of what he had heard in the dream dimension of life. (Sundkler 1961, 186–187)

There are three elements in this description that I suggest are critical to the composition and performance of *izihlabelelo zama-Nazaretha,* and that set them apart from what Sundkler calls the "hymn-carpentry" of the Christian mission: the relationship between words and rhythm; the human body, rather than writing, as the compositional medium; and the female voice as the vessel of transmission.

The female voice in song composition underscores the central position that young virgin girls occupy in *ibandla lamaNazaretha,* a position paralleled in pre-colonial Zulu communities (Muller 1999, chs. 2, 3, and 6). They have a special relationship, in myth and ritual, to the church founder. The articulation of the voice heard inside Shembe as female resurfaces in a comment made in one of the narratives about the sound of Isaiah Shembe's own voice at the time of his baptism by Pastor Lushigah of the African Baptist church on July 22, 1906: "After a time it became evident that this man (Shembe) did not stand by himself but that Jehova was with him. When they asked him to lead the service, he intoned the hymn of the Wesleyans, 'You suffered for me, eternal rock, that I may hide in thee, you wound of Jesus.' Then the diseases stood up. Shembe was singing with a very fine voice, even a girl would not have been able to sing like him" (Khaya Ndelu cited in Hexham and Oosthuizen 1996, Vol. 2, 32). Once again, it is the voice like that of a girl, but not quite, that signals the extraordinary spiritual powers of the prophet. This point ties to the earlier definition of *isihlabelelo* as the songs a mother sings to her children. Metaphorically, Isaiah takes the voice of a woman, a mother, and sings to his/her spiritual children.

There is one hymn in the hymnbook, Hymn 92, where Isaiah takes on the voice of a young girl. In English translation it reads, "I will dance the sacred dance with hope, I am a Nazarite maiden, I shall fear nothing, Because I am perfect (a virgin). . . ." While other Zulu-language composers claim that song composition occurs through the medium of dreams and visions (Ballantine 1999, Muller 1999), only Shembe hears these messages through the medium of a female voice, pointing once again to the special relationship Shembe had with his female membership.

Initially, the words and rhythms of these hymn visions were written down either by Shembe or an assistant. In time, his followers copied the written texts into their own books, which included hymns, miracle stories, prayers, sermons, and letters from Shembe. When Shembe's son Johannes Galilee assumed leadership, he had these texts transformed into a single book. Galilee himself had several compositional visions, and these songs were included in the published hymnal. University educated, the younger Shembe clearly understood the power and value of the book in European culture and the importance of having African literature available in the vernacular. W. H. Shepherd printed the first version of the

Nazarite hymnbook in Durban in 1940. That volume included 220 hymns; the more recent publication contains 242 hymns. Along with the Zulu translation of the Bible, *IziHlabelelo ZamaNazaretha* created a new set of practices and cultural truths outside of mission control. The hymnbook in particular constituted an innovative but more culturally coherent set of theological texts for people of African descent in twentieth-century KwaZulu Natal than the mission was ever able to provide.

Finally, it is significant that the images of song composition created in Galilee Shembe's dreams and visions differ markedly from those of his father. The images in Galilee's dreams/visions corresponded to his experience as a teacher: they came as words on a chalkboard. More recently, controversial Nazarite songwriter and arranger Nathoya Mbatha has had a vision of song composition that has shifted even further (see Muller 1999a, ch. 5 for further discussion): "When I am dreaming, or when I am just sleeping, it happens that I see myself in front of people, singing and all that. . . . When I wake up, I wake up and go to a keyboard or an organ or a tape if it's necessary, and tape what I have seen. . . . In the dream, it happens that I am with the choir, or I'm alone, sometimes in the forest or bush, seeing myself singing and a lot of people who are seated down. . . . They are just an audience" (Muller 1999a, 134). A century after Isaiah Shembe's experiences, Mbatha's vision is clearly modeled on a gospel-style performance, not connected to the world of the ancestors but emerging from the social space in which he longs to perform: on a stage in front of an audience. Here the young man is alone but he is dreaming of gospel performance stardom.

Nazarite Ritual

There are two frames in which *izihlabelelo* are habitually performed in *ibandla lamaNazaretha*. These two contexts seem to articulate to the cultural outsider what African-American intellectual and religious writer W.E.B. Du Bois would have called a double consciousness—the African simultaneously in the European world and embedded in his own African consciousness. Isaiah Shembe and his son Galilee conceived of religious worship in both the European congregational format (*inkhonzo*) of the Protestant church, with the book as the primary ritual object, and as African-derived sacred dance, with the body as the vessel of spiritual power. The way in which the hymns are performed in these two environments reflects these different modalities. In *inkhonzo* they are performed in the context of fixed liturgy read from a book. In sacred dance festivals or *umgido* the hymns are sung from memory. There is no visible presence of the book in this context.

I will qualify this distinction, however. Though on the one hand *inkhonzo* might seem to be a purely European invention borrowed by Isaiah and Galilee Shembe, Mthethwa (n.d.) argues that *ukukhonza* (to worship) was not uncommon in pre-colonial Zulu culture. This was the mode of interaction between a local king or paramount chief and his subjects. Those visiting the king/chief would sit quietly around the man while he exchanged words with the visitors. There would often be a pot of beer available and each person, including the king, would take a sip from the pot. The practice was equated with basking in the sun—the sun was the king, and the people basked in his presence. It was a practice that easily transferred into the mission structure of worship where members were expected to sit quietly while the minister preached. On the other hand, dance is an integral dimension of worship in the Psalm texts of the Old Testament. Once again, Zulu cultural memory is reinforced with the example and exhortations of the mission Bible.

Inkhonzo—*Congregational Worship*

In Paradis, the open-air temple at Ebuhleni, services are held every morning at 9 A.M., and in the evening at 6 P.M. The word *Ekuphakameni* means "elevated place" or "place of spiritual upliftment" and "heaven." Each time you come to Ebuhleni (the temporary site of Ekuphakameni) you enter the metaphorical gates, at which the Angel of the Lord stands, and walk to Paradis for the daily or Sabbath services. Once you are sitting inside the boundaries of Paradis you have the sense of being in a remarkably serene and exquisitely beautiful place. Trees form a canopy over the area; you hear the birds singing in an otherwise silent environment; and all inside in-

Shembe male follower sitting on his prayer mat in the Paradis temple at Ebuhleni with his Shembe hymnal and Zulu Bible, waiting for the service, Ebuhleni, August 1991.

habit a space of respect for each other and adoration of their leader. The sweet voices of the birds signal ancestral presence. Adorned in white prayer gowns, the *ibandla lamaNazaretha* community resembles the image of heaven Isaiah Shembe saw in his dreams and visions.

Members begin to gather at about 8:30 A.M. Clad in the white *imiNazaretha,* the young girls come with their heads draped in long white shawls, married women with the traditional top-knot adorned with Nazarite beadwork. Men typically wear bands of furry animal skin around their heads. All come bearing a handmade prayer mat, a Shembe hymnbook, and a Zulu Bible, both books often wrapped in a towel.

These services convey a deep sense of reverence. An aura of peace quite unusual in the larger political context permeates the scene. At about ten minutes to the hour, the bell rings. All members, wherever they are, kneel down in silent prayer when they hear the bell's first ringing. After the final ringing, everyone knows to gather their goods and to enter into Paradis through openings determined by gender and marital status. Within a periphery of white-painted stones, members sit in a circle around Shembe, men and

Woman member drums the rhythm of ukusina *at the Ama 14s' all-night meeting, KwaMashu F Section, November 1991.*

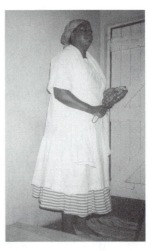

Woman shakes the bells to add to the rhythm of the dance.

boys on one side, virgin girls on the other, and married women and unmarried mothers seated directly opposite. Senior members of the community, including *abamshumayeli, abavangeli,* and *abakhokheli* (ministers, evangelists, and women leaders), take their places in the inner circle. The organ, introduced by third leader Amos Shembe into congregational worship in the late 1980s, sounds out through amplifiers attached to trees. It is situated at the boundary between the place for men and women, directly in front of Shembe. At nine o'clock one of the male leaders begins the liturgy for the Morning Prayer.

Morning Prayer

In this excerpt (CD TRACK 16) you hear three kinds of vocalization: the liturgy read by the leader, the responses of the congregation as recitation, and stanzas of the hymn sung for the morning prayer. The congregation hums together at the end, and goes into a time of collective prayer. The evangelist ends the prayer with *"Ameni."*

*Mrs. Nthini (at left) claps
to the rhythm of the dance.*

The Morning Prayer was written out by Isaiah Shembe but
printed by his son, Galilee, when the hymnal was first published in
1940. In the early years of the church, the services were conducted
according to the practices of the Wesleyan Separatist Church that
Isaiah had attended. It opened with prayer by a lay preacher, followed by a hymn, and a Bible passage read by a second preacher.
Another hymn was sung, and then the minister preached his sermon. The structure of the liturgy presented diverges from this early
pattern, with the solo voice of the leader dominant, interspersed
with single stanzas of the Morning Hymn and collectively recited
passages interspersed in the liturgy.

The text of the early part of the liturgy is based on the words of
Psalm 23, the Shepherd's Psalm, but rewritten to speak to the needs
of the local community. Liturgical portions are numbered. The
recorded excerpt is transcribed in Appendix 5. Translation by Bongani Mthethwa with Carol Muller.

Nazarite Hymns as Written Texts

Considering that the Zionists, *manyano* women, and *ibandla lama-
Nazaretha* are all religious communities whose constituency is
largely illiterate or only partially literate, it is perhaps surprising
that books, reading, and published liturgy occupy such a central

place in Nazarite daily and Sabbath ritual. From reading the text of the Morning Prayer and hearing the audio example it should be evident that *IziHlabelelo ZamaNazaretha,* the hymnal of *ibandla lama-Nazaretha,* is the key ritual object at this service. You may also have realized that this book is not read in quite the same way by Nazarites as it might be by those immersed in a culture of literacy. What you see by reading is not what you get in performance. If you look at the book without reading or understanding its Zulu texts, the Nazarite hymnal strongly resembles the format of standard Protestant hymn and prayer books—each hymn is divided into several stanzas of standard length and number of lines, and some have several stanzas with a repeating refrain. *Izihlabelelo,* however, are very rarely performed straight through, without seemingly endless cycles of repetition. It is in this repetition that the most sacred musical quality, a sense of rhythm, is articulated. As Pippin Oosthuizen (1967, 154–155) argued in his book on the Shembe hymns, "rhythm and word go together . . . the turning over and over of one idea in a sermon [or a hymn] is the rhythm of repetition."

The hymnbook contains more than just the songs. It opens with a photographic image of Isaiah Shembe. This photographic image, the representation of the founder, was believed by many followers in the early years to have the capacity to heal in the absence of the founder, who died before the hymnbook was published. Such interpretation of the photographic image of Shembe in the hymnal is much like his appearances in the dreams of members, that is, the seemingly magical experiences of new technologies are conflated with the equally extraordinary occurrences in which one's ancestors or Shembe himself appears in a dream.

The photograph of Shembe is followed by an index of hymn titles and three liturgical texts: the first for the Morning Prayers, the second for the Evening Prayers, and the third and most substantial for the Sabbath Prayers. As you heard on the recorded example, the liturgy is read out by a male leader in the congregational worship, with brief spoken responses from the congregation scattered throughout; all sing together the individual stanzas of hymns for each liturgical piece interspersed in the text; and finally the fragments of song are sung as a whole at the end of the liturgical reading. It is important to take note of the distinct differences in the mode of performance in each kind of vocal utterance. The main body of the liturgy is read as printed without repetition, while the hymn stanzas are sung with the greatest number of repetitions. Here a single line of text can be repeated for several minutes in multiple versions, which seems to signal the power of song in Nazarite spirituality. For it is through singing, not through the rapidly read liturgy, that each individual voice finds its own place in the larger ritual fabric. It is through song that members utter the inspired words of Shembe, and they do so with the most sacred of musical principles, a densely layered, overlapping, slow tempo, repeating rhythm. The words embody the rhythms; rhythm conveys the numinous and nonmaterial force of Nazarite spirituality (Oosthuizen 1967).

The texts themselves speak of a complex process of cultural and religious negotiation. I have already written about the way in which Isaiah Shembe named and sanctified the landscape with names derived from the Old and New Testaments. But Shembe goes further in the hymn texts by reconfiguring biblical narrative to coalesce with local experiences. This was revealed in his sermons but is most poignantly demonstrated in the words of *izihlabelelo*. Three examples illustrate how this negotiation is revealed in the *izihlabelelo* texts. In the first, Shembe uses a biblical text that is localized by the style of performance in some instances, or in both the style and text in other cases.

Hymn 152

1. *Jerusalema, Betlehema*　　　　1. Jerusalem, Bethlehem
Izazi zisitshelile　　　　　　　　The wisemen have told us
Umsindisi uselezelwe　　　　　　The Savior has been born
Ebetlehema eBetlehema.　　　　　In Bethlehem, in Bethlehem.

Hymn 58

1. *Baba wethu osezulwini*　　　　1. Our Father who is in heaven
Ngisebusweni bakho,　　　　　　I stand before you,
Aliphathwe ngobuNgcwele　　　　May your name be holy
Lelogama lakho.　　　　　　　　That name of yours.
CHORUS:

　Umoya wakho mawuze Nkosi　　　Let your spirit come, Lord,
　Ubaphilise abantu bakho.　　　　And heal your people.

Hymn 80

1. *Nkosi kuyisisusa sakho*
Ukwakhiwa komuzi wase Ntanda;
Namhla sesiyabonga
Ebusweni bakho.

1. Lord it is through your will
The Village of Ntanda was built;
Today we give thanks
In your presence.

2. *Nawe Betlehema Juda*
Muzi omncinyane,
Bongake kanye nathi,
Ngokwakhiwa kwakho.

2. Even you, Bethlehem of Judah,
The smallest village;
Give thanks with us,
Because you have been built.

5. *Yebo Betlehema Juda*
Muzi wakakhosazana,
Mawuhlobe ngeziqhamo
Umsinele uJehova.

5. Yes, Bethlehem of Judah,
Village of the maidens,
Be adorned with blossoms,
And dance for Jehovah.

The second text illustrates the way in which the style of the biblical Psalms has been absorbed into the Nazarite hymn. Compare, for example, Psalm 106 with Hymn 60:

Hymn 60
1. Give thanks to Jehovah
Because he is righteous
His mercy is everlasting,
Because he is righteous.

Psalm 106
1. Give thanks to the Lord
for he is good;
his love endures forever.

The third example introduces the political and economic struggles of African peoples into Nazarite theology:

Hymn 79

3. *Phakamisa amasango akho*
Singene sidumise,
Kade wawusimemeza
Uthi asizodumisa.

3. Lift up your gates
That we may enter and praise,
You have long been calling us
Saying we must come and praise.

4. *Phakamisa amasango akho*
Wozanini zizwe nonke,
Nize kudumisa uJehova
Amzini wase Mthwalume.

4. Lift up your gates!
Come, all nations,
Come and praise Jehovah
At the village of Mthwalume.

Hymn 120

1. *South Africa vuka*	1. South Africa, wake up!
Zokhele izikhuni zakho	Rekindle your fire logs
Zisondele zonke izizwe	So that all the nations may come closer
Ziwothe umlilo.	To warm themselves at your fire.

Inkhonzo Song Style

Several months after I began my field research in *ibandla lama-Nazaretha*, I was called to the office of church secretary Petros Dhlomo. He wanted to know how the work was proceeding. To test my assurance that all was well, he asked me to sing the melody of one or two of the more popular Nazarite hymns. I remember the panic that set in, not because I was unable to memorize a tune, but because I had been sitting among the virgin girls in temple worship and had never heard a single melody sung by those around me. The problem was not that there was no melody; it was that from my position in the temple, none of those whom I had captured on my tape recorder were singing a melody. Instead, they freely sang a range of "responses" to the call of the male song leader, who sang the melody but was seated in front of the male church members at some distance from where the young girls were located. I sang the melody as best I could, but it was difficult, because there was no one else to sing with me, to pick up parts of the melody and sing in a call-and-response pattern.

During worship, the men sang the melody, and the women improvised in word and tune, around the lower male voices. This gendered division of musical labor is described by South African musicologist Percival Kirby in his discussion of one of the oldest melodies in *izihlabelelo* sung to Isaiah Shembe's text, "Lalela Zulu."

Hymn 183

1. *Lalela Zulu*	1. Listen Zulu [nation]
Lalela abantu bengiphethe	Listen, hear our people nagging me
Ngezwe lethu.	About our land.

The song was recorded by Hugh Tracey, founder of the International Library of African Music (South Africa), perhaps as early as 1939 but issued on the commercial label Gallotone (South Africa) in the Sound of Africa Series in 1948. Kirby comments:

> There is no doubt that in Shembe's hymn, "Lalela Zulu," we have authentic Zulu choral music such as the early pioneers in Natal must have heard. This hymn is of great interest, for its music dates back at least to the days of Chief Mpande (1840–1872).
>
> The main melody is pentatonic, as might be expected, and it is executed by baritone voices. But at times, deeper voices, which normally sing in parallel with the others, double the melody in the lower octave. The "embroideries" sung by the women are of a comparatively free nature. (Kirby 1968, 249–250)

From the way Kirby describes this recording, shaped at least in part by Tracey's placement of the microphones to stress the melody in the lower voices, one might easily conclude that the "melody" was the most important musical parameter and the women's voices were merely ornamental. But five decades later, my own research among and recordings of Nazarite women singing suggests an alternative interpretation. On one hand, a series of compact discs and cassettes have been professionally recorded and sold in the commercial and Nazarite marketplaces in the last decade. For the most part, these embody the official sound of *izihlabelelo* along the lines of Tracey's recording, with a male leader who intones a melody and a relatively homogeneous choral response that overlaps with the line of the leader. On the other hand, the recordings I have made sitting among married women and unwed mothers in their all-night meetings, and among virgin girls in congregational (*inkhonzo*) contexts of hymn performance, provide a different perspective, suggesting that listeners' "readings" of a performance depend on where they are sitting in a service and what musical values they bring to the performance.

Nazarite Musical Examples

I have suggested that a basic distinction between the music of South Africa and the rest of the continent, particularly in the Western part of Africa, is that complexity in traditional African music was expressed in the human voice in South Africa rather than in the drumming ensembles so common to West Africa. As you listen to the traditional style of *izihlabelelo* on tracks 16–18 on the compact disc, think about what you consider the most outstanding musical characteristics of these performances. Look for call and response, cyclicity, overlapping phrases, tempo, rhythm, melody, cross-rhythm, syllabic treatment of text, melodic contour, bass voices, counterpoint, pentatonic vs. heptatonic scales, tone color, pitch treatment, and harmony.

How do the voices interact? What kinds of repetition do you hear? How do singers treat intonation, rhythm, and the relationships between voices? Has the music been written as a guide to singing, or is it freely improvised?

Now listen to an excerpt of *isicathamiya* [TRACKS 6–7], identify the outstanding musical characteristics, and compare the musical style of the male close harmony groups with that of Isaiah Shembe's *izihlabelelo*.

In the traditional *izihlabelelo* style, the "embroideries" sung by the women, freely woven in and around the "main" melody-words-rhythms intoned by the leader, are the sum total of the musical texture. Without the more homogeneous response of the lower voices described by Kirby, the musical texture created by the voices of girls and women is constituted from layers and layers of individual voices, freely playing with the rhythm of words, breaking up poetic phrases, repeating syllables, inserting vocables. The tempo is slow, the text is spun out syllable by syllable, fragment by fragment, overlapping, breaking off, starting up again, sometimes newly improvised, at other times copied from another line. In this frame of singing, each individual voice matters, each utterance contributes to the overall fabric of the song. The resulting effect of the interaction of voices is what Nazarite members call the rhythm of *izihlabelelo*. No two performances of a song are ever the same; your memory of each performance depends on what voices you could hear from wherever you were seated.

The Nazarites claim that this "rhythm" is what distinguishes their performance of *izihlabelelo* from any other kind of hymn singing in South African mission churches. If you are familiar with the religious singing of African Americans in the southern United States,

---

Comparing Musical Styles

Examples of African-American religious singing can be found on Smithsonian Folkways Wade in the Water Series, volume 2, 1994, copublished by the Smithsonian and National Public Radio. Even a group like Sweet Honey in the Rock, the a cappella women's ensemble from Washington, D.C., sings in a style that is similar to *ibandla lamaNazaretha,* though the Nazarites and the religious groups from the southern United States tend to sing in a much slower, more ponderous tempo. The idea of "singing in the Spirit" common to the Baptist churches in the United States has parallels in *ibandla lamaNazaretha,* both communities singing with a similar sense of rhythm.

---

you will probably hear some musical similarities between those of the South and those from *ibandla lamaNazaretha.*

Rhythmic articulation constitutes the substantive difference between mission and Nazarite practice. A typical mission hymn text would be sung straight through from beginning to end, with minimal repetition. In contrast, as has happened with African jazz (see West 2002 and Ballantine 1993), a Nazarite hymn is typically sung with far more improvisation from the church members and continually staggered entries through cycles of repetition. A member may take a fragment of the song text and improvise with the rhythm of the phrase, adding syllables, extending or contracting the phrase. There is also considerable overlapping of melodic material, resulting in an extremely dense musical texture. Members exercise enormous latitude in performance—far more so than we have become accustomed to, for example, in the *isicathamiya* choral performances of Joseph Shabalala and Ladysmith Black Mambazo. (As we discussed in Chapter Four, they adhere to a strict, one-line-each, leader-chorus format and, generally speaking, only the leader is allowed to improvise.)

The relative freedom of the female voice singing *izihlabelelo zamaNazaretha* works in stark contrast to the model of the civilizing mission, the European hymn. Poorly translated into vernacular languages, heedless of aesthetic sensibility, the mission hymn was ordered into four voices—soprano, alto, tenor, and bass—all required to move within a strictly controlled set of rules. Here we are reminded of Bokwe's biography of Ntsikana with transcriptions of four hymns interpolated into the written narrative. In contrast to the freedom of vocal utterance articulated in Shembe's hymns, the fixity of the four-part harmony in which Ntsikana set his hymns, albeit in his own language, speaks most profoundly of being bound into the project of the civilizing mission.

Significantly too, despite the model of a prophet leader like Ntsikana, Galilee Shembe chose not to have the hymns arranged in the mission model of four-part harmony when he codified the texts into book form, largely because that musical style is typically performed without any kind of body motion. According to Bongani Mthethwa (personal communication, 1991), there is a saying in *ibandla lamaNazaretha:* "*iculo elingasukumi lifile,*" which means a song that does not "stand up" (that is, make you dance) is dead.

Umgido: Festivals of Sacred Dance

The central importance and power of *umgido,* the festivals of sacred dance, cannot be overestimated in *ibandla lamaNazaretha.* Shembe introduced these dance festivals into his community as early as the 1920s. It was a radical position for an indigenous religious group, because even then the mission position was to forbid all forms of traditional dance in religious contexts. But as Esther Roberts reminds us from her research with Shembe in the 1930s, dance was one of the factors that contributed to the rapid growth of Shembe's movement in KwaZulu Natal from its earliest days, and the "concluding days of the [July] festival are devoted almost entirely to dancing. The red-skirted girls and the [boys] in kilts and pleated skirts usually play a more prominent part than the others" (Roberts 1936, 106).

Now that you have listened to the CD tracks with the traditional style for singing *izihlabelelo,* you might be wondering just what exactly excites the Nazarites about singing in this style. The music is slow and repetitive, it seems to take a long time to get through the words, and to the outsider, it seems to lack a good, toe-tapping beat. It is quite hard to connect emotionally to this musical style. If you were to go to Ebuhleni or one of the other Nazarite temples and watch *umgido,* you might begin to think the same thing about the dance festivals. Once you have seen an hour of the dance, with each of the groups represented in their visually stunning dance attire, it all begins to look the same. This was the kind of comment I over-heard made by one of the filmmakers when we were up on the holy mountain in January 1990.

This sense one has of being a complete outsider, of simply feeling that you are unable to make any meaningful engagement with a music or dance repertory is not uncommon when you participate in the world of music as a global phenomenon. To use this sense of alienation from the repertory productively, however, you must reflect on the purpose of *izihlabelelo zamaNazaretha* and *umgido.* While the dancers are visually spectacular, the goal of the performance is not to create a visual and musical spectacle, but rather to have as many members as possible participate in the process of singing and dancing together. To thread your voice into the larger fabric of song, to move your body in the same rhythms as the man, woman, boy, or girl standing on both sides, in front and behind you, and to do it in a style and manner that is culturally consistent is where the true power of this repertory lies.

This idea resonates with John Blacking's discussion of Zionist singing as having a more African than European sensibility that I mentioned earlier. Both Zionist singing, drumming, and body movement, and Nazarite song, using the words of their own founder and not a far-off European or American composer, naming places that people know locally, and articulating these words and sounds through the body moving in sync with hundreds of other bodies, some known and others complete strangers, is a radical gesture. But it is only significant to those who participate or who abide by similar sentiments. This sensibility is quite different from that of the popular music industry, which, in order to generate profits, has sought to find music with a common denominator and to reach the widest possible audience. In this commercial frame, the audience pays to have the performers move them emotionally, to perform aural and bodily tricks for them, and to be visually and aurally spectacular.

As cultural outsiders the closest we might come to engaging with the sounds of *ibandla lamaNazaretha* as performed for *inkhonzo* or *umgido* is to acquire some understanding of how the music and dance work and have meaning for its participants. For the Nazarites, dance is not just entertainment. It invokes the presence of the ancestors and its rhythm serves to unite the living with the dead. It is, in fact, a form of prayer. Oosthuizen claims in his 1967 work that "dancing before the Lord and repetitive singing are expressions of worship indigenous to the Zulu and foreign to the European. The sacred rhythm wants to come to expression in sacred dance. This is the way contact is made with the supernatural world. The pure expression of numinous power is in rhythm, poetry, music, and movements in dance" (1967, 154–155).

At the beginning of this chapter I gave a partial description of *umgido* on the mountain of Nhlangakaze, focusing for the most part on the uniforms worn and musical instruments used to accompany the singing and dancing of *ibandla lamaNazaretha*. In this section, we will spend a little more time thinking about the idea of rhythm, and the process of collective dance itself. Here I draw on my research with Nazarite women. I was extremely fortunate to have Khethiwe Mthethwa, Bongani Mthethwa's daughter, explain to me the process for participating in *umgido* of the married women in the early 1990s.

> The leader starts to sing—and everyone follows the leader of the song. After about a minute, she [and others] form a line and start to dance—very slowly, until all are in unison. And they dance following the song. The others—those who aren't dancing—start to clap, taking the rhythm of those who are dancing. When they have the good rhythm for that song, when the drum beater feels that those who are dancing and those who are clapping are in full unison, [s]he will take the cue and start to beat the drum, and have to pick up the right rhythm.
>
> After a very long time, maybe about ten minutes or so, again, the one who is blowing izimbomvu [long alpine horn-like instrument peculiar to *ibandla lamaNazaretha*] should blow it in a key that will be in harmony with the whole key used in the song.
>
> The people who are in control of the rhythm are the dancers, because those who are clapping look at the [dancers' feet]. And ac-

cording to the way they are dancing, they clap. The drumbeater too, will look at the way they dance, and beat according to the way they dance. If there is a foot that is stronger, maybe the right foot is stronger than the left that [beat] should be heard in the drum. So the strong beat is heard in the drum, so the drumbeater should be in unity with the dancers. Everything is in rhythm.

When the one who had started the song feels they've warmed up enough—the warm up is the repetition of the first two lines [of the hymn text] (that maybe about thirty minutes of the song), she'll change to the third and fourth lines of the song, which is faster and with more variations. When she changes, everything will be quiet. Everything breaks and they all listen to the changing.

Everyone will sing from the start. Then those clapping come in according to the right rhythm, and the drumbeater follows, and the blower comes in, and everything is in unity again. But faster this time. When the dance is at its climax, there may be a trumpet blower coming in, blowing according to the rhythm. (personal communication, December 1992)

This description shows *umgido* as a social and musical process. In Chapter One, I suggested that while there were many advantages to outsiders writing about African music, one of the problems was that quite often these outsiders only want to find out about the music and not about the music's connection to other dimensions of African art and life. In the last part of this section on *umgido* we discover a profound connection between the different expressive forms and spiritual practices embodied in *umgido* performance, particularly in its culmination in the pilgrimage to the holy mountain of Nhlangakaze. Walking to the mountain, singing, dancing, and the exquisite beadwork sewn together by Nazarite girls and women all combine conceptually and spiritually through the ideas of the path and the mountain.

Expressions of the Path

In Nazarite belief, walking to the mountain of Nhlangakaze earns one an imprint of the mountain on your feet. That imprint is recognized when you arrive at the gates of heaven. Those who have the mountain imprint, and their families, will be allowed to enter the gates of heaven; all others will be excluded.

Walking the path to the holy mountain is always accompanied by singing. Walking and singing are conceptually connected because both involve traversing a path. The path for physically walking is obvious, but the path for singing is perhaps not as clear. In Zulu, the word *indlela* is translated as "the way/path of the words." There is no melody without a text; because Zulu is a tonal language, all melodies are determined by the words of the text.

Women dancing *umgido* map out the symbolic pathways to heaven in a physical manner. Their dance steps, for example, are made from slow, controlled movements in which the feet move in a left-right, left-right-right-left duple rhythm. This is a highly rhythmic pattern derived from regular left-right walking in everyday life. Furthermore, dance is a form of prayer, the way in which the living invoke and invite the presence of the ancestors.

In women's singing for *umgido*, such as Khethiwe Mthethwa describes above, a transcription of the melodic paths sung by the leader and the rest of the women suggests that, through the medium of song, women symbolically climb the holy mountain. As Khethiwe's description suggests, in the typical performance of song for *umgido*, the leader begins the song by setting out the pitch, content, and shape of the melody. The women respond to this initiative by finding their individual vocal places on the melodic path. One hears several points of entry for these voices. The shape of the leader's melody is created by starting in the lower pitches and ascending through a series of melodic intervals that decrease in size. Then she levels out, repeating pitches in the high range, exploring the timbral possibilities of a repeating pitch. The other women join her in this exploration. On a recording, the leader's voice is submerged with the voices of the others for a few minutes, then she enters strongly again. This time she creates a kind of mirror image of the path she followed in starting the song. Here she takes the women back down in pitch to the starting note, with increasingly larger intervals. They all return to the original starting pitch. All the voices and instruments except the drum are silent until the leader takes the next couplet of text and starts the process over again, following the same melodic pathway.

Beadwork on a married woman's hat; the design is frequently in the shape of the mountain. Ebuhleni, September 1996.

A similar image—of a vertical ascent, a plateau, and a vertical descent—is commonly featured in the beadwork women create for their dance attire, particularly that worn by married women on their traditional hats, which consist of the weaving together of dried grass and a woman's own hair. This beadwork is traditionally given by a husband to his wife after the birth of their first child; the birth of a child signals the blessing of the ancestors and the incorporation of the wife into the husband's ancestral lineage. Bongani Mthethwa has written on the way in which this beadwork has been transformed in *ibandla lamaNazaretha* to signal a woman's spiritual relationship to Shembe rather than the romantic love of a man and woman. The colors signify particular spiritual qualities: white is purity, red is forgiveness. The outline of much of the women's beadwork is a kind of music writing that outlines the spiritual experience women have through song, another iteration of the sacred path.

Carefully examine the photographic image of the beadwork on the woman's hat. Imagine how you might transcribe the musical pathways created by a song leader and her community. Both have the diagonal ascent, leveling out, and diagonal descent. This image is filled in with a polyphonic mix of visual and vocal color, pattern, and texture; the straight lines of white beadwork resemble the nonmelodic instruments, the repetitive pulses of the drums, handclapping, and dancing feet; finally, there is the moment at the end of the textual couplet, in musical terms, a cadential moment, in which everything drops out except for the drumbeat. This moment of transition is signaled by the double strand of beads between the two mirror images of the beaded mountain that encircle the head of a woman. The musical transcription would repeat to complete the second couplet of a four-line stanza of text.

Recent Changes in *IziHlabelelo ZamaNazaretha*

In *ibandla lamaNazaretha,* spiritual and musical leadership are intertwined. Song is the vessel of spiritual power, so to be given new songs by the ancestors is a sign that an individual has been selected and blessed by the ancestors. Though Isaiah Shembe was best known outside his community for his abilities to heal the sick and to assist the needy, inside he is also warmly remembered for the song and dance repertory he bequeathed to his followers. His son Galilee left a much smaller body of songs but made his mark by compiling the Shembe repertory in a publishable book form. Amos Shembe, Galilee's brother, took the song repertory in a new direction: in the late 1980s he had Bongani Mthethwa introduce organ accompaniment into *inkhonzo* singing. This was not just because the organ is considered a church instrument; it was also an attempt to modernize the sounds of *izihlabelelo* in an effort to keep the next generation of Shembe youth interested in retaining their membership of *ibandla lamaNazaretha.*

To the outsider, bringing an organ into a church might not seem a particularly noteworthy event. But introducing a keyboard instrument with fixed pitch was a radical departure for the Nazarites. A note played on the organ always sounds the same, requiring everyone to tune to its pitch rather than finding the pitch that is comfortable for their voices. The organ clearly introduced a whole new way of performing *izihlabelelo zamaNazaretha* into the community. The new way of performing these treasured hymns caused enormous consternation among the older members of the community, and many did not approve of the aging leader's initiative.

Until Amos Shembe introduced the organ into congregational worship, freedom of voice, pitch, harmony, rhythm, and tonality were dependent on the vocal range and skill of each song leader for every new rendition of a hymn. While there was a song leader who intoned a call, the congregation freely responded, by listening to what was being sung around them. Without a fixed pitch reference point, members could explore the tone quality of a pitch, and it was easier to modulate upwards in the course of performance, gradually increasing the emotional intensity of the song. But with an organ and organist, the flexibility and freedom allowed the individual voice was curtailed, though not completely destroyed.

Bongani Mthethwa explained that the community was not accustomed to singing with keyboard accompaniment, and the song leaders continued to lead and not to submit to the pitch provided by the organ. This problem was solved in two ways. To accommodate the practices of song leaders, who determined starting pitch, tonality, modulations, and tempo, the organ was fitted with a pitch adjuster. In addition, Amos Shembe instructed Bongani Mthethwa to form a choir of young people who would sit around the organ and lead the Nazarite congregation.

Changes to the Hymn Repertory (see CD Tracks 18–22)

1. Congregation singing with organ accompaniment.

2. Bongani Mthethwa and KwaMashu Temple Choir, piano accompaniment to SATB arrangement. One of the consequences of the Kwa-Mashu choir and the organ accompaniment, in addition to Amos's concern for keeping the children of Shembe members active in *ibandla lamaNazaretha* in the early 1990s, was the spawning of Nazareth Baptist Youth for Shembe choirs, performing the classic repertory and South African gospel-style religious songs.

3. KwaMashu Youth Choir Gospel Style. This rendition was performed at the Blessing of Mshumayeli in KwaMashu in 1991. Compare the gospel rendition, or even Bongani Mthethwa's Youth Choir arrangements with *izihlabelelo* for *umgido*. This is where the difficulty lies, in the rhythm itself. It is hard to imagine dancing *umgido* to gospel arrangements. Although the music may appeal more to the uninitiated listener, it is a far cry from the rhythm of the older style.

4. KwaMashu Youth Choir Rehearsal of Classic "Makwaya." This piece uses tonic sol-fa.

*Shembe Youth Choir performs at Amos Shembe's funeral,
October 1995, at Ebuhleni.*

5. Youth choir rehearsal, singing in SATB style. The choir learns to sing in fixed voices. The style is less personal, lacking possibilities for improvisational exploration. The bodies have become stiff, at least for the more formal Shembe hymns.

6. Nathoya Mbatha. The "rhythm" of dance is gone: here is an individual performing with multi-track recording technology. He sings alone, makes his money alone, while giving praise to Amos Shembe for the miraculous way the project has succeeded.

In July 2002 I returned to Ebuhleni, primarily to get permission from Rev. Vimbeni Shembe to publish an English translation of the Zulu-language hymns of Shembe and to see what new music had appeared at the religious site. I was not disappointed. Blaring out at the edge of the village stores were startling new sounds of Shembe members loudly proclaiming their belief in Shembe. The volume of the music, the recording technology, and the acoustical space demanded by these new sounds all spoke to a newly found sense of place in the fully democratic South Africa of the early twenty-first century. The youth were no longer expressing their commitment to Shembe in the muted tones of twentieth-century Nazarite worship,

*The installation of fourth leader Rev. Vimbeni Shembe, iGospel,
southern KwaZulu Natal, December 1995.*

the softer tones of a docile black community under the apartheid
regime. As I suggested in Chapter Four might be the case with *isicathamiya,* the youth are claiming new public spaces for their voices,
and the volume has been turned all the way up. Nobody came to silence the blaring sounds of Shembe worship coming from the large
black speakers mounted on the sides of the store. Instead, there was
a steady stream of customers ready to buy the latest in the bright
sounds of Shembe gospel music. I happily joined the line to purchase.

REFERENCES

Blacking, John. *Music, Culture, and Experience.* Edited posthumously by
    Reginal Byron. Chicago: University of Chicago Press, 1997.
Doke, C. M., et al. *Zulu-English, English-Zulu Dictionary.* Johannesburg:
    University of the Witwatersrand Press, 1990.
Gaitskell, Deborah. "Devout Christianity? A Century of African Women's
    Christianity in South Africa." In *Women and Gender in Southern Africa
    until 1945,* edited by Cherryl Walker, 251–272. Cape Town: David
    Philip, 1990.

Gunner, Liz, and Mafika Gwala, eds. and transl. *Musho! Zulu Popular Praises*. East Lansing: Michigan State University Press, 1991.

Hexham, Irving, and G. C. Oosthuizen, eds. *The Story of Isaiah Shembe*. Translated by Hans-Jürgen Becken. Lewiston, NY: E. Mellen Press, c. 1996.

Hughes, Heather. "'A Lighthouse for African Womanhood:' Inanda Seminary, 1869–1945." In *Women and Gender in Southern Africa until 1945*, edited by Cherryl Walker, 197–220. Cape Town: David Philip, 1990.

Muller, Carol. *Rituals of Fertility and the Sacrifice of Desire: Nazarite Women's Performance in South Africa*. (CD Rom). Chicago: University of Chicago Press, 1999a.

Oosthuizen, G. C. E. *The Theology of a South African Messiah. An Analysis of the Hymnal of The Church of the Nazarites*. Leiden: E. J. Brill, 1967.

Papini, Robert. "Carl Faye's Transcript of Isaiah Shembe's Testimony of His Early Life and Calling," *Journal of Religion in Africa*, 29/3 (1999): 243–284.

Roberts, Esther. "Shembe: The Man and His Work." Unpublished M.A. Thesis, University of the Witwatersrand, 1936.

Sundkler, Bengt. *Bantu Prophets in South Africa*. London: Oxford University Press, 1961 (1948).

Tshabalala. *Shembe's Hymnbook Reconsidered, Its Sources and Significance*. Unpublished Masters Thesis, University of Aberdeen, Scotland, 1983.

Chapter Six

Final Reflections

I was born with the songs of Zulu rainmakers in my ears, they sang to end the drought, which burnt the land for ten years in South Africa. . . . I remember how my nanny would tell me that if I listened to the wind, I would hear the voices of my life. I listened and I heard Prof talk about justice, I heard Piet talk about hope, I heard Dubula Manzi, the old medicine man, talk about courage. I heard Maria [talk about love]. . . . These are the voices of my life, the voices of Africa; the voices I carry with me as Duma and I set out together to bring our country closer to each other. (Derived from The Power of One, *1992)*

The Power of South African Music

The Power of One is the name of the 1989 novel by Bryce Courtenay, and the 1992 Hollywood feature film directed by John G. Avildsen. It is an emotionally evocative narrative told in the first person by a young boy of English descent who is born on a farm in South Africa. The boy, PK, spends his early years with his best friend, a black South African whose mother is PK's nanny. PK is orphaned at the age of seven and sent to boarding school. It is in this school that the boy begins to witness many of the horrors of life in South Africa, initially under the racist policies of the British (prior to 1948), and later the even harsher system the white Afrikaner called "apartheid." PK meets up with a German piano professor after he goes to live with his grandfather, but the pianist is put into prison for failing to inform the British-controlled South African government that he was still in the country. While the "Prof" was away from Germany, the Nazis killed his family (including his grandson, who was the same age as PK) because they stood up against Hitler. Taught to box by a black South African prisoner (played by Morgan Freeman) the young man is instilled with a burning desire to seek justice for all South Africans. Prof and the young boy decide to work with the prisoner to compose a song for all the black prisoners to sing for an important white official who is to visit the prison. Because most whites do not understand African languages, they are not aware that the words of the song speak to a pan-African unity. The narrative is simple, perhaps a little idealistic, and certainly open to much critique. That is not my purpose here.

The Power of One celebrates the idea of "one" in several ways. It is about the capacity of an individual like PK to make a difference in the lives of so many. It speaks of the impact of a single song in forging unity between people of different languages and cultures, albeit of a single race. And it speaks to the power of song as a force of national reconciliation and unity. To conclude this book, I use the story of the *Power of One* to restate themes of the film that resonate with this book on the one hand, and to address questions that the personal style I have used in writing this text might raise on the other hand. In a very real sense, we might wonder how one person's experiences and story might speak to larger historical, musical, social, even political processes. Can one person's narrative represent anything larger than itself? I begin by highlighting themes in the film that are generated in the narrative of this book and then address the question of larger representation.

The Human Voice

The film opens with an unaccompanied solo voice, echoing through the vast expanses of the map of Africa, which is represented in a hand-drawn outline of the African continent. The map is almost empty—a few animals are scattered on its surface. We can interpret the image from several perspectives. It could represent the lack of knowledge the average film viewer has of the African continent; it might reference the way in which the first European colonists saw the continent—as *terra nubilus*—land without inhabitants, open to occupation. The map may even symbolize a desire to start afresh in a post-colonial world, expunging the horrors of the past, a desire that can ultimately not be realized. At the very least, the map opens up to the story of a white boy born in Africa.

In South Africa it is the human voice and not the drum that signals the sounds of place and identity in this film. The singing voice is, nonetheless, a hybrid. By hybrid I am not simply referring to a natural category, but one often shaped by struggle and emerging out of violence and silence. Throughout the film, PK's narrative voice intermingles with the singing voices of black South Africans. These are human voices that have encountered European tradition, absorbed it, and made it sound South African by incorporating local languages, timbres, and intonations germane to the region. The real South African voice is not pure, but a voice in constant encounter with other voices, other languages, other sounds. Its authenticity lies in its peculiar kind of hybridity, and a constantly evolving sound, structure, and timbre.

Colonial History

Running over the map at the start of the film are printed words, words that tell of the arrival of Europeans in that part of the world: the French, the Dutch, and the Germans who left Europe in the 1680s because of religious persecution and traveled to South Africa. They spent 250 years fighting with the English (and local Africans, though the filmmaker does not mention this) for control of the land. At this moment, the soloist is incorporated into a mixed-voice choir, singing in a call-and-response structure. Throughout the film, the words are foreign to the American viewer—mostly in Zulu, or sung simply as sounds that evoke a particular kind of ambience—but the sounds are arranged in a familiar structure. Very soon, we hear the autobiographical voice of PK as he begins the story of his evolving relationship to South Africa, and indeed, of his sense of being South African rather than English. The voice starts out as British in accent, but gradually changes in the film to sound more typically white South African, shaped by its interaction with the sounds of Afrikaans, Xhosa, and Zulu, among other languages spoken in the region and in the natural world.

The Body

An integral part of achieving political liberation in 1994 was the recuperation of the human body. The body beaten, abused, even destroyed under apartheid is very much alive in musical performance. Even singing, which in our world often uses only the voice, emphasizes the body. Group singing in the film consistently involves exuberant clapping, body swaying, and eye contact. As we read in Chapter Five and could see in the *Gumboots!* video, the body is a central dimension of South African performance for many of its citizens. Singing is a very physical act.

Song

The song composed by the pianist and PK serves to resolve differences—not by forcing everyone into a monophonic rendition, or even one in the four-part harmony of Caluza's Quartet, the 1930s recording used in the sound track. Rather, the composition allows for call and response, for several groups to sing their own melodies in a larger harmony with other groups. Each sings their part and does it in their own way, but ultimately, the voices blend together to create a rich musical texture. Different voices weave their parts into a single entity. Singing the song, voices engaged with each other, becomes a metaphor for nation building. Singing this song gives each singer a glimpse into the political possibilities of unity in diversity, of "many cultures, one nation," the idea that underpinned the birth of the "new South Africa" in the 1990s.

Middle Class Mission Music

Reuben Caluza's Double Quartet traveled to England from the city of Durban to record their music in the 1930s (see Erlmann 1991 recording). This recorded example is drawn from the scholarly reissue of this historic recording by ethnomusicologist Veit Erlmann. It is a remarkable document. If you can locate the compact disc, listen closely to the excerpt, for it encapsulates a moment of encounter: black South Africans encountering the culture of American missionaries in KwaZulu Natal. If you listen to the piano accompaniment on other tracks of the compact disc, you will hear echoes of secular ragtime. If you focus on the voices, you hear the SATB arrangements of the mission hymn brought to South Africa and introduced to black South Africans as the model, the *isawundi* (sound), of civilized music. In this recording, the voices seem a little strained, the African voice striving to assimilate into European ways. By the end of the twentieth century, African voices have found a comfortable place for themselves in the "classic" repertory of Europe.

European classical music is definitely more commonly sung in black communities than by those of European descent in South Africa. This begs the question about the nationality of, for example, Handel's *Messiah* in the twenty-first century. We can easily identify its European origins, but with less certainty, its consumption and performance in the contemporary world. In the early 1990s Sam Tshabalala, who worked for Radio Zulu at the time, translated the text of *The Messiah* into the Zulu language. This translation was performed on national television, live in City Halls in several communities, and on radio for South Africans. To whose culture does *The Messiah* belong? In South Africa the answer is a complicated one, suggesting, as the film does in other ways, that in South Africa racial and cultural stereotyping becomes a messy process.

Transnational Collaboration

Borrowing of culture from beyond South Africa's geopolitical borders has certainly characterized the history of South African musical traditions in the twentieth century. Some of the outside culture has been assimilated because it was imposed, some in more neutral forms of borrowing. In the film we are shown the compositional process of the unity song. It was a combination of the European classical skills of the German Prof, the Zulu language and conducting skills of PK, and most certainly the words were the ideas of the prisoner who taught PK to box. Like Paul Simon's *Graceland* project, the song in the film is an interracial, intergenerational, and intercultural musical collaboration, a pooling of resources, some times more equitably than others. There are times in the twentieth century when borrowing has come through human copies of recorded objects that have traveled from the global metropolitan centers—New York City, Los Angeles, London, and Paris—to South Africa. There is ample evidence of this process in Chapter Three. Without access to appropriate models locally, South Africans have copied, imitated, and typically transformed the foreign sounds into local languages.

Africa as Resource

We learn from the film that Africa is not just a place of copies and appropriations. In the mind of the highly cultured German pianist, Africa is also a resource, not to be exploited but valued. He urges PK to learn to read the signs of the natural world as a resource for original thought. PK heeds the pianist's advice, and it is this capacity to read the signs of the natural world in South Africa that enables him to define himself as South African rather than British. But it is also the specificity of his experiences living in South Africa that mark him as different from his British compatriots.

Global Travel

PK comes to know the German pianist because he is a global traveler, performing his skilled interpretations of European classical music the world over. He stops over in South Africa and has to stay a while because his travel is interrupted by the events unfolding in Europe in what we now call World War II. So one of the primary forms of cultural encounter is through the world travels of performers from Europe and the United States. But it is not only the Europeans coming to South Africa. Later in the film, PK is granted a fellowship to study at Oxford University in England. Unlike others, however, PK ultimately turns down the scholarship to forge a place for himself and others in South Africa. The point is that various forms of travel have shaped South African culture, both internationally and within the country, between town and countryside. We saw in Chapters Three and Four how music has created the connective tissue in these travels, either as live or mediated performance.

Individual Versus Collective

Each time we are taken into the township of Alexandra or into the prison in Barberton in the film, we are shown images of black South Africans performing. Here all performance is live and collective, there are no individual musicians walking the streets alone; even the pennywhistle players in the middle of the film are performing as a group. Each plays an individual melody, but all perform on the same common ground. We know from Chapter Four that individual musicians were quite common on the streets of South Africa in this time period, but what the filmmaker is presenting to us is a stereotype of African performance—that it is always collective. It is a stereotype projected from within the black community and outside of it, and it can at times be quite difficult for individual musicians to record their music alone.

Orality and Literacy

PK recalls at the start of the film that in his early childhood he was taught by his mother about the ways of England, in which there were books and music, and by his nanny whose knowledge of Africa came directly from the wisdom of her people. One of the ways in which PK is urged to help his fellow South Africans in Alexandra township is through literacy training, specifically by teaching a group of people to read English. The idea is that to engage with the contemporary world, to be able to read its signs, one has to have a command of the English language, as both spoken and written language. But the prisoners are not taught the song of unity by reading, though the piece was written, but rather through forms of oral and aural transmission. They learned by listening. In Chapters

Three and Five we caught a glimpse of the coexistence and at times tensions between orality and literacy, core characteristics of South African performance in the twentieth century.

The Peculiarity of the Hybrid

Finally, we have learned that South African identity and its musical performance in the post-colonial world is a hybrid identity, not purely African or European. In fact, neither European nor African makes complete sense in South Africa; both have been somewhat redefined in contact with the other. There are, too, multiple forms of national identity. As we saw in Chapter Two, the meaning of the word *nation* has shifted dramatically for some in South Africa; no doubt for others it still retains something of its nineteenth-century inflection—the Zulus belong to the Zulu nation, the Afrikaners to the Afrikaans nation. For others, just to be South African and not culturally or racially categorized is an adequate category of identity.

South Africa in Africa

You might be wondering, what exactly is the nature of South Africa's relationship to the continent of Africa? For so long, it seemed to have remained isolated, cut off from internal travel and engagement. To meet other Africans, South Africans often had to travel abroad, to England, Europe, or the United States. While Africa has certainly opened itself up to South Africans since the early 1990s, and South Africa has had to open its borders to people from other parts of Africa, the relationship is tenuous and, at times, fragile.

This is beautifully illustrated for me in a compact disc, *South Africa—Rainbow Nation* (1996). Ostensibly a celebration of the African-ness of all South Africans, it is a CD of only four or five songs. One is titled "Viva Madiba" (Long Live Mandela), a song in praise of Mandela as the father of the nation; a second is a reissue of Miriam Makeba's now famous "Click Song," sung in the New York City Town Hall in the early 1960s. That song begins with Miriam Makeba's youthful voice telling the story of the place of the song in her "native land," of the "African peoples" in that land. In that story, African was the opposite of European. But "African" now means something else because, as *The Power of One* suggests, all people born in Africa are indeed Africans, regardless of skin color or culture. The trouble now is how to define South Africa's relationship to the "Africa" beyond its borders. This CD embodies the complexity of that relationship: the CD is cut in the shape of Africa, but it is the South African flag that covers the entire continent. The question remains: to what extent will South Africa now become the dominant force in Africa, musically, culturally, economically, and politically? It is a question that many grapple with, both inside and outside of South Africa. Not everyone is comfortable with the consequences of that kind of role and responsibility.

Finally, what is the power of one ethnomusicologist in conveying a sense of South African music and culture in the twentieth century for readers in far-flung places? How representative are my experiences as a white English-speaking South African woman now living in the United States? It has to be said that they are quite peculiar. In my generation, few white South Africans ever crossed the boundaries between white urban spaces and black townships. Then again, that is not unique to South Africa. Racial, linguistic, class, and social differences are clearly marked on the landscapes of many cities and rural areas around the world. My hope is that through reading this book you have opened your minds to the experiences of South Africans I have encountered and written about; that your ears are tuned to the music these men and women have made, a small portion of which is available on the compact disc; and that you have participated at least imaginatively and from a distance in the vibrant and always changing musical traditions of twentieth-century South Africa.

REFERENCES

Avildsen, John. *The Power of One.* Burbank, CA: Warner Studios, 1992.
Kruger, Kevin, and Dan Hill (Producers). *South Africa: Rainbow Nation.* Pretoria: Mac-V, 1996.
Powell, Aubrey (Director). *Gumboots! An Explosion of Spirit and Song.* Chatsworth, CA: Image Entertainment, 2000.
Simon, Paul. *Graceland.* Burbank, CA: Warner Brothers, 1996 [1986].

Appendix One

A Guide to African Music: A Music of Encounters

African Music: Early Encounters

The earliest written record of sub-Saharan African peoples is mention of "pygmies" in the account of a Fourth-Dynasty Egyptian expedition to discover the source of the Nile. This record is preserved in the tomb of Pharaoh Nefrikare, and was composed by Herkouf, the Pharaoh's commander. Herkouf tells that they went into "a great forest west of the Mountains of the Moon and discovered there a people of the trees, a tiny people who sing and dance to their god, a dance such as had never been seen before" (Turnbull 1968, 15). The Pharaoh ordered the expedition to return with one of these small people. The next mention of pygmies is in Homer's Illiad, in which the "Pygmaean race" is mentioned as having been killed by the men of Troy, though again it is not clear if Homer's is a mythical reference (Turnbull 1968, 15).

Though not depicting musical performance as such, Bushman paintings, some of which are 25,000 to 27,000 years old, have images of ritual performances and of trance dances. In fact, much of this very old artwork on the rock faces of mountains in southern Africa is thought to articulate the relationship between the spirit world and the everyday life of hunter-gatherers in Southern Africa. Communication between those spheres is induced by song or chant performance (Lewis-Williams and Dowson 1994 and National Geographic DVDs on Africa). The last Bushman rock painters died in the nineteenth century.

In the late 1860s, German linguist Dr. W.H.I. Bleek and his sister-in-law, Lucy Lloyd, began work with a small group of Cape Bushman convicts, two of whom were prolific storytellers and song performers. They produced a

12,000-page record of the stories, prayers, and songs of the Cape Bushman as recounted by these people (Lewis-Williams 2002). One can only speculate on the age of some of the myths and narratives recounted in this collection though it is thought that the Bushmen have inhabited South Africa for at least 20,000 years.

Hanno's *Periplus* provides another example of an early Western voyage of discovery. Dating to about 500 B.C.E., it survived as a tablet housed in a temple at Carthage, inscribed in a Phoenician language. This account makes brief reference to African musical performance on an island on the West coast of Africa: "We could discover nothing in the day time except trees; but in the night we saw many fires burning, and heard the sound of pipes, cymbals, drums, and confused shouts. We were then afraid, and our diviners ordered us to abandon the island" (Palmer 1931, 2, cited in McCall 1998, 74). Hanno's mention of musical performance is unusual because most ancient narratives of voyages to Africa provide little such information; travelers did not go ashore and engage with indigenous peoples at the time.

The first real records of encounters with African musical performance come from Arabic traders from Mediterranean and Middle Eastern coastal cities. The earliest such account mentions music at the Ghanaian royal courts in 1067. "The beginning of a royal audience is announced by the beating of a kind of drum which they call deba, made of a long piece of hollowed wood. The people gather when they hear this sound" (Davidson 1964, 72, cited in McCall 1997, 75).

The fourteenth-century account of Moroccan traveler Ibn Battuta, who visited the capital of the Malian empire, is particularly important because it provides written documentation of contemporary oral history, which claims the existence of griots in that region dating back seven centuries. On returning to his home, Battuta dictated a narrative on his encounters with these griots (Hale 1998, 3; McCall 1997). From the fifteenth century numerous Portuguese, Spanish, and English traders traveled into the heart of Africa. Vasco da Gama, who traveled around the southernmost tip of Africa, made brief reference to musical performance on the Kenyan coast.

The earliest known report of South African indigenous performance was that recorded by Portuguese explorer Vasco da Gama in his diary about his travels around the South African coast in 1497. This is the first known written description of flutes made of reeds played by "Hottentots," indigenous South Africans living on the Western coast of the Cape, near the contemporary town of Mossel Bay. They played on four- or five-reed pipes for the Portuguese travelers. A report by Peter van Meerhoff in 1661 provides the most comprehensive account of these performances. He describes a group of between one hundred and two hundred flute players, each with a hollow reed in hand, dancing in a circle while blowing their instruments. In the center of the circle was a man grasping a long stick. The reeds were played in harmony with each other, and sounded like trumpets (Kirby 1968, 135–136).

In the seventeenth and eighteenth centuries, numerous missionaries and traders, the Portuguese in Congo, and the French and Dutch in Guinea, produced writings about African music, usually disparaging. In the nineteenth century, the idea of Africa and its music in the European mind was definitely one of wild savagery (see McCall 1998). In contrast, South African ethnomusicologist, Percival Kirby, undertook groundbreaking archival and ethnographic research into South African musical instruments in the 1920s. Kirby examined the earliest known documents, some as early as the late fifteenth century, describing the instruments, their social uses and value. The book he published (1968 [1934]) is a remarkable resource for the instrumental traditions of African peoples as practiced in South Africa in the early twentieth century; the written records from much earlier suggest that some of these traditions might be traced back several centuries.

In tandem with Kirby's research, British-born musicologist Hugh Tracey began recording the traditional music of Africa, starting in South and Central Africa in the 1930s, and ultimately producing the remarkable *Sound of Africa* series. This is a collection of 200 LP records, which are meticulously documented. They represent many musical traditions that are no longer practiced in contemporary Africa.

A handful of nineteenth-century writings on African music include written transcriptions, that is, visual representations of what African music sounded like to the writers. Thomas Bowdich, a writer working for the British African Company, traveled to West Africa to negotiate with the Ashanti. He published a book on that experience, including a chapter on Ashanti music that contains two Ashanti songs transcribed by Bowdich. For his insight into the limitations of European notational symbols to convey Ashanti musical sensibility, and the detail he provides about the musical life of Ashanti people, he may qualify as the first real ethnomusicologist to have worked in sub-Saharan Africa (McCall 1998, 88–89).

A second study is a wonderful piece of nineteenth-century collaborative African musicology about musical life among the Ijebu, part of the Yoruba, in Nigeria. The piece comprises the memories of an African man named Osifekunde (Joachim was his "Christian" name), who was captured by pirates and sold as a slave. Osifekunde ended up in Brazil; thirty years later, he told his story to ethnologist M.A.P. D'Azevac-Macaya. The interviews with Osifekunde took several weeks, and produced the first written account of Yoruba culture. Included in this narrative is a brief section on music with transcriptions of songs performed by Osifekunde (see Lloyd 1968, 277–280, cited in McCall 1998, 89–91).

Other Europeans left musical transcriptions, but perhaps the most significant in shaping European and American ideas of African music in the twentieth century was the music scholar Richard Wallaschek, who published a book in 1893 titled *Primitive Music: An Inquiry into the Origin and Development of Music, Songs, Instruments, Dances and Pantomimes of the Savage Races.* In this text, influential for European comparative musicologists of the later nineteenth and early twentieth centuries, Wallaschek incorporated nineteenth century ideas of social Darwinism into a theory of "primitive" music. Wallaschek used these theories in an attempt to give value to the music of primitive people, countering beliefs current in Europe that the music of primitive peoples like Africans was not to be considered music at all. Wallaschek argued that rather than just being an object of aesthetic pleasure, primitive music was integrally connected to everyday social life. However, his view of African music was that it was music of an earlier stage of human development, and that European music, the music of the present, signaled a higher level of human and cultural development (McCall 1998, 93–97).

Encounters with African Music in the Twentieth Century

This account of the history of African music has privileged written documents over oral narrative as sources of African musical history; the voices of African scholars and individuals have largely remained silent. This should not be interpreted to mean that African people have not had ideas or theories of musical performance in their societies, or that they have had no means of recording or representing their music.

Africans in contact with the Arab world in North Africa for example, have had their own music theorists for centuries (see, for example, Wright 1978 and Farmer 1957, both cited by Shelemay 1998, 146–147). Unfortunately, there has been very little systematic search, recovery, or analysis of African music writing in sub-Saharan Africa. This means that as outsiders to these performance cultures, we may need to look in different places for these records or forms of representation.

The best-developed example of indigenous African musical notation has been written about by ethnomusicologist Kay Shelemay (all informa-

tion on Ethiopia here is derived from Shelemay 1998, 146–151). Shelemay studied the musical notation of the Ethiopian Christian church.
(Ethiopia became a Christian country in the fourth century, and by the
sixth, had a literature and script in the language known as Ge'ez.)

While the earliest parchment texts in Ge'ez derive from the sixth century, the system of music writing emerged much later, in the mid-sixteenth
century, following a Muslim invasion of Christian churches and monaster-
ies (1529–1541). Ethiopian church clerics devised a notational system to
create written records of the liturgy. Historical sources suggest that the system of notation may have been developed from extant notations that were
obliterated by the Muslims in this period. This system of music writing
continues to be used and taught in contemporary Ethiopia though it has
always operated in conjunction with a vibrant oral tradition; the practice
of committing to memory the musical performance is an integral part of
monastic training.

In the twentieth century, other kinds of musical notations have been
used and created for African musical performance. Tonic sol-fa, the system of notation using the syllables do re mi fa sol la ti do, has been deeply
integrated into choral rehearsal and performance in South Africa (Muller
1999, ch. 5) and parts of East Africa (Gunderson 1991). I have heard
tonic sol-fa criticized by black South Africans because it is limited for the
study of instrumental music.

Several African countries created national orchestras in a bid to foster a
sense of national unity once they gained independence from European
colonial powers beginning in the 1950s. This has frequently entailed gathering into a single entity many regional musicians who play diverse styles
and use a range of languages and dialects. Completely new hybrid music
and dance styles have emerged out of this process, necessitating the creation of an innovative notational system to accommodate musical and linguistic diversity. Standard Western notation has not proved fully adequate
for the task, often requiring modification to accommodate specific musical
qualities not germane to the European classical or popular tradition. The
Ethiopian National Orchestra has developed a complex notational system
using pictographs to represent musical elements. For example, a turtle
placed above a musical note indicates a slow tempo (Shelemay 1983).

Though art music is not a focus of this book, a small but significant
number of European- and American-trained composers from Africa have
sought to express themselves through the medium of written compositions. Writing art music is a struggle for the African composer, because
many outside of Africa expect their music to sound ethnically African.
Nigerian ethnomusicologist and composer Akin Euba has been at the

forefront of the struggle to find a legitimate compositional space for intra-cultural composers like himself. To this end he has been one of the organizers of a biannual gathering of composers and scholars at City University in London. Mzilikazi Khumalo (Msibi, unpublished) is one of a handful of South African art composers. Like Euba (Omojola 2001), he has experimented with the problems of combining African traditional musical aesthetics with the forms and aesthetics of European art music. Both have grappled with the challenges inherent in performing African music on western instruments like the piano or in the symphony orchestra format. White South African Kevin Volans (Taylor 1995) experimented with the sounds of traditional music in his *mbira* works of the 1980s. Using transcriptions of *mbira* music, he "classicized" the sounds by performing the transcriptions on retuned harpsichords. The American group the Kronos Quartet has made a significant contribution to these intracultural compositional experiments by commissioning new work by African composers, then performing and recording the music for wider consumption.

Oral performance, either transmitted live or recorded in the media of sound and video, remains the most vibrant source of African contemporary and historical performance. In the scholarly world outside of Africa, however, written and recorded words and sounds have been given greater status than those contained in human memory. Human memory, it is claimed, is not as reliable as the written document. While this might be true of individual memories in Europe and the United States, where technologies of writing and computing have become the memory banks of many, it is not the case in parts of Africa that have for centuries nurtured and sustained the human capacity for good memory.

The most outstanding example of the capacity to remember and transmit cultural history is that embodied in the *griot/griottes,* or *jeli/jeliya* traditions of West Africa. Manding musicians come from the countries of Mali, Guinea, and Senegambia. The history of their musical traditions, particularly those performed with words accompanied on the *kora,* are documented by Charry (2000), Duran (1994), Hale (1998), and Knight (ca. 1986). Manding *jeli/griots* claim that their ancestry can be traced as far back as the thirteenth century. As mentioned earlier, these oral traditions can be verified by the Arabic documents written in the fourteenth century by Ibn Battuta who first saw griots at the court of Mandinkan ruler Mansa Sulayman (1341–1360). *Griots/jelis* function as genealogists, historians, spokespeople, diplomats, musicians, teachers, warriors, praise singers, masters of ceremonies, and advisers (Hale 1998).

Appendix Two

Key Dates in South African History

c. 100,000 B.C.	San people settle in Southern Africa
c. 500 A.D.	Bantu speaking people to present day KwaZulu Natal
1487	Portuguese explorer Bartholemeu Dias sails around Cape of Good Hope
1498	Portuguese Vasco da Gama records passing encounters with Cape, KwaZulu Natal, and Mozambique
c. 1500	Basotho people settle in present day Lesotho
1652	Dutch (Boer) settlement in Table Bay (Cape Town), as refreshment station, Cape also called "Tavern of the Seas"
1688	French Huguenots arrive in the Cape
c. 1690	Boers move into hinterland outside of Cape Town
c. 1750	Nguni people in Swaziland
1779	Boer fight Xhosa at Great Fish River in Eastern Cape
1795	British capture Cape Town from Dutch
1815	Shaka seizes power in KwaZulu part of KwaZulu Natal, *mfecane/difeqane* (forced migration) begins
1820	British settlers to Eastern Cape, may not import slaves
1828	Ordinance 50 allows freedom of movement for "Coloureds," may own land and work where they wish
1830s	Voortrekkers (Dutch farmers) begin Great Trek from Cape northwards
1833	Slavery abolished in British Empire
1838	Boers defeat Zulus at Battle of Blood River
1840s	First missionaries to KwaZulu Natal
1843	Natal a British colony
1847–1849	British settlers come to Natal
1851	First sugar cane production in Natal
1852	Boers create Boer Republic of Transvaal, recognized by Britain

1854	Britain recognizes independent Republic of Orange Free State
1857	Diamonds discovered in Griqualand West (now Kimberley); start of industrial revolution in South Africa
1858	British defeat Xhosa after great cattle killing
1860	Indian indentured laborers arrive from India to work sugar cane fields in KwaZulu Natal
1868	British annex Basotholand (Lesotho)
1871	British annex Griqualand West with 50,000 fortune seekers, African labor needed for mines
1875	Formation of Genootskap van Regte Afrikaners (Society of True Afrikaners) an association of those of European descent, wanting Afrikaans to be recognized as official language
1877	British annex Transvaal Republic
1879	Anglo-Zulu War, British ultimately gain control of Zululand
1881	Boers defeat British; Transvaal becomes South African Republic
1886	Gold discovered on Witwatersrand, gold rush, Americans and British arrive in droves
1887	British annex Zululand, Zulu king Cetswayo exiled to island of St. Helena
1891	Indian Immigration Law in Natal Colony controls all aspects of Indian life
1893	Indian lawyer M. K. Gandhi arrives in South Africa, establishes Natal Indian Congress to resist discrimination against Indians
1896	Pass laws introduced to control movement of black miners
1898	Tensions between British and Boers over miners' rights to franchise
1899–1902	Anglo-Boer War, British burn Boer farms, put Boer women and children into concentration camps, 26,000 die in camps
1902	Transvaal and Orange Free State republics annexed by British, economic reconstruction by British
1904	60,000 Chinese indentured laborers imported to gold mines, mostly repatriated
1905	Abdullah Abdurahman becomes president of African Political Organization founded in 1902, in Cape
1908	Gandhi leads passive resistance campaign against pass laws for Indians

1910   Union of South Africa, blacks denied vote; Lesotho and
        Swaziland became British Protectorates

1912   South African Native National Congress, forerunner of the
        African National Congress (ANC), formed by John Dube

1913   Native Lands Act restricts black ownership of land to 8 percent

1918   Broederbond, secret society of powerful Afrikaners similar to Ku
        Klux Klan in the U.S., formed to protect interests of Afrikaners

1919   Black Industrial and Commercial Workers Union formed

1921   South African Communist Party founded, campaigns against pass
        laws

1922   Army crushes white miners wanting job reservation

1923   First Urban Areas Act restricting entry of Africans into urban areas

1924   Hertzog, champion of poor whites, workers, and Afrikaner
        nationalism, becomes Prime Minister

1925   Afrikaans replaces Dutch as second official language

1936   Native Trust and Land Act transfers African and Coloured people
        from Cape Voters' Roll to separate list; increases land allocated to
        native reserves from 8 to 13 percent

1939   Split among whites over support of Europeans in war, some
        Afrikaners turn support to Nazis, English support Allies

1943   ANC Youth League formed, includes Nelson Mandela, Robert
        Sobukwe, Walter Sizulu, and Oliver Tambo

1946   India wins United Nations vote of censure against South Africa
        for discrimination against Indians in Natal

1948   Nationalist Party wins over the United Party, Afrikaner
        Nationalists to power

1949   Prohibition of Mixed Marriages

1950   Immorality Act, forbids sexual relations between whites and any
        people of color; Population Registration Act introduces legalized
        racial classification: Whites, Coloured, Native, and Asiatic; Group
        Areas Act divides the country into residential areas based on
        racial classification; Suppression of Communism Act defines
        communist as anyone hostile to the government; South African
        Communist Party dissolves, many join the ANC

1951   Government legislation to remove Coloureds from Voters' Roll;
        Bantu Authorities Act creates tribal and territorial authorities,
        retribalizing African population

1952   Native Laws Amendment Act extends influx control to all urban
        areas and to black women; Defiance Campaign begins

1953   Public Safety Act enables governor general to declare states of
        emergency and rule by decree

1954   Native Resettlement Act allows for forced removal of black
        residents from Sophiatown, Johannesburg, over five years

1955   ANC Freedom Charter, drawn up by the Congress of the People,
        adopted

1956   South African Amendment Act removes 45,000 Coloured votes
        from electoral rolls; Industrial Coalition Act reserves certain
        skilled jobs for whites

1957   Union Jack removed as dual official flag of South Africa

1958   First all-white election, National Party wins large majority; women
        protest the pass laws, about 2000 arrested

1959   State President Hendrik Verwoerd launches independent
        "homelands" project; Extension of University Education Bill
        exludes all nonwhites from white universities, creates separate
        universities for blacks, Indians, and Coloureds; Pan Africanist
        Congress (PAC) formed

1960   Police fire on PAC-inspired march against Pass laws, Sharpeville
        Massacre, 60 killed, 178 wounded; UN Security Council call to
        end apartheid

1961   South Africa proclaimed a republic; Albert Luthuli receives
        Nobel Peace Prize; treason trial of Mandela and other members
        of ANC ends after four years, all found guilty

1963   General Law Amendment Act allows police to arrest and detain
        suspects for 90 days without trial; police capture ANC
        underground leadership including Nelson Mandela, Govan
        Mbeki, Walter Sizulu, charged with sabotage (punishable by
        death without appeal); Transkei becomes self-governing

1964   Mandela and others sentenced to life in prison; South Africa
        banned from Olympic Games participation

1965   Bantu Laws Amendment Act denies 7 million black people the
        right to live inside South Africa

1967   Defense Amendment Act requires white South African men to
        undertake military service; Terrorism Act defines terrorism as
        anything that threatens law and order, gives unlimited powers to
        arrest, detain, and hold trials without jury

1968   Black Consciousness Movement constituted with Steve Biko as
        first president

1969   Bureau of State Security established with wide investigative
        powers, newspapers may not report activities of Bureau

1970   Bantu Homelands Citizenship Act makes all black South Africans
        citizens of a tribal homeland, regardless of their place of birth

1970–1980s	Union activity, anti-apartheid activity, South African Defense Force activity in surrounding countries
1972	Bophutatswana, Ciskei, and Lebowa independent homelands, with KwaZulu part of KwaZulu Natal as semi-autonomous
1976	Television comes to South Africa; Soweto uprising: school children protest Afrikaans as medium of instruction, police fire on children, months of protest countrywide
1977	Steve Biko detained under Terrorism Act and dies of brain injuries suffered in custody
1983	United Democratic Front (UDF) formed to coordinate resistance
1984	Archbishop Desmond Tutu awarded Nobel Peace Prize
1985	Political protesters fired on, indefinite State of Emergency declared; Congress of South African Trade Unions (COSATU) formed
1986	Pass Laws, Prohibition of Mixed Marriages, and Prohibition of Political Interference Acts all abolished
1987	Political turbulence in KwaZulu Natal intensifies
1988	Church leaders begin to assume place as spokesmen for political organizations
1990	State President De Klerk unbans political organizations including ANC and PAC, announces release of Mandela; Separate Amenities Act repealed; State of Emergency lifted
1994	First free democratic elections held, Nelson Mandela elected first black president of South Africa
1998	Thabo Mbeki voted in as second black South African president

Appendix Three

Selected Websites:
South Africa and Its Music

These sites are intended to give you starting points in your investigation of South Africa and its music. There is much more available in cyberspace.

South African History

http://www.robben-island.org.za
http://www.sahistory.org.za

South African Record Companies: Commercial and Archival

http://www.gallo.co.za
http://www.mg.co.za (archive)
http://www.oneworld.co.za
http://www.sabc.co.za
http://www.3rdearmusic.com

South African Music and Musicians

http://www.africanmusic.org
http://www.afribeat.com
http://www.afropop.org
http://www.allaboutjazz.com
http://www.cama.org.za
http://www.johnnyclegg.com
http://www.music.org.za

http://www.putumayo.com
http://www.sheer.co.za
http://www.tunokwe.com

South African Tourism

http://www.owls.co.za
http://www.robben-island.org.za

Purchasing South African Music

Most of the material discussed in the book is available through the major online webstores including amazon.com or barnesandnoble.com.

If you wish to purchase South African music when you travel to South Africa, there are numerous places that now sell South African recordings, but the best collection available is in the International Departures Lounge in the Johannesburg International Airport. In addition, if outside South Africa:

http://www.epinions.com has limited stock of major musicians
http://www.kalahari.net has some stock
http://www.oneworld.co.za has more stock on display, but you cannot
    purchase online from the United States
http://www.nextag.com has limited stock of major musicians

Appendix Four

Themes Common to the Study
of African Music: 1980s to Present

The study of music in Africa and the study of African music has largely been categorized in two ways: by geographical region and by concept or theme. In this section, I highlight the materials referenced at the end of the book as they pertain to these two kinds of discussion.

There are a few works listed that provide a general overview of the study of contemporary African culture (Barber 1986, 1997 a and b; Drewal 1991; Fabian 1997; Hannerz 1997; Thompson 1979). The recently published *Garland Encyclopedia of World Music: Africa* (Stone 1998) provides overview chapters on five musical regions: West Africa, North Africa, East Africa, Central Africa, and Southern Africa (see Dje-dje 1998, Wendt 1998, Cooke 1998, Kubik 1998, and Kaemmer 1998 respectively; see also Langlois 1996 and Danielson 1996 for additional North African material; Allen 1996 and Coplan 1998 for South Africa). The Garland volume provides additional pieces on individual countries but the coverage is not consistent for the entire continent. Although this volume contains a compact disc, the recordings are rather limited. They will need to be supplemented with commercially produced sound and video recordings. There are several other volumes that are concerned with popular and traditional music of the continent generally (Bender 1991, Bergman 1985, Broughton et al. 1994, Euba 1988, Ewens 1991, M. Floyd 1999, Graham 1988 and 1992, Mensah 1998, Njoku 1998, Nketia 1982 and 1998, Roberts 1998, Schmidt 1994, Stapleton and May 1990, Stewart 1992). Impey (1998) covers African popular music generally, including discussion of festivals, and the impact of the music industry on African performance. Generally speaking, I shall discuss the literature and recordings on African musical performance as follows: Arabic influences on North Africa; the pygmy sounds of Central Africa; the *griot-jeli* and drumming traditions of West Africa; the loss of Africans to the slave trade and African music in diaspora; competitiveness and the impact of Arabic music from Egypt on East Africa; the *mbira* traditions of southern Africa; and vocal music of South Africa. I have selected these themes because they have emerged out of the literature published since 1980.

West Africa

Perhaps because of the significant presence of Africans forced into the Americas through the slave trade, much of what is popularly known in the United States about African music comes from West Africa, the site of much of the slave trade. Frequently, all of African musical production is subsumed under what is specific to the Western part of the continent. For example, in the introduction to his landmark study on African drumming and sociability, ethnomusicologist John Chernoff commented in the early 1970s that the most common perception about African music outside the continent is that it was a continent of drummers. Three decades later, the stereotype of Africa remains one of drums and drummers. For those interested in drumming, there are several books and videos that explain drumming techniques as well as the social elements pertaining to drumming ensembles particularly in Nigeria and Ghana (Chernoff 1979, Euba 1990, Locke 1990, Nzewi et al. 2001). For discussion of West African *griot/jeli* traditions, see Charry 2000, Diawara 1997, Duran 1995 and 1994, Eyre 2000, Hale 1998, Jegede 1994, and Knight 1991. Additional pieces on West African popular culture, art music, and individual musicians include: Avorgbedor 2001, Collins 1992, Grebner 1997, Omojola 1997, Schmidt 1994a and b, Veal 2000, and Waterman 1997.

East Africa

There are three broad themes in writing about musical performance in East Africa. The sociability of African (and particularly Ghanaian) drumming ensembles is countered with the stress on competition (see Gunderson and Barz 2000). The impact of religious belief is another theme: for Islam and North African musical culture on the East African coastline see Askew 1997 and Fargion 1999; both Askew and Fargion also have pieces in Gunderson and Barz (2000); for the impact of gospel and mission choir music see Barz in Gunderson and Barz (2000). Additional work in popular music focuses on the guitar (see Kaye 1998, Schmidt 1994a). Fargion's work is specifically focused on women in Taraab as performers and composers.

North Africa

Aside from the general introductory material on music in North Africa (Langlois 1996, Wendt 1998), and music and Islam (Shiloah 1995), there is some discussion of music and trance in the popular imagination (Langlois 1998). My focus in North Africa is with musical performance in two countries: Algeria and Egypt, and with issues of gender, popular culture, and ethnography. The key works referred to are: Schade-Poulsen (1999) on men and Algerian popular music, and Danielson (1997) on a powerful woman singer and radio broadcaster, mother of the Arab world, Umm Kulthum.

Central Africa

There are two broad strands of music research on Central Africa in the last two decades: the popular music scene, amply covered in the general texts on African traditional and popular musics cited above, and the music of the so-called pygmies native to the central African rainforest. The pygmies have long captured the imagination of Africans and non-Africans alike. Considered some of the original inhabitants of the continent, their relationship to non-Africans has not always been so positive. Turnbull conducted landmark ethnography with a group of pygmies in the 1950s (Turnbull 1962, recently reissued). Michelle Kisliuk (1998) and Steven Feld (2000) have produced the most recent work. Feld's writing outlines the often exploitative relationship of the non-Africans to pygmy sound recordings, first produced by Turnbull and ethnomusicologist Hugo Zemp. Numerous popular musicians have used the evocative sounds of pygmy peoples to enhance their own musical performance. These include Herbie Hancock, Madonna, and Zap Mama.

Southern Africa

Several general works relate to music in southern Africa, though my main focus is obviously on the country called South Africa. Zimbabwe, and the *mbira* as both traditional and popular instrument and musical style, is written about by Berliner (1978), Brown (1998), and Turino (2000, 1998). Wells (1994) writes on traditional music in Lesotho, and Vail and White (1997) have a fascinating piece on the oral transmission of simple work-song in Mozambique. A general overview of South African popular music is provided by Coplan (1985 and 1998). Individual genres of performance include pennywhistle *Kwela* (Allen 2000), South African jazz and vaudeville (Ballantine 1993, Coplan 1985, McGregor 1995, Muller 2001 and 1996, and Rasmussen 2000 and 1999), *maskanda* (Davies 1994 and Muller 1999), gumboot dance (Muller and Fargion 1999), and *isicathamiya* (Erlmann 1999, 1995, and 1993 and Meintjes 1990). Women musicians have been the specific focus of several pieces (James 1999, Makeba 1987, Muller 2001, 2000, 1999, and 1996) and male musicians have been given some special attention as well (Ballantine 1999, 1996, and 1993, Erlmann 1999, and Rasmussen 1999).

Appendix Five

Discussion of Musical Examples on Compact Disc

Sathima Bea Benjamin, Tracks 1–5

These five tracks have been selected to convey the profound sense of connection many people of color in South Africa felt between their own struggles against racial oppression and those of African Americans in the United States in the twentieth century. Musical performance, and jazz specifically, was a key cultural medium through which the connection in struggle was articulated. The first track is a traditional African American spiritual, a song Benjamin began all of her live performances with in the 1980s. This is an excerpt of a particularly evocative and heart rending performance. The second track evokes the historical connection, made largely through sound recordings and Hollywood films that Sathima and her peers heard and watched in postwar Cape Town. "I Only Have Eyes for You" is performed by Cape Town musicians in 1999. They remember playing the song in those early years as an integral part of Cape culture. Three of Benjamin's own compositions follow. "Windsong" is a song that evokes memories of what it was like to live in Cape Town, the windy city. The memories were particularly poignant while Benjamin and Abdullah Ibrahim lived in exile in New York City, unable to return to the "Mother City" until the early 1990s. "Nations in Me" and "Africa" carry deep feelings about the struggle in South Africa, about a longing for Africa and a vision of a new nation. The latter song is remarkably prophetic for its time, a period in South African political history, the early 1980s, when there seemed to be little hope for the kind of political transformation that seemed so miraculous in the early 1990s.

TRACK 1: "Sometimes I Feel Like a Motherless Child"
Traditional
Public domain

Vocals: Sathima Bea Benjamin
Drums/Percussion: Billy Higgins
Recorded: Rudy van Gelder Studios, 1985
Reissued: Rasmussen, 2001

TRACK 2: "I Only Have Eyes for You"
Harry Warren and Al Dubin
Remick Music Corporation (ASCAP)
Vocals: Sathima Bea Benjamin
Piano: Henry February
Bass: Basil Moses
Drums: Vincent Pavitt
Arrangement: Sathima Bea Benjamin
Recorded: Cape Town, 1999
Reissued: Rasmussen, 2001

TRACK 3: "Windsong"
Sathima Bea Benjamin
Ekapa R.P.M. Publishers (ASCAP)
Vocals: Sathima Bea Benjamin
Piano: Kenny Barron
Bass: Buster Williams
Drums: Billy Higgins
Recorded: Rudy Van Gelder Studios, 1985
Reissued: Rasmussen, 2001

TRACK 4: "Nations in Me, New Nation-a-Coming"
Sathima Bea Benjamin
Ekapa R.P.M. Publishers (ASCAP)
Vocals: Sathima Bea Benjamin
Piano: Onaje Allen Gumbs
Sax and flute: Carlos Ward
Bass: Buster Williams
Drums: Billy Higgins
Arrangement: Sathima Bea Benjamin
Recorded: Rudy Van Gelder Studios, 1983
Reissued: Rasmussen, 2001

TRACK 5: "Africa"
Sathima Bea Benjamin

Ekapa R.P.M. Publishers (ASCAP)
Vocals: Sathima Bea Benjamin
Piano: Onaje Allen Gumbs
Bass: Buster Williams
Drums: Billy Higgins
Arrangement: Sathima Bea Benjamin
Recorded: Rudy van Gelder Studios, 1983
Reissued: Rasmussen, 2001

Isicathamiya, Tracks 6–7

These two tracks are field recordings of rehearsals of *isicathamiya*. The first example is a recording of one *isicathamiya* group performing at the all-night choir competitions held weekly in the YMCA Hall on Beatrice Street, Durban. The group starts out at the back of the hall, and slowly moves forward. Their stepping is quiet at the start, as they move forward to the stage, where the judges are seated. The overall performance moves from soft stepping, synchronized, catlike movements of singers, onto the stage, where the group leader stands in front of the rest of the singers. You can hear the group's supporters applauding at intervals throughout the performance. On a couple of occasions, the applause signals support for a woman—girlfriend or wife—who has approached one of the singers, and claimed him for herself. She stakes her claim by giving him some money, or putting a piece of her own jewelry onto his uniform. About two-thirds of the way through the performance, the singers start to dance together, stepping on the wooden stage in a more pronounced manner. At the end of the song with steps, they form a line and proceed off the stage to the back of the hall.

On Track 7, Traditional Music Association co-founder Paulus Msimango explains to me what is unusual about this group: they have a woman alto. It is hard to really distinguish her voice from the male singers.

TRACK 6: Beatrice Street YMCA, Durban
Field recording by Carol Muller, Durban, 1996
Isicathamiya "Praktisa"

TRACK 7: Xolo Homeboys rehearsal
Field recording by Carol Muller, Durban, 1996
Explanation by Paulus Msimango (now deceased)

Tracks 8–15, Zulu *Maskanda* and Gumboot Dance

These eight tracks provide a detailed soundscape of *maskanda* performance, both as a highly skilled singer-songwriter guitar tradition (Thami Vilakazi) in the style of *isiZulu,* and as the Zulu *maskanda* sounds used to accompany gumboot dance. The maskanda style represented here, embodied in the guitar, violin, and concertina, emerged from the southern coastal region of KwaZulu Natal, and is known as *Umzansi.*

Blanket Mkhize's guitar playing harkens back to an earlier style, *ukuvamba* (vamping chords), rather than the *ukupika* (picking style) of Thami Vilakazi. Blanket's guitar playing includes the scraping sounds that harken back to the friction musical bow, and forward to the use of the violin, so I have placed his friction style of guitar playing next to the track with the violin playing.

While the musicians who accompany gumboot dance do so by providing a basic rhythmic groove, a largely improvised, heavily repetitive cyclical accompaniment, Thami Vilakazi's *maskanda* style has reached the height of excellent *maskanda* performance. His music is discussed further in the specific tracks below.

TRACK 8: Blanket Mkhize
Field recording by Carol Muller, Durban, 1996
Zulu *maskanda* guitar with comb

TRACK 9: Friend of Blanket Mkhize
Field recording by Carol Muller, Durban, 1996
Zulu *maskanda* concertina

TRACK 10: Friend of Blanket Mkhize
Field recording by Carol Muller, Durban, 1996
Zulu *maskanda* violin

TRACK 11: "Chuning"
Field recording by Carol Muller, Durban, December 14, 1994
Thami Vilakazi, composer and guitarist

The "chuning" here reminds me of the chimes of grandfather clocks present in many white homes in South Africa in my childhood.

TRACK 12: "Awusho Ndodana"
Field recording by Carol Muller, Durban, December 14, 1994

Thami Vilakazi, composer and guitarist
Song translation: Sazi Dlamini

Indodana yami	*My Son*
Awusho ndodana uyitholeph'indawo	Say my son, where did you find it?
Awusho ndodana uyitholeph'indawo	
Awusho mfana wami uyitholeph'indawo	Say, my boy, where did you find it?
Awusho ndodana uyitholeph'indawo	Say my son, where have you found a place?
Awusho ndodana uyitholeph'indawo	
Awusho mfana wami uyitholeph'indawo	Say my boy, where did you find it?
Awusho ndodana uyitholeph'indawo	
Musukufihla ndodana	Out with it, my son
Iqondo liyabaqed'abantu	This [sexual disease] wipes out people
Musukufihla mfana wami	Out with it my son
Iqondo likuqondile	The disease is on top of you
Musukufihla mfana wami	Out with it my boy
Ilumbo liyabathath'abantu	The affliction takes people away
emhlabeni bo	from the face of the earth
Abanye babo abasekho emhlabeni	Some of them are no longer on this earth
Abanye babo bayagula	Some of them are ill
Balel'esibedlela	They are sleeping in the hospital
Abanye babo abasekho emhlabeni	Some of them . . .
Abanye babo bayagula	
Balel'esbedlela	
Abanye babo abasekho emhlabeni	
Abanye babo bayagula	
Balel'esbedlela	
Awusho ndodana uyitholeph'indawo	Say my son, where did you find it?

[Self Praises]

Zasha phela madoda kuChakide	Men, its burning from Chakide
Ugobekanje bethi bamkakile	Bent like this, they say they have surrounded him
Kwamphosel'uhlamvu	Threw a grain down
Bathi bayaluthatha	They try to pick it up
Bataphuna isitingi senkukhu	They soil their hands with chicken shit
uChakide waphuma kanje	Chakide comes out on the other side
Kwath'angilale [A saying]	[With laughter] I nearly fell sleep
Umahlalel'okade wahlala	The longtime unemployed
Evuk'ekuseni ath'uyemsebenzini	He woke in the morning saying he was going to work
Kant'uyeshebeeni abuyelapho	But he was going to the shebeen and from there
Ayifak'induku	He wielded a stick
Athi kadulelephi izolo	Saying, "Where did you sleep last night?"
Ungabaleki uze ngala	Don't run this way
Uma esekushaya wena	When he's beating you
Uzongixabanisa	You will cause a quarrel
Kubesengathi ubulele kwami	It will seem like you spent a night with me
Kanti angikwazi	Whereas I don't know you
Wangiphika futhi ngikweshela	You refused me when I proposed to you
Hah!	Hah!
Ji!	Ji!
Usehleli phezulu-ke manje	Now he's right on top
UChakide ekhanda kulendoda	Chakide on top of this man's head
Ilibele ukumvimba ubala	Trying in vain to stop him [Chakide]
Abangani bayo	His friends
Bayayibuza ukuthi	Are asking
Ubani lapho wemfowethu	"Who is that there, my brother?"
Hayi khululekani nina khohlwani yimina	"No, you relax and forget about me."
Khon'uChakide la	"It is Chakide here."

TRACK 13: "Kungcono Khona"
Field recording by Carol Muller, Durban, December 14, 1994

Thami Vilakazi, composer and guitarist
Song translation: Sazi Dlamini

Kungcono khona ngizihlalele	It's better that I stay like this
Kunalento engiyibonayo	Than what I am seeing
Kungcono khona ngihlalele Baba	It's better that I stay like this, father
Kunalento engiyibonayo	
Ngilunge mina ngizihlalele	
Kuna lento engiyibonayo	
Kungcono khona ngizihlalele	
Kunalento engiyibonayo	
Kungcono khona ngihlelel Baba	
Kunalento engiyibonayo	
Kungcone khona ngizihlalele	
Kunalento engiyibonayo	
Ngilunge mina ngizihlalele Baba	
Kuna lento engiyibonayo	

[Story]

Akenithulenini phela kenginixoxele	Be quiet while I tell you a story
Ngitholiphepha lapha incwadi encane	I received a paper, a short letter
Ngisukenaye lomuntu la Ethekweni	Having left Durban with this person
Ngimuse ekhaya afik'agilimkhuba	Taking her home only for her to break taboos
Aqomabafana lababelusa izinkomo	Falling in love with herdboys
Ngitheng'isidwaba	I bought the skirt for marriage
Ngithi ngithengelumakhoti	Saying I am buying for the bride
Athi isidwaba siyamusinda	She says the skirt is heavy
Ngeke asifake	She won't wear it
Usekhohliwe ukuthi ufun'umendo	She's forgotten she seeks marriage
Ucabang'ukweqa manje ashon'eGoli	She's contemplating running off to Johannesburg
Uthenengakeqi nje wabanjwa ubaba	But before doing so, my father caught her
Eshuk'igudu la emva kwendlu ngenhla	Rolling a joint behind the house

Wakhuz'ibhadi ubab'ebon'imikhuba	My father was appalled at the spectacle
Abizumana ukuba azombukisa	He called my mother to see for herself
Kuthe kunjalo-ke washaya wachitha	Immediately she ran away
Umakhot'wami lona esebhek'eGoli	My bride to Johannesburg
Uma ngithi ngiyabuza ukuthi kwenzenjani	When I asked her what is wrong
Ahleke kancane nje athi gwegwegwe	She just laughs a little, gwegwegwe
Unginika malini njengoba wangithath'eThekwini	What do you give me having taken me from Durban
Wathi uyongithengel'inyama	Saying you are going to buy me meat
Kanti uyongidlis'imfino	But feeding me wild spinach
Awukahle phela khoti ukutheth'ekhaya	Hold on a little, my bride, lower your voice at home
Ubab'uzothini ngoba usafika emzini	What will my father say? You are new in the family
Anginamsebenzi mina ngizobuyel'ekhaya	I don't care, I will go back home
Yeyeni webantu kanti eThekweni kunjani	Oh my, my, how then is Durban?

[Self Praises]

Zasha phela madoda kuChakide	Men, its burning for Chakide
uPhumekanje bathi bamkakile	He went like this when they surrounded him
Wabaphosela uhlamvu	He threw them a kernel
Bathi bayalunqaka	When they caught it
Kanti bathinta isitingi senkhukhu	They touched chicken shit
UChakide waphuma kanje	Chakide comes out the other side
Yini le sekhanda lakho wena?	What's that on your head?
Izinwele zami	It's my hair
Uhleli phezulu wethu?	Is he on top brother?
Ungabe usayiphath	Don't mention it.
Ngilunge mina ngizihlalele Baba	I am alright as I am, Father
Kunalento engiyibonayo	Better than what I am seeing around me.
Ngilunge mina ngizihlalele Baba	
Kunalento engiyibonay	

TRACK 14: *Maskanda* group accompaniment for gumboot dance, without dancers
Field recording by Carol Muller, Durban, September 1996
Guitar: Blanket Mkhize
Violin, concertina: friends of Blanket Mkhize

TRACK 15: *Maskanda* accompaniment for gumboot dance, with dancers
Field recording by Carol Muller, Durban, September 1996
Guitar: Blanket Mkhize
Violin, concertina: friends of Blanket Mkhize
Dancers: Mkhize and sons

Shembe Liturgy, Tracks 16–17

The first track provides an excerpt of congregational liturgy, hymn singing, and prayers taken from a morning service held at Ebuhleni in September 1996. The last track has the "Ameni! Oyincwele" calls, which translated mean Amen, He is Holy. These are the words used to praise the person of Shembe when he joins the congregation on the Sabbath, and other occasions, after the liturgical part of the service is complete.

TRACK 16: *Ibandla lamaNazaretha,* Liturgy for Morning Prayers
Field Recording, Carol Muller, September 1996, Ebuhleni
Excerpt of liturgy in Zulu and English translation. We are about 6 minutes into the liturgical recitation and singing:

31. *Uma wenake uyisizukulwana sika Adam no Eva, okwathiwa kuye ensimini yase Eden lima, ulinde, ubonakala uthabatha isimo sobunja uyazethuka wena ngokungathandi ukusebenza.*

31. If you then are of the generation of Adam and Eve, to whom it was said in the Garden of Eden, plough and watch, you insult yourself by not wanting to work, and are seen to take on the form of a dog.

32. ISILANDELO SEBANDLA (chanted in call and response)
      (0:07) *Nkulunkulu onamandla onke,*
      Yise wabo bonke abamkhonzayo,
      Busisa ukuvuka kwethu kwanamhlanje,
      Usigcine ngomsa wakhe. Amen.
32. CONGREGATIONAL RESPONSE
      God almighty

Father of all those who worship him
Bless our awakening this day
And keep us in your mercy. Amen.

33. (0:19) *Ngokuba kwathiwa umuntu uyokudla umvuzo wezithukuthuku zezandla zakhe, washo uThixo ka Adam.*

33. For it was said that a human being shall eat of the product of the sweat of his hands, thus said the God of Adam.

34. *Wathi uNkulunkulu ngokuqinisa umuntu uyokudla ejulukile. Uyawaphikisa wena lamazwi na? Uyathokoza yini ngawe uNkulunkulu uma udla ukudla ungakusebenzanga ungakujulukelanga ebusweni bakho.*

34. God said emphatically that a human being shall eat only after sweating. Do you oppose these words? Does God rejoice over you when he sees you eating food you have not labored for by the sweat of your brow?

35. (0:38) *Uthanda ukudla ungakujulukelanga. Ubeka isono phezu kwabakuncishayo kanti isono sakho.*

35. You like to eat food that you have not sweated for. You blame those who deny you, when it is rather your own fault.

36. *Amehlo ka Nkulunkulu ayathokoza yini ngawe, uma udla ukudla ungakujulukelanga ukwebile loko kudla.*

36. Do the eyes of God rejoice in you? If you eat food that you have not sweated for, you have stolen that food.

37. ISIHLABELELO (0:52)
Owasinikela ebuhlungwini bazo,
Ngenxa yezono zethu.
Mbukhishwe ubuhlungu bazo, (last two lines repeat)
Ngalelo gama lakho.

37. HYMN
To whose poison you handed us over
Because of our sins.
Remove their poison
Through that name of yours.

38. ISIHLABELELO
Ibusise Nkosi Baba,
Imisebenzi yezandla zethu,
Singadingi singesweli, (last two lines repeat)
Thina bantu bakho.

38. HYMN
    Bless Lord, our Father
    The work of our hands
    That we will have neither need nor want
    We who are your people.

39. *Unkulunkulu akathokozi uma ebona dula ukudla ungakusebenzanga nakancane. Noma uyitombazana uyivila uyavama ukuthakaza ngokuthatha izinto zamanye amantombazane. Wenake ungeneleni esimilweni esibi kangaka na? Sokuba uNkulunkulu akubone usosizini nobuso bakho bunyukubele ngenxa yokulamba.*

39. God does not rejoice if he sees you eating food for which you have not performed anything, even the smallest amount of work. Even you, lazy girl, you frequently make a nuisance of yourself by taking the belongings of other girls. Why have you taken on such bad character? God sees you in sorrow and your face haggard from hunger.

TRACK 17: *Ibandla lamaNazaretha* "Ameni! Oyincwele!"
Spoken at the end of the liturgy
Field recording, Carol Muller, Ebuhleni, September 1996

Shembe Hymns and Gospel Songs, Tracks 18–22

The remaining five tracks focus on Shembe hymns and represent transformations in the traditional style of performance to hymn singing accompanied on the organ. These arrangements of the hymns in four-part harmony (soprano, alto, tenor, and bass), sung by a youth choir, are intended to help members learn to sing with organ accompaniment, and to foster the creation of a new repertory of gospel style songs sung to and about Shembe (rather than Jesus, for example).

In Track 18, the traditional leader of congregational singing begins singing the song by coming in on the pitch comfortable for his voice. The organist is required to find where the leader has pitched his voice, and to then add chordal accompaniment to this singing. In Track 19, we hear the youth choir formed by first church organist Bongani Mthethwa. He has arranged one of the hymns in four-part harmony and plays a more conventional piano introduction and accompaniment for the singing. The next track gives an example of the same youth choir preparing to compete in the annual Youth Choir competition for Shembe members. Here they are learning the more "classical" repertory (that is, conventional four-part harmony) by first learning to sing the piece using solfege, that is, learning pitch using do re mi fa sol la ti do. The next track has a melody you probably know—it is from the Christmas carol "Joy to the World," transformed into a four-part harmony arrangement with Zulu language words that pertain to praise of Shembe. The last track provides an excerpt from a commercial recording made by church member Nathoya Mbatha in a studio using a keyboard and multitrack recording technique. He is transforming the song style to suit a more youthful audience.

TRACK 18: Nazarite Hymn Singing with Organ Accompaniment
Field recording, Carol Muller, Ebuhleni, July 1991

TRACK 19: Nazarite Hymn with Piano Accompaniment, arranged in SATB
Field recording, Bongani Mthethwa, ca. 1989, used with permission

TRACK 20: Youth Choir Rehearsal singing in Solfege (do re mi fa sol la ti do)
Field recording, Carol Muller, Durban, November 1991

TRACK 21: Youth Choir Performance in "Classic" Style
Field recording, Carol Muller, Durban, July 1991

TRACK 22: Nathoya Mbatha's Gospel Version of Shembe Hymn
Mbatha recording used with permission from Mbatha and Rev. Shembe, recorded Richards Bay, ca. 1995

Glossary

a cappella   sung without instrumental accompaniment

African Jazz and Variety   a traveling show produced starting in 1952 by white impresario Alfred Herbert using black and Coloured musicians performing African-inspired jazz and variety

Afrikaans   language that emerged out of colonial encounter in South Africa, largely derived from Dutch, first written in Arabic by Cape Muslim clerics.

Afrikaner   people of European descent who speak Afrikaans

amadoda   Zulu word meaning "men"

amadoubles   team performances of gumboot dance routines

amantombazane   Zulu word for "girls"

apartheid   the system of racial segregation legislated by the Afrikaner Nationalists in 1948 in South Africa

Asian   in the apartheid structure in South Africa, Asian largely referred to people from India and Japan; the Chinese came as laborers and intermarried with those called "Coloured"

Bantu (languages)   "bantu" literally means "people." Bantu languages in South Africa include Zulu, Xhosa, Ndebele, and North and South Sotho

Bantustan   the name for a black homeland in the apartheid days, the rural reserves where all people of a particular ethnic group were forced to live

Bhaca   a largely Zulu speaking people, who live in southern KwaZulu Natal

bioscope   the colloquial name for movie theater

call and response   a format of performance common in Africa, in which a soloist calls a melodic line, and a group responds, usually by repeating what the soloist has called

Chakide   a cunning mythical being, like a trickster, in Zulu mythology

chuning   the tuning of a Zulu guitar or concertina

Coloured   those defined as of "mixed" race

Coloured Jazz and Variety   similar to African Jazz and Variety, but focused on traditions coming out of Cape Town's working class Coloured communities

concertina   a small, simple, and less expensive version of a piano accordion

Ebuhleni   the current Shembe headquarters

Ekuphakameni   the original Shembe headquarters, also used to refer to heaven

Ethiopianism   a late nineteenth-century form of religious independence which allowed for varying degrees of assimilation of European culture; begun in response to mission Christianity

ethnomusicology   the field of musicology that examines music as a cultural practice, and which historically is concerned with music outside of Europe

fanakalo   the language of command developed among linguistically diverse migrant workers, especially in the mines of South Africa

fundamental   the basic pitch, usually in the lower register, that produces overtones/partials

ghoema   drum performance by slaves from Indonesia and Malaysia in eighteenth and nineteenth century Cape Town; spawned *ghommaliedjes,* songs with a mixture of Dutch and Malay origins, sung in the Cape

gospel music   in South Africa, gospel music takes its cue from the United States, but is sung in local languages, and has its own body of locally composed songs

Graceland   the controversial album by Paul Simon and several other musicians released in 1986

griot/griotte   a traditional poet-historian-musician in West Africa

gumboot dance   a neo-traditional dance form developed on the mines by the amaBhaca migrant workers

IBA (Independent Broadcast Authority) established to help South African radio and television become more focused on South African music and culture, and to more fairly represent South Africans in its broadcasting

ibandla lamaNazaretha the congregation of Nazaretha, the religious group founded by Isaiah Shembe

ibombing the loud, almost shouting vocal style of early *isicathamiya*

imbongi a Zulu praise poet (like a griot)

imiNazaretha the white prayer gown worn by followers of Shembe that identifies them as Nazaretha

inkhonzo congregational worship style among followers of Shembe

isangoma traditional healer

isicathamiya the close harmony, SATB-style performance of Zulu-speaking male migrant workers

isicathulo literally means shoe, also refers to the elite styles of gumboot dance

isingles improvised solo dancing by gumboot dancers

isishameni style of song and dance from the Colenso region of KwaZulu Natal

isiZulu style of *maskanda* performance from northern KwaZulu Natal

isteps the dance routines of *isicathamiya* performers

izihlabelelo zamaNazaretha the hymns of the Nazaretha composed by Isaiah and Galilee Shembe and compiled into a hymnal in 1940

kam Blanket Mkhize plays guitar with a hair comb that he rubs against the strings, much like a violin is scraped

khoi short for Khoi-khoi or Khoisan, the indigenous peoples of South Africa

King Kong the first African musical with black South African performers, musicians, and narrative; performed in South Africa, and London in late 1950s

Klopskamer the headquarters of each performing troupe in Cape Town's New Year's celebrations

kora   a West African harp-like instrument

kwela   a pennywhistle style of performance developed on the streets by young boys in South Africa in the 1940s

langarm   literally "long arm," refers to ballroom dance in Cape Town

makwaya   a Zulu version of the word "choir"; refers to mission-derived choral performance

marabi   popular music developed in working-class drinking establishments; the forerunner of South African jazz

maskanda   literally means "musician," refers to Zulu musicians using European instruments

mbaqanga   originally called "African jazz," refers to studio-produced Zulu music from the early 1960s continuing through to contemporary popular music scene

mbira   a generic term for the Central African "thumb piano," a metal-tongued instrument popular in Zimbabwe

mbube   literally means "lion"; refers to early prototype of *isicathamiya*

moppie   upbeat comic song sung by working-class Coloured people from Cape Town, often in New Year's festivities

mqashiyo   style of popular music in Johannesburg townships and on radio

music culture   all the cultural elements that make up a musical performance, including the social organization of a performance, beliefs about that performance, its material culture, and its history

mvangeli   evangelist in *ibandla lamaNazaretha*

nagtroepe   night troupes who entertain communities in Cape Town at New Year's

Nhlangakaze   literally means "the first or great reed," name of holy mountain of Shembe

Nguni   collective term for Bantu-speaking peoples in South Africa, including the Zulu, Xhosa, Swazi, Pedi, and Sotho

ngoma   a dance, song, healing, drumming complex, also refers to particular style of song and dance among Zulu-speaking men

Nkosi sikelel'iAfrika a song composed by Enoch Sontonga that was the official anthem of the African National Congress, and has now been combined with "Die Stem," the old South African anthem, to create a new anthem for a democractic South Africa

Ohlange the valley in which Isaiah Shembe created his first community in KwaZulu Natal

overtones/partials tones produced by a resonant lower register fundamental tone, common in musical bow playing

Paradis the name of the Shembe open-air temple

passbook/"dompas" the document required by all black and Coloured South Africans if they were to live in the urban areas in the apartheid era

ramkie small three- or four-stringed guitar, usually plucked; developed by Khoi people in the eighteenth century

Shembe, Isaiah founder of *ibandla lamaNazaretha;* succeeded by son, Johannes Galilee; succeeded by Galilee's brother Amos; and present leader Vimbeni; Londa Shembe, son of J. G. Shembe, sought to lead after death of J. G., but was murdered

Sun City the casino in the South African homeland of Bophutatswana where foreign musicians played when they were not supposed to travel to South Africa

township places close to major urban areas where black South Africans established living quarters

Township Jazz show from late 1950s created by white South African, but performed by black South Africans and featuring the transformed sounds of American music to suit local taste

tradition also **invented tradition**, how cultural ways are transmitted from one generation to the next; if they are invented, it is usually a cultural practice that is self-consciously fashioned at a specific moment in time to meet a political need, such as defining a newly constituted nation

ukusina sacred dance in *ibandla lamaNazaretha*

umgido festivals of sacred dance in *ibandla lamaNazaretha*

umshumayeli preacher in *ibandla lamaNazaretha*

umzansi the area south of the city of Durban

wimoweh   the word used to replace "mbube" when the song traveled to the United States in the 1950s

Xhosa   a language and people who speak one of the "click" languages, related to the Zulu language; Nelson Mandela is Xhosa-speaking

Zionist   religious independent movement arose out of the Zions Kerk and also related to Zion City in Illinois, United States

Zulu   those who speak Zulu as a first language and who identify culturally as "Zulu"

References

BOOKS AND JOURNAL ARTICLES

Allen, Lara. "An Archive of Black South African Popular Music: Recently Released Reissues." *British Journal of Ethnomusicology,* 5 (1996): 177–180.

_____. "Kwela: The Structure and Sound of Pennywhistle Music." In *Composing the Music of Africa: Composition, Interpretation, and Realization,* edited by Malcolm Floyd, 227–264. Brookfield, VT: Ashgate, 1999.

Anderson, Benedict. *Imagined Communities: On the Origins and Spread of Nationalism.* London: Verso, 1983.

Andersson, Muff. *Music in the Mix: The Story of South African Popular Music.* Johannesburg: Ravan Press, 1981.

Askew, Kelly. *Performing the Nation: Swahili Musical and Cultural Politics in Tanzania.* Chicago: University of Chicago Press, 2002.

Avorgbedor, Daniel. "'It's a Great Song!' Halo Performance as Literary Production." *Research in African Literatures,* 32/2 (2001): 17–43.

Baines, Gary. "Catalyst or Detonator? Local Music Quotas and the Current South African Music 'Explosion.'" *Social Dynamics,* 24/1 (1998): 66–87.

Ballantine, Christopher. "Looking to the USA: The Politics of Male Close-Harmony Song and Style in South Africa During the 1940s and 1950s." *Popular Music,* 18/1 (1999): 1–17.

_____. "Joseph Shabalala: Chronicles of an African Composer." *British Journal of Ethnomusicology,* 5/2 (1996): 1–37.

_____. *Marabi Nights: Early South African Jazz and Vaudeville.* Johannesburg: Ravan, 1993.

Barber, Karen, ed. *Readings in African Popular Culture.* Bloomington: Indiana University Press, 1997a.

_____. "Preliminary Notes on Audiences in Africa." *Africa,* 67/3 (1997b): 347–362.

_____. "Popular Arts in Africa." *African Studies Review,* 30/3 (1986): 1–78.

Bender, Wolfgang. *Sweet Mother: Modern African Music*. Chicago: University of Chicago Press, 1991.

Bergman, Billy. *African Pop: Goodtime Kings*. Dorset, UK: Blandford Press, 1985.

Berliner, Paul. *The Soul of Mbira: Music and Traditions of the Shona People of Zimbabwe*. Berkeley: University of California Press, 1978.

Bickford Smith, Victoria, Elizabeth van Heyningen, and Nigel Worden, eds. *Cape Town in the Twentieth Century*. Cape Town: David Philip, 1999.

Blacking, John. *Music, Culture, and Experience*. Edited posthumously by Reginal Byron. Chicago: University of Chicago Press, 1997?

Broughton, Simon, et al., eds. *World Music: The Rough Guide*. New York: Penguin Books, 1999.

Brown, Ernest. "The Guitar and the Mbira: Resilience, Assimilation, and Pan-Africanism in Zimbabwean Music." *World of Music*, 36/2 (1994): 73–117.

Bryant, A. *Zulu-English Dictionary*. Unpublished Manuscript in Killie Campbell Library, University of Natal, South Africa, n.d.

Chamber of Mines. *1920 Miner's Companion in Zulu*. Johannesburg: Central News Agency, 1920.

———. *1938 Miner's Companion in English, Afrikaans, Sesutho, and Mine Kaffir*. Johannesburg: Central News Agency, 1938.

———. *The Miner's Dictionary in English, Afrikaans, and Fanakalo*. Johannesburg: Central News Agency, 1974.

Chapman, Michael. *Southern African Literatures*. London: Longmans, 1996.

Charry, Eric. "The Grand Mande Guitar Tradition of the Western Sahel and Savannah." *World of Music*, 36/2 (1994): 21–61.

———. *Mande Music: Traditional and Modern Music of the Maninka and Mandinka of Western Africa*. Chicago: University of Chicago Press, 2000.

Chernoff, John. *African Rhythm and African Sensibility: Aesthetics and Social Action in African Musical Idioms*. Chicago: University of Chicago Press, 1979.

Cockrell, Dale. "Of Gospel Hymns, Minstrel Shows, and Jubilee Singers: Toward Some Black South African Musics." *American Music*, 5/4 (1987): 417–432.

Collins, John. *West African Pop Roots*. Philadelphia: Temple University Press, 1992.

Comaroff, Jean. *Body of Power, Spirit of Resistance*. Chicago: University of Chicago Press, 1985.

Cooke, Peter. "East Africa: An Introduction." In *The Garland Encyclopedia of World Music: Africa,* edited by Ruth Stone, 598–609. New York: Garland, 1998.

Coplan, David. "Popular Music in South Africa." In *The Garland Encyclopedia of World Music: Africa,* edited by Ruth Stone, 759–780. New York: Garland, 1998.

_____. *In The Time of Cannibals: Word Music of South Africa's Basotho Migrants.* Chicago: University of Chicago Press, 1994.

_____. "Ethnomusicology and the Meaning of Tradition." In *Ethnomusicology and Modern Music History,* edited by Stephen Blum, et al., 34–60. Urbana: University of Illinois Press, 1991.

_____. *In Township Tonight! South Africa's Black City Music and Theatre.* New York: Longmans, 1985.

Danielson, Virginia. *The Voice of Egypt: Umm Kulthum, Arabic Song, and Egyptian Society in the Twentieth Century.* Chicago: University of Chicago Press, 1997.

_____. "New Nightingales of the Nile: Popular Music in Egypt Since the 1970s." *Popular Music,* 15/3 (1996): 299–311.

Davidson, Basil. *The African Past: Chronicles from Antiquity to Modern Times.* NY: Grosser and Dunlap, 1964.

Davies, Nollene. "The Guitar in Zulu Maskanda Tradition." *World of Music,* 36/2 (1994): 118–137.

De Certeau, Michel. *The Practice of Everyday Life.* Translated by Steven Randall. Los Angeles: University of California Press, 1988 [1984].

Dje-dje, Jacqueline. "West Africa: An Introduction." In *The Garland Encyclopedia of World Music: Africa,* edited by Ruth Stone, 442–470. New York: Garland, 1998.

Diawara, Mamadou. "Mande Oral Popular Culture Revisited by the Electronic Media." In *Readings in African Popular Culture,* edited by Karen Barber, 40–47. Bloomington: Indiana University Press, 1997.

Doke, C. M., et al. *Zulu-English, English-Zulu Dictionary.* Johannesburg: University of the Witwatersrand Press, 1990.

Drewal, Margaret. "The State of Research on Performance in Africa." *African Studies Review,* 34/3 (1991): 1–64.

Duran, Lucy. "Birds of Wasulu: Freedom of Expression and Expressions of Freedom in the Popular Music of Southern Mali." *British Journal of Ethnomusicology,* 4 (1995): 101–134.

_____. "Music Created by God." In *World Music: The Rough Guide.* Edited by Simon Broughton, et al., 243–259. New York: Penguin Books, 1999 (1994).

Erlmann, Veit. *Music, Modernity, and the Global Imagination.* New York: Oxford University Press, 1999.

_____. *Nightsong: Performance, Power, and Practice in Black South African Performance.* Chicago: Chicago University Press, 1996.

_____. *African Stars: Studies in Black South African Performance.* Chicago: Chicago University Press, 1991.

Euba, Akin. "Text Setting in African Composition." *Research in African Literatures,* 32/2 (2001): 119–133.

_____. *Yoruba Drumming: The Dundun Tradition.* Bayreuth, Germany: Eckhard Breitinger, 1990.

_____. *Essays on Music in Africa.* Bayreuth, Germany: IWALEWA Haus, Bayreuth University Press, 1988.

Ewens, Graeme. *Africa O-Ye! A Celebration of African Music.* London: Guinness, 1991.

Eyre, Banning. *In Griot Time: An American Guitarist in Mali.* Philadelphia: Temple University Press, 2000.

Fabian, Johannes. "Popular Culture in Africa: Findings and Conjectures." In *Readings in African Popular Culture,* edited by Karen Barber, 18–28. Bloomington: Indiana University Press, 1997.

Fargion, Janet Topp. "Consumer-Led Creation: Taarab Music Composition in Zanzibar." In *Composing the Music of Africa: Composition, Interpretation, and Realization,* edited by Malcolm Floyd. Brookfield, VT: Ashgate, 1999.

Farmer, Henry George. "The Music of Islam." In *The New Oxford History of Music, Vol. 1,* edited by Egon Wellesz, 421–477. Oxford: Oxford University Press, 1957.

Feld, Steven. "The Poetics and Politics of Pygmy Pop." In *Western Music and Its Others,* edited by Georgina Born and Desmond Hesmondhalgh, 254–279. Berkeley: University of California Press, 2000.

Floyd, Malcolm. *Composing the Music of Africa: Composition, Interpretation, and Realization.* Brookfield, VT: Ashgate, 1999.

Floyd, Samuel. *The Power of Black Music: Interpreting Its History from Africa to the United States.* New York: Oxford University Press, 1995.

Gaitskell, Deborah. "Devout Christianity? A Century of African Women's Christianity in South Africa." In *Women and Gender in Southern Africa until 1945,* edited by Cherryl Walker, 251–272. Cape Town: David Philip, 1990.

Garafalo, Reebee. *Rockin' the Boat: Mass Music and Mass Movements.* Boston: South End Press, 1992.

Gassert, Richard. "Bop 'Til You Drop: An Oral Study of Popular Music Cultures in Cape Town from the Late 1940s to the Early 1960s." Unpublished Honors Essay, University of Cape Town, 1988.

Gunner, Liz, ed. *Politics and Performance: Theater, Poetry, and Performance in Southern Africa.* Johannesburg: Witwatersrand University Press, 2001.

Gunner, Liz, and Mafika Gwala, eds. and transl. *Musho! Zulu Popular Praises.* East Lansing: Michigan State University Press, 1991.

Gutsche, Thelma. *The History and Social Significance of Motion Pictures in South Africa.* Cape Town: Howard Timmons, 1972.

Hadebe, Jonney. Program notes for South African Railways Gumboot Dance performance. ND.

Hajdu, David. *Lush Life: A Biography of Billy Strayhorn.* New York: Farrar, 1996.

Hale, Thomas. *Griots and Griottes: Masters of Words and Music.* Bloomington: Indiana University Press, 1998.

Hamm, Charles. *Putting Popular Music in Its Place.* Cambridge: Cambridge University Press, 1995.

Hannerz, Ulf. "Sophiatown: The View from Afar." In *Readings in African Popular Culture,* edited by Karen Barber, 164–170. Bloomington: Indiana University Press, 1997.

Hexham, Irving, ed. *The Scriptures of the AmaNazaretha of Ekuphakameni: Selected Writings of the Zulu Prophets Isaiah and Londa Shembe.* Translated by Londa Shembe and Hans-Jürgen Becken, with an essay by G. C. Oosthuizen. Calgary: University of Calgary Press, 1994.

Hexham, Irving, and Robert Papini, eds. *The Catechism of the Nazarites and Related Writings.* Translated by Hans-Jürgen Becken and Phyllis Zungu. Lewiston, NY: E. Mellen Press, 2002.

Hexham, Irving, and G. C. Oosthuizen, eds. *The Story of Isaiah Shembe.* Translated by Hans-Jürgen Becken. Lewiston, NY: E. Mellen Press, c. 1996.

Hofmeyr, Isabel. "John Bunyan, His Chair, and a Few Other Relics: Orality, Literacy, and the Limits of Area Studies." In *African Words, African Voices: Critical Practices in Oral History,* edited by Luise White, et al., 78–90. Bloomington: Indiana University Press, 2001.

Holiday, Billie, and William Dufty. *Lady Sing the Blues: The Searing Autobiography of an American Musical Legend.* New York: Penguin, 1984 [1956].

Hughes, Heather. "'A Lighthouse for African Womanhood': Inanda Seminary, 1869–1945." In *Women and Gender in Southern Africa until 1945,* edited by Cherryl Walker, 197–220. Cape Town: David Philip, 1990.

Impey, Angela. "Popular Music in Africa." In *The Garland Encyclopedia of World Music: Africa,* edited by Ruth Stone, 415–437. New York: Garland, 1998.

International Library of African Music. *Proceedings of the [South African] Symposiae on Ethnomusicology.* Grahamstown: Rhodes University, 1980ff.

James, Deborah. *Songs of the Women Migrants: Performance and Identity in South Africa.* Edinburgh: Edinburgh University Press, 1999.

Jegede, Tunde. *African Classical Music and the Griot Tradition.* London: Diabate Arts, 1994.

Kaemmer, John. "Southern Africa: An Introduction." In *The Garland Encyclopedia of World Music: Africa,* edited by Ruth Stone, 700–721. New York: Garland, 1998.

Kaye, Andrew. "The Guitar in Africa." In *The Garland Encyclopedia of World Music: Africa,* edited by Ruth Stone, 350–369. New York: Garland, 1998.

Kiernan, Jim. "Canticles of Zion: Song as Word and Action in Zulu Zionist Discourse." *Journal of Religion in Africa,* 20/2 (1990): 169–179.

Kirby, Percival. *The Musical Instruments of the Native Races of South Africa.* Johannesburg: Witwatersrand University Press, 1968 (1934).

Kisliuk, Michelle. *Seize the Dance! BaAka Musical Life and the Ethnography of Performance.* Oxford: Oxford University Press, 1988.

Knight, Roderic. "Music Out of Africa: Mande Jaliya in Paris." *World of Music,* 33/1 (1991): 52–69.

Kubik, Gerhard. *Africa and the Blues.* Jackson: University Press of Mississippi, 1999.

_____. "Central Africa: An Introduction." In *The Garland Encyclopedia of World Music: Africa,* edited by Ruth Stone, 650–680. New York: Garland, 1998.

Langlois, Tony. "The Gnawa of Oujda: Music at the Margins in Morocco." *World of Music,* 40/1 (1998): 135–156.

_____. "The Local and the Global in North African Popular Music." *Popular Music,* 15/3 (1996): 259–273.

Layne, Valmont. "A History of Dance and Jazz Band Performance in the Western Cape in the Post-1945 Era." Unpublished M.A. Thesis, University of Cape Town, 1995.

Lewis-Williams, J. David. *A Cosmos in Stone: Interpreting Religion and Society Through Rock Art.* New York: Alta Mira, 1994.

Lipsitz, George. *Dangerous Crossroads: Popular Music, Postmodernism, and the Poetics of Place.* New York: Verso, 1994.

Lloyd, P. C. "Osifekunde of Ijebu." In *Africa Remembered: Narratives by West Africans from the Era of the Slave Trade,* edited by Philip Curtin, 217–288. Madison: University of Wisconsin Press, 1968 (1845).

Locke, David. *Drum Damba: Talking Drum Lessons.* Crown Point, IN: White Cliffs Media, 1990.

Makeba, Miriam, with James Hall. *Makeba: My Story.* New York: New American Library, 1987.

Martin, Denis-Constant. *Coon Carnival: Cape Town, Past and Present.* Cape Town: David Philip, 1999.

McCall, John. "The Representation of African Music in Early Documents." In *The Garland Encyclopedia of World Music: Africa,* edited by Ruth Stone, 74–99. New York: Garland, 1998.

McCord, Margaret. *The Calling of Katie Makanya.* Cape Town: David Philip, 1995.

McGregor, Maxine. *Chris McGregor and the Brotherhood of Breath.* Flint, MI: Bamberger Books, 1995.

McMurtry, Mervyn. "'Doing Their Own Thane': The Critical Reception of Umabatha, Welcome Msomi's Macbeth." *Ilha do Desterro,* 36 (1999): 309–336.

Meintjes, Louise. *Sound of Africa! Making Zulu Music in a South African Studio.* Durham: Duke University Press, 2003.

_____. "Paul Simon's *Graceland,* South Africa and the Mediation of Musical Meaning." *Ethnomusicology,* 34 (1990): 37–73.

Mensah, Atta. "Compositional Processes in African Music." In *The Garland Encyclopedia of World Music: Africa,* edited by Ruth Stone, 208–231. New York: Garland, 1998.

_____. "Jazz—The Round Trip." *Jazzforschun—Jazz Research,* 3/4 (1972): 124–137.

Molefe, Z. B., and Mike Mzileni. *A Common Hunger to Sing: A Tribute to South Africa's Black Women of Song 1950–1990.* Cape Town: Kwela Books, 1997.

Moodie, Dunbar. "Mine Culture and Miner's Identity on the South African Gold Mines." In *Town and Countryside in the Transvaal: Capitalist Penetration and Popular Response,* edited by Belinda Bozzoli, 176–197. Johannesburg: Ravan Press, 1983.

Msibi, Sikelela. Unpublished essay, "Mzilikazi Khumalo."

Mthethwa, Bongani. Incomplete Doctoral Dissertation on *Syncretism in the Hymns of Ibandla LamaNazaretha.* Durban: University of Natal, n.d.

Muller, Carol, ed., translated by Bongani Mthethwa, assisted by Sazi Dlamini and Carol Muller. *The Hymns of the Nazaretha. Composed by Isaiah and Galilee Shembe.* Pietermartizburg: University of Natal Press, forthcoming.

_____. "Archiving Africanness in Sacred Song." *Ethnomusicology,* 46/3 (2002): 409–430.

_____. "Capturing the 'Spirit of Africa' in the Jazz Singing of South African–born Sathima Bea Benjamin." *Research in African Literatures,* 32/3 (2001): 133–152.

_____. "Sathima Bea Benjamin, Exile and the 'Southern Touch' in Jazz Creation and Performance." *African Languages and Culture*, 9/2 (1996): 127–144.

_____. *Rituals of Fertility and the Sacrifice of Desire: Nazarite Women's Performance in South Africa*. (CD Rom). Chicago: University of Chicago Press, 1999a.

_____. "Chakide—The Teller of Secrets: Space, Song, and Story in Zulu Maskanda Performance." In *Oral Performance and Literature in Southern Africa*, edited by Duncan Brown, 220–234. New York: Oxford University Press, 1999.

Muller, Carol, and Janet Topp Fargion. "Gumboots, Migrants, and Fred Astaire: South African Worker Dance and Musical Style." *African Music*, vol. 714 (1999): 88–109.

Murray, Jon, Jeff Williams, and Richard Everist. *Lonely Planet South Africa, Lesotho, and Swaziland*. London: Lonely Planet Publications, 3d, 1998.

Nasson, Bill. "'She Preferred Living in a Cave with Harry the Snake-catcher': Towards an Oral History of Popular Leisure and Class Expression in District Six, Cape Town, c. 1920s–1950s." In *Holding Their Ground: Class, Locality, and Culture in 19th and 20th Century South Africa*, edited by P. Bonner, et al., 286–295. Johannesburg: Witwatersrand University Press, 1989.

Nixon, Michael. The World of Jazz in Inner Cape Town, 1940–1960. *Proceedings of the Symposium on Ethnomusicology No. 14, July 1997*. Grahamstown: International Library of African Music, 19–23.

Nixon, Rob. *Homelands, Harlem, and Hollywood: South African Culture and the World Beyond*. New York: Routledge, 1994.

Njoku, J A-K. "Art Composed Music in Africa." In *The Garland Encyclopedia of World Music: Africa*, edited by Ruth Stone, 232–253. New York: Garland, 1998.

Nketia, Kwabena. "The Scholarly Study of African Music: A Historical Review." In *The Garland Encyclopedia of World Music: Africa*, edited by Ruth Stone, 13–73. New York: Garland, 1998.

_____. *The Music of Africa*. London: Victor Gollancz, 1982.

Nkosi, Lewis. *Home and Exile and Other Selections*. New York: Longmans, 1965.

Nutall, Sarah, and Cheryl Michaels, eds. *Senses of Culture*. London: Oxford University Press, 2000.

Nzewi, Meki, et al. "Beyond Song Texts—The Lingual Fundamentals of African Drum Music." *Research in African Literatures*, 32/2 (2001): 90–104.

Omojola, Bode. "African Pianism as an Intercultural Compositional

Framework: A Study of the Piano Works of Akin Euba." *Research in African Literatures,* 32/2 (2001): 153–173.

_____. *Nigerian Art Music, with an Introductory Study of Ghanaian Art Music.* Ibadan and Beyreuth, Germany: Bayreuth Studies in African Music, 1997.

Oosthuizen, G. C. E. *The Theology of a South African Messiah., An Analysis of the Hymnal of The Church of the Nazarites.* Leiden: E. J. Brill, 1967.

Palma, H. R. *The Carthaganian Voyage to West Africa in 500 B.C.* Bathurst, Western Cape, South Africa: J. M. Lawani, 1931.

Papini, Robert. "Carl Faye's Transcript of Isaiah Shembe's Testimony of His Early Life and Calling." *Journal of Religion in Africa,* 29/3 (1999): 243–284.

Pewa, Elliot. "Musical Competition." Unpublished M.A. Thesis, University of Natal, 1994.

Philips, Ray. *The Bantu in the City: A Study of Cultural Adjustment on the Witwatersrand.* London: Faber and Faber, 1938.

Pongweni, Alec. "The Chimurenga Songs of the Zimbabwean War of Liberation." In Barber, Karen, ed. *Readings in African Popular Culture,* edited by Karen Barber, 63–72. Bloomington: Indiana University Press, 1997.

Ranger, Terence. "Protestant Missions in Africa: The Dialectic of Conversion in the American Methodist Episcopal Church in Eastern Zimbabwe, 1900–1950." In Thomas Blakely et al. (eds.) *Religion in Africa.* London: Heinemann and James Currey, 1994.

Rasmussen, Lars. *Abdullah Ibrahim: A Discography.* Copenhagen: The Booktrader, 1999.

_____. *Sathima Bea Benjamin: Embracing Jazz.* Copenhagen: The Booktrader, 2000.

Reader's Digest. *Illustrated History of South Africa: The Real Story. Expanded third edition, completely updated.* Cape Town: Reader's Digest, 1994.

Richmond, Simon, et al. *Lonely Planet: South Africa, Lesotho, and Swaziland.* Victoria, Australia: Lonely Planet Publications, 2002.

Roberts, Esther. "Shembe: The Man and His Work." Unpublished M.A. Thesis, University of the Witwatersrand, 1936.

Roberts, John S. *Black Music of Two Worlds: Africa, Caribbean, Latin, and African American Traditions.* New York: Schirmer, 1998 (1972).

Rossi, Michael. "Perspectives on Saxophone Performance Practices in South Africa." *IAJE Jazz Research Proceedings Yearbook XXXI* (2001): 12–18.

Rycroft, David. "Stylistic Evidence in Zulu Song." In *Essays on Music and History in Africa,* edited by K. P. Wachsmann, 213–241. Evanston, IN: Northwestern University Press, 1971.

Sarno, Louis. *Bayaka: The Extraordinary Music of the Babenzele Pygmies.* New York: Ellipsis Arts, 1995.

Schade-Poulsen, Marc. *Men and Popular Music in Algeria: The Social Significance of Rai.* Austin: University of Texas Press, 1999.

Schmidt, Cynthia. "The Guitar in Africa: Issues and Research." *World of Music,* 36/2 (1994): 3–20.

_____. "Interview with John Collins on Cultural Policy, Folklore, and the Recording Industry in Ghana." *World of Music,* 36/2 (1994): 138–147.

Shelemay, Kay. "Notation and Oral Tradition." In *The Garland Encyclopedia of World Music: Africa,* edited by Ruth Stone, 147–163. New York: Garland, 1998.

_____. *Music, Ritual, and Falasha History.* East Lansing: Michigan State University Press, 1989.

Shelemay, K., and P. Jeffrey. *Ethiopian Christian Liturgical Change: An Anthology.* 3 Vols. Madison, WI: A-R Editions, 1993.

Shembe, Galilee, ed. *IziHlabelelo ZamaNazaretha.* Durban: WG Shepherd, 1940.

Shifrin, Thelma. "South Africa: Idealism or Blackmail?" *Musical America,* July 1989: 21.

Shiloah, Ammon. *Music in the World of Islam: A Socio-Cultural Study.* Detroit: Wayne State University, 1995.

South African Library. *The Book of Books: Catalogue of an Exhibition of Bibles Held in the South African Library, June–September 1986.* Cape Town: South African Library, 1986.

Stapleton, Chris, and Chris May. *African Rock: Pop Music of a Continent.* New York: Obelisk, 1990.

Stewart, Gary. *Rumba on the River: A History of the Popular Music of the Two Congos.* London: Verso, 2000.

_____. *Breakout! Profiles in African Rhythm.* Chicago: University of Chicago Press, 1992.

Stone, Ruth, ed. *The Garland Encyclopedia of World Music: Africa.* New York: Garland, 1998.

Sundkler, Bengt. *Bantu Prophets in South Africa.* London: Oxford University Press, 1961 [1948].

Taylor, Timothy. *Global Pop: World Music, World Markets.* New York: Routledge, 1997.

Thomas, Jeff. *Ingoma Dancers and Their Response to Town: A Study of Ingoma Dance Troupes among Zulu Migrant Workers in Durban.* Unpublished M.A. Thesis, University of Natal, Durban, 1988.

Thompson, Robert F. *African Art in Motion.* Los Angeles: University of California Press, 1979.

Tomaselli, Keyan. "Mandela, MTV, Television and Apartheid." *Popular Music and Society,* 17/2 (1993): 1–19.

Tracey, Hugh. *African Dances of the Witwatersrand Gold Mines.* Johannesburg: African Music Society, 1952.

Trewhela, Ralph. *Song Safari.* Johannesburg: Limelight Press, 1980.

Tshabalala, Mbuyisazwe. *Shembe's Hymnbook Reconsidered, Its Sources and Significance.* Unpublished Masters Thesis, University of Aberdeen, Scotland, 1983.

Tucker, Percy. *Just the Ticket! My 50 Years in Show Business.* Johannesburg: Jonathan Ball Publishers, 1997.

Turino, Thomas. "The Mbira, Worldbeat, and the International Imagination." *World of Music,* 40/2 (1998): 85–106.

_____. *Nationalists, Cosmoplitans, and Popular Music in Zimbabwe.* Chicago: University of Chicago Press, 2001.

Turnbull, Colin. *The Forest People.* New York: Touchstone, 1962.

Vail, Leroy, and Landeg White. "Plantation Protest: The History of a Mozambican Song." In *Readings in African Popular Culture,* edited by Karen Barber, 54–62. Bloomington: Indiana University Press, 1997.

Veal, Michael. *Fela: The Life and Times of a Musical Icon.* Philadelphia: Temple University Press, 2000.

Wallaschek, Richard. *Primitive Music: An Inquiry into the Origin and Development of Music, Songs, Instruments, Dances, and Pantomimes of Savage Races.* London: Longmans, Green, 893.

Waterman, Christopher. "'Our Tradition Is a Very Modern Tradition': Popular Music and the Construction of Pan-Yoruba Identity." In *Readings in African Popular Culture,* edited by Karen Barber, 48–53. Bloomington: Indiana University Press, 1997.

Watkins, Lee. "Tracking Down the Narrative: The Poetics of Identity in Rap Music and Hip-hop Culture in Cape Town." Unpublished M.A. Thesis, University of Natal, Durban, 1999.

Wells, Robin. *An Introduction to the Music of the Basotho.* Morija: Morija Museum Press, 1994.

Wendt, Caroline Card. "North Africa: An Introduction." In *The Garland Encyclopedia of World Music: Africa,* edited by Ruth Stone, 532–548. New York: Garland, 1998.

White, Luise, Stephan F. Miescher, and David William Cohen, eds. *African Words, African Voices: Critical Practices in Oral History.* Bloomington: Indiana University Press, 2001.

Zaretti, Joan. *Carnegie Hall Presents Global Encounters. South African Sounds, Teacher's Guide and Accompanying Compact Discs.* New York: Carnegie Hall Education Department, 2002.

Zonk! An African People's Magazine, various issues.

VIDEO RECORDINGS ON AFRICAN MUSIC
(PLACE AND NAME OF U.S. DISTRIBUTOR GIVEN)

Absa, Mousa Sene. *Ca Twiste a Popenguine.* San Francisco: California Newsreel, 1993.

Anderson, John. *King of Jazz.* Hollywood, CA: MGM Studios, 1930.

Austin, Chris. *Brother with Perfect Timing.* New York: Rhapsody Films, 1988.

Ba, Ndiouga Moctar. *You Africa! Youssou N'Dour and Super Etoile: The African Tour.* San Francisco: California Newsreel, 1994.

Balmer, Paul. *Africa I Remember: A Musical Synthesis of Two Cultures.* New York: Filmmakers Library, 1995.

Bausch, Ike Brooks. *Zonk!* Vancouver, BC: Villon Films, 1994.

BBC Productions. *Under African Skies: Mali, the Music of Life.* Princeton: Films for the Humanities and Sciences, 1997.

Bischoff, Peter. *Listen to the Silence: A Film about African Cross-Rhythms as Seen through Ghanaian Music.* Princeton: Films for the Humanities and Sciences, 1996.

Bowey, John. *African Wave: South African Music and Its Influences.* Princeton: Films for the Humanities, 1998.

Cut Above Productions. *African Wave: South African Music and Its Influences.* Princeton: Films for the Humanities and Sciences, 1998.

De Villiers, Violane. *Mizike Mama.* New York: Interama Video Classics, 1992.

Drewal, Margaret. *Yoruba Ritual. Accompanying Video to Yoruba Ritual: Performers, Play, Agency.* Bloomington: Indiana University Press, 1992.

Erlmann, Veit. *Nightsong: Performance, Power, and Practice in South Africa.* (Accompanies book of same title.) Chicago: University of Chicago Press, 1996.

Genini, Izzi. *Gnaouas (Morocco).* New York: Icarus, First Run Films, 1990.

Gibson, Angus, and Jo Mennell (Directors). *Mandela, Son of Africa, Father of a Nation.* Marina Del Ray, CA: Lion's Gate Films, 1996.

Hirsch, Lee. *Amandla! Revolution in Four Part Harmony.* Santa Monica, CA: Artisan Entertainment, 2002.

Haydon, Geoffrey, and Dennis Marks. *Repercussions: A Celebration of African-American Music.* Chicago: Home Vision, 1994.

Knight, Roderic. *Jali Nyama Suso: Kora Player of the Gambia.* Tivoli, NY: Original Music, 1992.

_____. *Music of the Mande.* Tivoli, NY: Original Music, 1992.

Kubik, Gerhard. *African Guitar: Solo Finger-Style Guitar Music, Composers and Performers.* Cambridge, MA: Rounder Records (US distributors), 1995.

Little Steven and Arthur Baker. *Sun City: Artists United Against Apartheid.* New York: Manhattan Records, 1985.

Lough, Robin. *African Sanctus: David Fanshawe's African Journey.* Robin Lough & Associates, 1994.

Marre, Jeremy. *Rhythm of Resistance: The Black Music of South Africa.* Newton, NJ: Shanachie Records, 1988.

_____. *Graceland: Recounting the Journey of a Legendary Music Recording.* Los Angeles: Rhino Entertainment, 1998.

Morin, Bertrand. *The Lost City of Zimbabwe.* Princeton: Films for the Humanities and Sciences, 1993.

Noble, Nigel. *Voices of Sarafina! Songs of Hope and Freedom.* New York: New Yorker Video, 1988.

Nofal, Emil. *Song of Africa.* Vancouver, BC: Villon Films, 1994.

Powell, Aubrey. *Gumboots! An Explosion of Spirit and Song.* Chatsworth, CA: Image Entertainment, 2000.

Raeburn, Michael. *Zimbabwe: Music with a Past.* Princeton: Films for the Humanities and Sciences, 1997.

Ralulimi, Albert, and Rob Allingham (Producers). *Township Swing Jazz, Vols. 1 and 2.* Johannesburg: Gallo Records (Archival Reissue), 1991.

Rosellini, Jim. *Diro and His Talking Musical Bow; Adama, the Fulani Magician; Dance of the Bella.* Santa Cruz, CA: African Family Films, 1996.

Schmitz, Oliver. *Mapantsula.* San Francisco: California Newsreel, 1990.

Simon, Paul. *Graceland: The African Concert.* New York: Warner Brothers, 1988.

Simon, Sylvan. *Rio Rita!* Hollywood, CA: MGM Studios, 1942 [1930].

Singh, Avant. *Sarafina!* Hollywood, CA: Miramax, n.d.

Smith, Larry. 1990. *Dagbamba Praise Names and Dances, Stories and Drummer Language.* Crown Point, IN: White Cliffs Media, 1990.

_____. *Dagbamba Praise Names.* (This and preceding video accompany David Locke's *Drum Damba: Talking Drum Lessons,* op. cit.) Crown Point IN: White Cliffs Media, 1990.

Soule, Beatrice, and Eric Millot. *Djabote: Senegalese Drumming and Song from Master Drummer Doudou N'Diaye Rose.* Montpelier, VT: Multicultural Media (now defunct), 1993.

Toepke, Alvaro. *The Language You Cry In: The Story of a Mende Song.* San Francisco: California Newsreel, 1999.

A Voice of Egypt: Umm Khulthum. Waltham, MA: Filmmakers Collaborative, 1997.

Yamamato, Hiroshi. *Smithsonian/Folkways Video Anthology of Music and Dance of Africa. Africa, Vols. 1–3.* Japan: Victor, 1996.

Zantzinger, Gei. *Songs of the Adventurers (Lesotho).* DeVault, PA: Constant Springs Productions, 1987.

_____. *Mbira dza Vadzimu: Dambatsoko: An Old Cult Center.* University Park, PA: Penn State University Media Sales, 1978.

_____. *Mbira dza Vadzimu: Urban and Rural Ceremonies.* University Park, PA: Penn State University Media Sales, 1978.

_____. *The 1973 Mgodo wa Mbanguzi.* University Park, PA: Penn State University Media Sales, 1974.

SOUND RECORDINGS CITED AND RECOMMENDED

Benjamin, Sathima. *Cape Town Love.* Cape Town: Ekapa (South Africa), 1999.

_____. *Windsong.* New York: Ekapa, 1985.

Caluza, Reuben. *Caluza's Double Quartet: 1930.* Sleeve Notes by Veit Erlmann. Wiltshire, England: Heritage Records, 1992.

From Marabi to Disco: 42 Years of Township Music. Johannesburg: Gallo, 1994.

Indestructible Beat of Soweto. Newton, NJ: Shanachie Records, 1987.

Inspiration, The. Philadelphia: University of Pennsylvania, 1996.

Juluka: Universal Men. Johannesburg: EMI Music, 1992.

King Kong Original Cast: All African Jazz Opera. Johannesburg: Gallo, 1996.

Kramer, David. *Klassic Kramer.* Cape Town: Blik Music, 1996.

Leeukop Prisoners Choir: Going Home. Johannesburg: Gallo, n.d.

Monk, Thelonius. *Solo Monk: Original Recording Remastered.* New York: Sony, 2003.

Simon, Paul. *Graceland.* New York: Warner Brothers, 1986, 1996.

Soweto String Quartet. *Zebra Crossing.* Johannesburg: BMG Records, 1994.

Long Walk to Freedom: A Celebration of Four Decades of South African Music. London: Wrasse Records, 2002.

The Rough Guide to South African Jazz. London: Rough Guide, 2000.

Township Jazz and Jive. Music Collection International, n.p., 1997.

Index